W9-ACX-202

Exhibitions: Universal Marketing Tools

Cassell/Associated Business Programmes Marketing Library

Editors
Franklin A. Colborn and Aubrey Wilson

Exhibitions: Universal Marketing Tools

ALFRED ALLES DIC, DIPL ING, C ENG, M I MECH E

A HALSTED PRESS BOOK

JOHN WILEY & SONS
New York

CARL A. RUDISILL LIBRARY
LENOIR RHYNE COLLEGE

To Lala

658.82

ALse

89238

June 1974

English Language Edition, except U.S.A.
published by
Associated Business Programmes Ltd.
17 Buckingham Gate, London SW1
Distributed by
Cassell and Co. Ltd.
35 Red Lion Square, London WC1R 4SJ

Published in the U.S.A.
by Halsted Press, a Division
of John Wiley & Sons, Inc.
New York

Library of Congress Number 73–1796

First published 1973

© Alfred Alles 1973

This book has been printed in Great Britain
by The Anchor Press Ltd. and bound by
Wm. Brendon & Son Ltd., both of Tiptree, Essex

ISBN 0 470–02332–5

Contents

FIGURES AND TABLES IN THE TEXT

FIGURES

TABLES

Introduction

Throughout the centuries markets, fairs, trade fairs and exhibitions have been the places of exchange of goods offered by a multiplicity of sellers and appraised, acquired or rejected by a multitude of buyers.

If marketing started in the market place and exhibitions claim to be directly descended from the great markets which became great trade fairs, then it is only appropriate that exhibitions should be studied for what they are—marketing tools. According to Ezekiel XXVII at the international fair regularly held at Tyre, the following goods were offered by suppliers from twelve different countries:

> Silver, iron, bright iron, tin, lead, brass vessels.
> Coral, agate, precious stones, ivory, ebony.
> Wheat, honey, wine, cassia, calamus, spices.
> Fine linen, white wool, purple, embroidery.
> Blue clothes, precious clothes for chariots, chests of apparel.
> Slaves, horses, mules, lambs, rams, goats.

In the middle ages great fairs were held in towns, usually once or twice a year, and were attended by merchants from all parts of Europe. They were in fact international market places as distinct from local markets attended mostly by craftsmen offering their own products. Wine from the Rhine, silks and spices from the East, woollens from Flanders and armour from Lombardy were carried across Europe on trade routes crossing frontiers and connecting towns and cities.

Market laws dealing with fairs and markets came into being in the ninth century, were applied by special courts and heavy penalties were imposed for transgressions.

The markets and great fairs which in the eleventh century and twelfth century reflected the revival of trade, proliferated in the thirteenth century to such an extent that legal restrictions were imposed on their activities. The Leipzig Fair claims a foundation date of 1165 and its subsequent development from market place to samples fair and to general and industrial exhibition became a model for many followers. Frankfurt was enfranchised to become a centre of trade fairs under a royal decree of 1240.

Industrial exhibitions made their debut in the sixteenth century, when an exhibition which is regarded as the first of this kind, was held in the town hall of Nuremberg in 1569. Exhibitions of industrial arts were held in Paris in 1683 and 1763, and in Britain the Society of Arts exhibited prize winning designs, models and machines in 1761.

In France, recovering from the aftermath of the revolution, the commissioners of the formerly royal factories of Sevres porcelain, Gobelin tapestries and Savonneries carpets, in 1797 mounted an exhibition of these products to stimulate sales of accumulated stocks and to alleviate unemployment. During the following fifty years of the Napoleonic regime and the restoration, a series of industrial exhibitions followed, most of which showed unmistakable signs of a campaign aimed against British industry.*

In other parts of Europe and in America similar industrial exhibitions were held during this period, whilst Britain remained somewhat aloof, although a number of local exhibitions connected with the Mechanics Institute movement took place.

Then came the Great Exhibition of 1851.

It displayed to the world the achievements of British manufacturers, but it also revealed that newcomers to the international industrial scene are developing their skills with considerable speed. The International Exhibition held in Paris in 1867 and what was seen there prompted the setting up of a Commons Select Committee to enquire into the shortcomings of technical education in Britain and indirectly led to the foundation of Whitworth Scholarships.

The Crystal Palace exhibition of 1851 initiated the era of great international exhibitions and world fairs, an era which is still with us. The displays of engineering achievements seen at industrial exhibitions have contributed as much as the engineers who created them to changes in our environment, have

* In 1970 the impact of a long scheduled British industrial exhibition in the Argentine—BA 70 as it was called, was suddenly almost pre-empted by a French exhibition Francia 70 announced at very short notice and scheduled to end only eight days before the opening of BA 70.

brought about direct changes in urban developments and have influenced styles and fashions of buildings, of furniture and of articles of everyday use.

Following the display of Japanese buildings at the Philadelphia 1876 and San Francisco 1894 fairs, Japanese design elements made their appearance in interior house decorations and furniture. The classic style façades of the Chicago Columbian exposition in 1893 is held responsible for generating in America the propensity for pseudo-classical architecture and columned buildings.

Exhibition buildings transformed town centres and stimulated the creation of new districts. The Crystal Palace, first erected in Hyde Park was then moved to Sydenham, the 1862 exhibition buildings erected in South Kensington were then moved and re-erected at Alexandra Palace. The Paris Trocadero of the 1878 exhibition, the Eiffel Tower the central feature of the 1889 exhibition, the Grand Palais, Petit Palais and the Alexander III bridge of the 1900 exhibition are still in use. In Brussels permanent buildings erected for the 1953 exhibition were later used for the annual Brussels Trade Fair.

In 1951 the Festival of Britain and the Brussels 1958, Montreal 1967 and Osaka 1970 world fairs all made their mark and left behind some of their buildings and their influences. The speedways serving the Hanover Fair and its complex of exhibition buildings and those of Düsseldorf, Frankfurt, Paris, Turin, and many others, are all witness to the exhibition activities which continue unabated all over the world.

In London we also have the Earls Court and Olympia complexes until recently proudly displaying their functional obsolescence, but now overtaken by events.

Definitions of Industrial Exhibitions
Industrial exhibitions or rather exhibitions serving industrial markets have suffered for a long time, and still do, from the misunderstanding and misinterpretation of their purpose and of their capability.

A great many of these misconceptions both pronounced *ex cathedra* and published in textbooks stray down one common line of thought: they confuse activity with objectives. But a theoretical misconception of a phenomenon does not necessarily impair its effective manifestation, as is proved by the Flat Earth Society. In the case of exhibitions the fact is that if the proponents of these definitions acted in accordance with their own maxims there would not be much wrong with exhibitions providing they were fully exploited. If, according to one definition, exhibitions are sales promotion functions, one could hardly find a better sales promotion medium for industrial products than exhibitions. Another definition is that they are three-dimensional advertisements. This one is more difficult, because further on in this study the assertion is made that the ineffective use of an exhibition reduces it to not more than a three-dimensional advertisement, the implication being that this is not such an honour for an exhibition. However, one could argue that even for 3-D advertisements an exhibition can do more than any other medium. Most industrial objects can be shown in their natural size and shape, if they make a noise it can be heard, they can be smelled, touched, if not too heavy lifted, and rather unlikely but possible—tasted, they can move under their own power, they can be taken to pieces and re-assembled, they can be operated, demonstrated, tested to destruction, they can have almost anything done to them. To offer all that the exhibition must be a good advertising medium.

No new definition or concept has been ever proposed without provoking modifications, additions, paraphrases, shortened and expanded versions and now and then condemnations as utter nonsense, and this is as it should be, lest they be taken too seriously and become dogmas.

There are many *definitions of marketing* made by economists, sociologists, academics, industrialists and marketing practitioners and they range from the simple and somewhat derogatory statement that 'marketing is nothing more than a glamorous name for selling' to that of an 'all-embracing system with technical and social functions aiming at ensuring a profitable life and growth of businesses'. The plethora of these definitions shows at least one common denominator: whatever *marketing* is to different people, it is to all a *management precept*.

If it is accepted that economic survival and development is the supreme corporate goal, then the effective application of marketing concepts and techniques is not only a prerequisite to achieving that goal but also a measure of management performance.

The effective application of techniques implies the use of the best available tools and it is the aim of this study to demonstrate that:

for the overwhelming majority of industrial products exhibitions are excellent *universal marketing tools*

the systematic use and exploitation of exhibitions can bring very high benefits and rewards.

One of the assertions of this study is that a disturbing proportion of exhibition activities is undertaken and carried out without a full awareness of marketing concept criteria. This applies as much to a great number of exhibition enterprises, as to exhibitors participating in them and visitors visiting them. It seems, therefore appropriate to examine the facilities and opportunities which exhibitions can offer to prospective exhibitors and visitors and to review them critically against the bench marks of recognised marketing functions and activities. A scrutiny of a list of marketing activities will show that an exhibitor can carry out the following main marketing functions: sales operations, sales promotion and advertising.

Background information and intelligence can be gathered for the functions of marketing research, sales planning and physical distribution. The exhibition effort can be regarded as a special promotion function although its scope, as will be seen, goes far beyond that definition. The function of selling is a normal exhibition activity.

The functional elements of distributing sales aids can be carried out effectively, training of salesmen can be a subsidiary activity and the impression created by a competent exhibition effort may well attract potential employees. At some exhibitions the exhibitor may find buying opportunities, he can select sources of supply, negotiate prices, terms and delivery terms and place orders. Product service capability could be physically provided, and service capability can be displayed and demonstrated.

A visitor can select sources of supply, he can negotiate prices and place orders, he can visit customers and ascertain their needs and pursue product and market intelligence tasks.

Apart from these orthodox marketing activities, an exhibition can be used as an observation laboratory of functional marketing behaviour, of manifestations of talents, of techniques, of establishing rapport, of conflict-creating behaviour. These observations can be made on the exhibitors' stand and on other stands, and valuable insights can be gained into conditions and situations which could not be expected to be observed by busy personnel, and are rarely reported on.

An exhibition is also a very good observation post for the study of the following phenomena: group behaviour in special situations; reactions to extraneous conditions of rain, sleet, cold or heat and their influence on the change of intentions to visit indoor stands or outdoor areas and vice versa; different types of stance adopted by stand personnel towards different types of visitors; the influence of the time of day on length of visits to stands.

The Structure of Industrial Exhibitions
Expanding the proposition that marketing is a management precept and that exhibitions are marketing tools, this study aims at providing an analysis of the structure of exhibitions and an assessment of the suitability of that structure for the achievement of marketing objectives. It is addressed to marketing executives in the hope that it will assist them in the integration and co-ordination of exhibitions into their marketing system as one of its elements.

The study develops the outline of a systematic procedure for selecting exhibitions for participation and visiting in three steps of assessments: first the definition of marketing motives for exhibiting or visiting, second the location of exhibitions which would serve these motives and third the selection of exhibitions in which participation or visiting can be implemented.

The analysis of the structural elements of industrial exhibitions discusses classification problems, titles and aims and examines the functions and importance of the exhibition catalogue. Brief comments are made on the inclusion of management interests in the programmes of exhibitions in the USA.

The versatility of industrial exhibitions as marketing tools stems from the variety of marketing objectives it can serve and from the range of marketing techniques which can be employed. The question of the effectiveness of exhibitions is one of the badly misunderstood areas of the subject. The bad musician blames his instrument for a bad performance, the clumsy craftsman blames his tools for a spoiled piece of work, and the disappointed exhibitor blames the exhibition for unsatisfactory results. He does not stop to ask whether he has selected the most suitable exhibition and whether he has made the best use of the exhibition.

A high-powered racing car driven at 20 mph on a country lane does not cease to be a racing car, nor does a small runabout become a racing car because it is driven around a race track. How the effectiveness of an exhibition or, as it will be described in the text, its *marketing merit* can be assessed qualitatively and quantitatively from the point of view of exhibitors and visitors, is discussed in this study.

Many years of experience and the continuous observation of ineffectual manifestations of exhibition efforts and of indifferent and negative attitudes to exhibitions leads one to the conclusion that there can be only two reasons for such a state of affairs. Either a great number of firms engaged in the marketing of industrial goods misunderstand or fail to appreciate the value and use of *exhibitions as marketing tools*, or that it is not the tool which is misunderstood but the *concept of marketing*. The study suggests that for all exhibition activities marketing motives should be the moving spirit and the basis for decisions. A range of *principal and subsidiary marketing motives* is reviewed and their merits discussed.

The complexity of international or multi-market activities and the difficulty of reconciling the variety of available exhibitions with marketing strategies often baffles those charged with the task. Managements authorising computer programmes and times for the solution of problems whose claim for attention is rather the weight of the paperwork they generate, than their fundamental influence on the business, react with incredulity when a request is made for help in the solution of such marketing problems as participating in exhibitions. The versatility and adaptability of exhibitions to a variety of marketing tasks is accompanied by one very special feature—their time dependence. Exhibitions have a date dependence and a duration time dependence. *Exhibition time elements* and *time classification elements* are discussed in the context of a time management concept. Exhibitions activities are a unique mixture of free ranging design inspiration and meticulous organisation, of a galaxy of technical aids and of person to person contacts, of publicity stunts and scientific lectures.

Exhibition activities are discussed in terms of a *material non-personal structure and personal activities.*

The subjects of *stand design*, *exhibits* and *stand personnel* come within the orbit of that discussion. Qualifications of a stand manager, of stand personnel and the categories of their duties are considered and a reflection on *exhibition manners* is included. Person to person contacts and exchanges of information are the main human communication functions of an exhibition effort. These contacts and exchanges take place in a specific environment partly controlled or manipulated by the exhibitor and aimed at the receiver—the visitor. The effectiveness of the exchanges depends therefore on people, their personalities and their behaviour.

In the exhibition situation the simple final person to person confrontation is influenced and complicated by the *exhibition environment* in which both *marketing merits* and *buying mandates* can involve more than one specific product or service and in which competitive merits can be compared with greater ease and in a shorter time than in normal trading conditions.

The most frequent confrontation is that between the exhibitor-seller and the visitor-buyer.

This confrontation is illustrated by a *peripheral influence diagram* and the *transposition process* of industrial products and the changing roles of buyers and sellers are reviewed.

Visiting Industrial Exhibitions

Textbooks on marketing subjects usually deal with exhibitions in a few paragraphs and at the most in a few pages. Perceptive authors write that exhibitions are badly understood and ill-used forms of sales promotion, others warn prospective exhibitors of the dangers and temptations of exhibitions and are very explicit in explaining what not to do. Most authors advise prospective exhibitors to select the right exhibition for his products, to use competent people to man the stand and to count the number of visitors to their stand. Usually, the interests of visitors are hardly considered, except for fleeting remarks about their comfort.

An extensive literature is available on the subject of exhibitions but the texts deal mainly with techniques of exhibiting from the viewpoint of the exhibitor. The subjects often discussed with great expertise and on the basis of long experience are: stand design, display, presentation, graphics, lighting.

Some texts emphasise the best ways and means of attracting visitors, some mention visitors' needs, but only from the point of view of the visitor as a customer or potential customer of the exhibitor. That the visitor is in his own right a customer of the exhibition enterprise, without whom it could not exist, is seldom mentioned. The visitor and his marketing interests are discussed in this study and the attendance figures for individual exhibitions in which visitors are counted in thousands, ten of thousands and even hundreds of thousands justify that discussion. The chapter on visiting exhibitions discusses the marketing interests of visitors, the planning of visiting tasks, and the character of *visiting contacts*.

Publicity and Public Relations

The importance of publicity and public relations and their contribution to the exhibition effort are discussed at length. The attitudes of technical people to publicity are examined and the case is presented for the exhibition as an excellent publicity and public relations medium.

Intelligence

Of all sources of intelligence the exhibition is the most openly legal and ethical one. Products are displayed, demonstrated, tested, information is imparted by means of sales and technical literature, verbally, by films, lectures, discussions. You are invited to partake of that feast of information, the only limitations seem to be your capacity to do so.

Intelligence tasks and the subject of exhibition merit intelligence are discussed at length.

The Proliferation of Exhibitions

The proliferation of exhibitions is an international phenomenon noticeable particularly at two ends of the size scale of exhibitions. At one end many small often short-lived exhibitions appear on the scene, undistinguishable from each other except by their location and slight differences in their small-minded ambitions. At the other end large exhibition enterprises erect bigger, better and more magnificent exhibition halls and fiercely compete for top place in the international exhibition world and for the patronage of long-contract exhibitors.

The proliferation of exhibitions puts a great premium on any systematic approach to selection and participation. Exhibitions have become very big business graduating from being a marketing medium for other industries to being an important industry providing a marketable service. Some exhibition enterprises clearly display their acceptance and practice of marketing concepts, others sell their exhibitions like patent medicines were once sold, wrapped in alluring promises of colossal success if partaken of and dire results if rejected.

In fact the reverse occurs, dire results come from taking the medicine. This surfeit of exhibitions creates a general aura of perplexity before the event and of disillusionment after it which unfortunately affects the attitude to other excellent and important exhibitions, both large and small, which serve a marketing purpose and serve it well.

Many British manufacturers participate in exhibitions abroad, but a very great number of medium and small companies do not. It is immaterial for the end result, whether the abstention from international exhibitions is based on rational arguments of lack of material or human resources, or a matter of vague feelings that not much would be gained by participation and visits, or simply on inertia and on a 'we know best' attitude. The fact is that the competitors of these firms can visit such international exhibitions in their own countries and in great numbers do so. The fact that arrangements for a visit to Paris or Brussels or Amsterdam can be made more simply and quickly than to Scotland or Wales is not always appreciated by those who still consider exports as a 'foreign' activity.

It is a matter for speculation (and it could be a subject for a research study) to what extent the absence of truly international industrial exhibitions in Britain during the last twenty years, deprived British engineers of the impact and stimulus of competitive designs and technical developments and to what extent the prolific growth of the main European exhibitions contributed to the more successful export performances of many European engineering products.

Internationalisation of Industrial Exhibitions

The conceptual separation of home and export markets based on selling as an end function and on a geographical territory as a market area, when applied to industrial products was a misconception even before the advent of marketing as a management concept.

It emphasised the differences between the two markets as if each domestic national market was one homogenous unit which must be compared with another, a foreign, homogenous national unit. Analysts who took great pains to examine, dissect and classify the various sectors of the domestic market retreated into generalisations and summary treatment of foreign markets. It is only recently that the similarities of market sectors at home and in foreign countries are recognised as more significant, from a marketing point of view, than the differences which they will obviously show by being located in different national environments. Inevitably the same home-export discrimination was applied to exhibitions. The difficulties to be overcome when exhibiting abroad were mostly explained in terms of deviations from established home practice with the implied assumption of the effectiveness of that home practice.

When marketing became recognised as a concept and selling as one of its functions and when in parallel exporting became a function of international marketing, exhibitors and visitors looked up and noted that international exhibitions in their domestic market showed marked affinities to similar exhibitions in other countries. The standards of stand design, types of visitors, methods of display were similar in their general aspects, although there were differences in approach as a result of national characteristics.

Marketing Capabilities of Industrial Exhibitions

This study is concerned with industrial exhibitions and the terms industrial suffers from the shortcomings of most portmanteau terms—the outside is quite impressive but you never know what really is inside until you open it.

If we look at manufacturing industries in their wide array from abrasive discs to zip fasteners, we invariably find that some form of engineering is an integral part of these industries. In most industries several kinds of engineering operate in active partnership such as mechanical and electrical, chemical and civil, electronic and pneumatic, or in other more complex and involved inter-relations. Engineering enters industries in their embrionic stage when they emerge from the phase of scientific or inventive concepts, it then has an all-pervading presence in their manufacturing stage and is still with them in the shape of operational, maintenance and service activities when the products of industries are in the hands of customers and users.

Engineering is therefore deeply involved in the industrial marketing system and so are engineers irrespective of whether they are aware of the involvement in a marketing sense, or not.

If industrial marketing is to succeed in its task, if its efforts are to produce the right response in the market, it is just as important for those practising marketing to know about engineering and engineers, as it is for engineers to understand marketing and those practising it, and for both parties it is imperative that they should continue to enlarge their mutual understanding with an open mind.

The marketing capabilities of industrial exhibitions serve the great range of industrial products from one end of miniature components to the other of giant structures and machines, they also serve scientific disciplines and technologies. They were in the past and they still are the showrooms for new developments, new services and new concepts. They enable, develop and on occasions restore contacts between people with different national, social, educational or pro-fessional background.

At an exhibition the exhibitor is the host, the visitor is the guest; this is a sufficient first qualification. One may become a seller and the other a buyer; that is why most of them came to the exhibition. Exhibitions serve small firms and large ones and it is not always the large ones who secure the best results. These are the opportunities.

There are also problems mostly of uncertainty. But uncertainty need not inhibit initiative and planning. If you exhibit, you aim at exposure, if you exhibit efficiently you can achieve maximum exposure. Under certain circum-stances you may prefer optimum exposure instead.

Check Lists. A systematic approach to exhibiting and visiting exhibitions involves the participants in *motivation, discrimination* and *selection* processes which must be completed before actual exhibition activities can be initiated and implemented. Very often these processes have to be applied in areas of insufficient information, complexity or perhaps unfamiliarity.

To assist in these processes, the elements of the subjects discussed in this study are arranged in check lists placed at the end of relevant sections. These check lists can be used for *monitoring* of activities and materials by means of simple item checking, they can be used for *yes-no decisions* and where approp-riate for *rating, ranking* or *weighting* procedures. The lists have *individual* validity but they can also be used *sequentially* and several can be arranged in *matrix* formation and in that form they can be used for *optimum selection* or *optimum solution* purposes. In practice the addition of auxiliary check lists with suitable ranges of monetary values, real time periods and actual dates would enable the use of check lists matrices for *expenditure budgeting* and *function cost analysis*. In view of the great variety of exhibitions, exhibitors and visitors and of the diversity of their needs, the check lists are intentionally designed to be no more than a guide to a possible method of procedure which can be adapted to individual requirements.

No book can take the place of first hand experience but if this study assists in the making of decisions and points the way to systematic exploration, it has fulfilled its purpose.

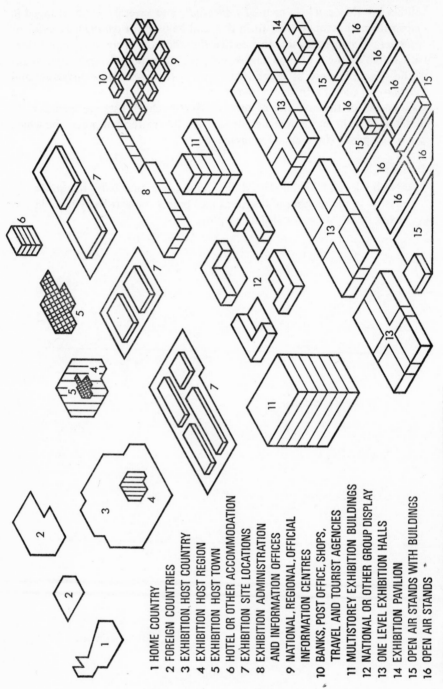

1 HOME COUNTRY
2 FOREIGN COUNTRIES
3 EXHIBITION HOST COUNTRY
4 EXHIBITION HOST REGION
5 EXHIBITION HOST TOWN
6 HOTEL OR OTHER ACCOMMODATION
7 EXHIBITION SITE LOCATIONS
8 EXHIBITION ADMINISTRATION
  AND INFORMATION OFFICES
9 NATIONAL, REGIONAL, OFFICIAL
  INFORMATION CENTRES
10 BANKS, POST OFFICE, SHOPS,
  TRAVEL AND TOURIST AGENCIES
11 MULTISTOREY EXHIBITION BUILDINGS
12 NATIONAL OR OTHER GROUP DISPLAY
13 ONE LEVEL EXHIBITION HALLS
14 EXHIBITION PAVILION
15 OPEN AIR STANDS WITH BUILDINGS
16 OPEN AIR STANDS

FIGURE 1. TOPOGRAPHY OF AN EXHIBITION

Item

1. HOME COUNTRY = country of residence of exhibitor or of visitor to exhibition, country in which the headquarters of an exhibitor's or visitor's organisation is located. The distance of the home country from the exhibition host country and the available travel and transport facilities will influence the time and cost factors involved in exhibiting or visiting.

2. FOREIGN COUNTRY = any country outside exhibitor's or visitor's home country and outside exhibition host country. The location of a foreign country in relation to the home country and to the exhibition host country and its marketing merits for the exhibitor or visitor may influence the decision to combine exhibition activities with visits to a foreign country.

3. EXHIBITION HOST COUNTRY = country in which exhibition is held.

4. EXHIBITION HOST REGION = a region of the exhibition host country in which exhibition is held and with identifiable market characteristics or marketing merits.

5. EXHIBITION HOST TOWN = the town or city in which exhibition is held. The town or city may have its own general marketing merits e.g. a capital city, a commercial centre, an industrial centre, on the other hand it may have no other marketing merit than being a host to the exhibition.

6. HOTEL or other ACCOMMODATION = the location of available hotel or other accommodation in relation to the exhibition site and also the quality of the available facilities can be an important time, transport and fatigue factor as well as a cost factor particularly where such accommodation is only available at a distance from the exhibition site.

7. EXHIBITION SITE LOCATIONS = exhibition halls or display areas can be dispersed over more than one location and the distances between these locations and the available transport and travel facilities can be a serious time and fatigue factor.

Items from 8 to 16 constitute exhibition stands and facilities which can vary in scope, site and quality and which can be only assessed individually for each exhibition.

TABLE 1. GLOSSARY OF TERMS USED IN FIGURE 1

PART ONE

The Structure of Exhibitions

The physical structure and the *topography* of a typical international industrial exhibition is shown diagrammatically in Fig. 1, p. 22, and the definitions used are interpreted in the glossary Table 1. The titles of exhibitions, their aims, their time classifications, the significance of the geographical location and the importance of the exhibition catalogue are discussed in nine sections of this chapter. Individual elements of the exhibition structure which require attention and scrutiny are examined to provide a basis for the review of motives for exhibiting and visiting, for the evaluation of merits of exhibitions and for the final selection and decision taking procedure.

1. Classification of Exhibitions

The pursuit of exhibition activities by both exhibitors and visitors would be greatly assisted by a classification system, that is by an orderly arrangement of facts relating to the conduct of the exhibition business. To be workable such a classification system must have a clearly stated practical purpose and to be effective its objectives must be limited to that purpose.

An attempt to classify current exhibitions and trade fairs produces great difficulties if the requirements of a genuine classification system are to be met.

The interests of exhibitors and visitors would require the classification system to enable them:

> to locate all exhibitions nominally suitable for defined objectives and tasks by virtue of:
>> the exhibition aims and programme
>> the exhibition time and location
> to assess the respective merits of these exhibitions in relation to exhibitors/visitors objectives, resources and restraints
> to make a final selection of suitable venues.

On first thought it would seem that the suitability of an exhibition can be ascertain from its published titled and programme of activities and that the importance of an exhibition can be measured by its capacity to attract an optimum attendance of exhibitors and visitors of the right calibre. Here we encounter the first difficulty in the form of the duality of the basic interests of exhibitors and visitors, in their role as buyers and sellers and of the interaction of these two interests.

However the motives of both exhibitors and visitors are by no means all of a simple buying or selling character, nor are the merits of exhibitions merely a matter of counting exhibitors and visitors.

The growing interdependence of national economics is reflected in the growing internationalisation of many exhibitions which traditionally had a regional or national character.

Exhibits seen at truly international exhibitions bear witness to the decline of frontiers as economic and political obstacles to the manufacturing and marketing activities of one firm in several countries, and to the increasing number of products including components and accessories made in different countries. Mergers, conglomerates, horizontal and vertical integration activities on an international scale also become evident, be it obliquely by virtue of the displayed range of goods, be it manifestly by means of a deliberate display of the international capabilities of a new combination of enterprises.

In the wake of this internationalisation many minor ventures delude exhibitors, visitors and mostly themselves by placing the 'international' tag in front of whatever title their effort has. Their reputation and future business would be much better served if they declared what they really are, which is mostly a small exhibition of specialised interest, and if they exploited a well defined market segment on sound marketing principles. They could then plan for steady growth, instead of suffering a painful descent on the sharp edges of a seesaw diagram of regression.

World Fairs are perhaps the unintentional expression of an ultimate marketing concept attitude as they serve a universe of exhibitors, users and consumers, combining the display of the fulfilment of current needs with a hopeful if sometimes optimistic look into a brighter future. Their futuramas have an air of technological forecasting. They have the potential power to influence the market place in matters of taste, fashion and awareness of technologies. Their remoteness from direct or immediate purchasing possibilities perhaps adds some credibility to the professions of the participating exhibitors to serve no one but the customer.

The titles of recent world fairs such as 'man and his world' of the Montreal Expo '67 or 'Harmony for Mankind' of the Osaka Expo '70 disclose at least their ambitious aims, if not always their actual achievements. The influence of great world fairs as an international sociological and economo-political phenomenon would deserve a full scale study, quite beyond the framework of this book.

Due to their gigantic size and scope only treasurers of very large corporations and of national coffers can provide the resources required to meet the expense of participating.

General Trade Fairs and Exhibitions usually combine industrial and consumer goods and in some cases also agricultural equipment and produce. The great majority are known by the town or region in which they are held, whilst their scope and aim as declared in the prospectus may change from time to time. Many general trade fairs are held twice a year mostly in spring and autumn.

The majority of general trade fairs are *international* events, but there are also *national* events such as the Swiss Industries Fair in Basle, the Swiss National Autumn Fair in Lausanne and the German Industries Exhibition in West Berlin.

Examples of general trade fairs and exhibitions of declared *regional* character are: Lake Constance Fair in Friedrichshafen, International Mediterranean Fair in Palermo, Provincial Exhibition in Quebec City.

Many general fairs originated as *samples fairs*, some still retain that title, some like the Leipzig Fair only the symbol. Examples of general trade fairs serving the exchange of goods between two countries, mostly neighbours, are the Anglo-Dutch Exhibition held in Ipswich and the Franco-British Trade Fair held in Dieppe.

The *combination of industrial and consumer goods* in one trade fair has many critics, but seems justified for small or compact markets, which are perhaps remote from the mainstream of trade and commerce. From a buying point of view such a general fair enables buyers who may be dealing in both types of goods to survey the offering. From a selling point of view, the country or region can display all it has to offer in a better and more effective manner, than it could do for separate sectors of its capacity.

In sophisticated markets general trade fairs develop into a conglomeration of specialised sections, catering for industrial, consumer durables and consumer goods. They become in effect a number of separate specialised exhibitions sharing the same exhibition grounds and the same date and time.

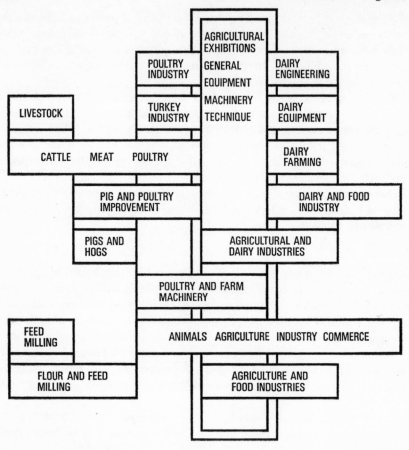

TABLE 2. AGRICULTURAL AND AGRICULTURE AFFINITY EXHIBITIONS

The table shows exhibitions directly linked to the main body of general agricultural exhibitions, with definite affinity to agriculture and including the term agriculture in their title.

Table 3 shows exhibitions of a secondary affinity resulting from a direct connection of food to agriculture.

TABLE 3. FOOD EXHIBITIONS AND FOOD AFFINITY EXHIBITIONS

The table shows exhibitions directly linked with the main body of general food exhibitions, and with more or less close affinities to food as an industrial concept. Food exhibitions have a primary affinity to agricultural exhibitions thus providing the link between the two groups.

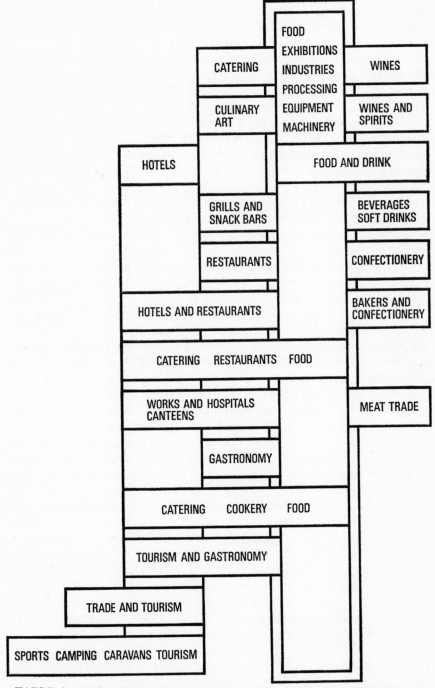

TABLE 3. FOOD EXHIBITIONS AND FOOD AFFINITY EXHIBITIONS

The arguments for and against such general ventures are many and varied. Local pride and organisers' ambitions, trade associations' and other interests enter into the controversy, the existence of exhibition halls or the plans to build new ones, the granting or threat of withdrawal of municipal subsidies play their role. The merits of alternative solutions from the point of view of the marketing interests of the customers namely exhibitors and visitors seem to remain somewhere in the background instead of being the primary consideration. *Local exhibitions* are mostly organised by trade associations with specialised interests or by trading or manufacturing groups with common interests within a defined geographical area. Often the emphasis is not so much on actual products as on a display of manufacturing, subcontracting or servicing facilities. Such local exhibitions are also used by firms from outside the area, displaying their local distribution, spares depot and service facilities. In highly industrialised areas firms of national or even international standing participate in local exhibitions to display their capacity to supply auxiliary products, particularly of consumable character such as lubricants, cleaning materials, abrasives, small tools, etc., and occasionally they use the occasion for recruiting local agents and representatives. Contacts made during such exhibitions are usually in the area of medium level buying decisions and decision influences and of a small to medium bracket of expenditure budgets.

Agricultural fairs and exhibitions are one of the oldest manifestations of marketing techniques and even today they occupy a numerically leading position in the total multitude of all types of exhibitions. They range in importance from not more than a glorified local cattle market to *great international exhibitions* covering livestock, produce and equipment. They have also produced a number of *specialised* offshoots and divisions into separate livestock, produce and machinery exhibitions. Even the most international of them retain a strong regional or local flavour and there is little doubt that their natural propensity to seasonal timing has influenced the not always rational following of other exhibitions into the same crowded seasons.

As the industrialisation of agriculture has grown over the years, so have the entries of equipment, implements and, lately of aids to administration and management.

The potential scope of agricultural fairs and exhibitions as marketing targets, reaches into a great variety of sectors of the economy. At one end of the spectrum there are buckets, brushes, gifts and toys; at the other bulldozers and silos. Biological, environmental and soil sciences are involved, and so are aspects of human and animal health and comfort. The interrelations with forestry, horticulture are natural, the affinity to food production obvious. A schematic representation of these relations is shown in Tables 2 and 3.

Consumer and Industrial Exhibition titles are based on the most popular and facile market classification of exhibitions into consumer goods and industrial goods events. The division is unambiguous for such goods as turbines and cosmetics but it loses validity for trade fairs combining the two kinds of goods and for goods on the border line of the division or those straddling it or changing from one sector to another depending on application. Many general trade fairs with half yearly frequency devote the spring fair to consumer goods and the autumn fair to industrial products or vice versa. However at the so-called consumer durables end of the range the dividing lines between consumer and industrial goods become somewhat blurred and some products make their way from one category to another. The high technical content and service requirements of some consumer durables brings them much nearer to the family of industrial products. On the other hand many industrial products like fasteners, hand tools, consumable tools, are by their nature more consumable than industrial. The crossing and re-crossing of the imaginary consumer-industrial frontier by such products as do-it-yourself equipment or packaging containers, further clouds the issue. Apart from organisational and structural differences of the industrial and consumer environment, buyers in both sectors seem to be motivated as much by emotions as by cold assessments and in the final, person to person, encounter show more similarities than differences in their purchasing behaviour.

General Industrial Exhibitions and Specialised Exhibitions cover industrial products and services in a range depending on the aim and programme of the individual event. As they are the main subject of this study they are dealt with in detail in the chapters on exhibition titles and those following.

Exhibitions within Exhibitions are special displays within the general framework of an exhibition and can range from modest information stands to grandiose national pavilions. Trade associations, industrial or commercial groupings, regional or municipal authorities, governments and government departments, utilities, public services, Chambers of Commerce, display their activities and services connected in some way with the aims of an exhibition. Large corporations with multi-product or multi-market activities have self-contained sections or pavilions displaying the whole range of their products and offerings.

Congresses, Conferences, Conventions, Symposia are in many cases organised as events complementing established exhibitions, in others these meetings of people are the main events and exhibitions are an appendage to them. The relative importance of the two elements in such combined activities range widely. A gathering of scientists of great eminence is taken by suppliers of relevant instruments or equipment as an opportunity to show their wares and to offer lavish hospitality.

An exhibition displaying new technological concepts or important innovations is taken as an opportunity for serious discussions of the problems involved.

Between these two types of initiatives there are combinations ranging from some equipment and a lot of lectures, through half equipment and half lectures, to a few lectures and a great mass of equipment.

An apocryphal story relates that some black sheep of the exhibition fauna organise exhibitions on the basis of conferences to which they invite as speakers executives of companies which they then persuade to take stands in the exhibition hall which in the event remains half empty.

World Trade Centres are complexes of buildings occupied by rent paying firms of international provenance, by government agencies, purchasing missions, and other official or semi-official bodies concerned with international marketing activities.

Although essentially designed as information exchange centres, these complexes usually include exhibition facilities of permanent or temporary character.

The most prominent of these centres in the course of completion is the New York World Trade Centre which is reputed to be a £240 million project. The architectural features of the centre are breath-taking and so are the estimates of 50,000 people who will work in the centre and of 80,000 visitors daily. Whether these numerical estimates will be realised, remains to be seen, but what is more important is whether the international marketing opportunities created by comprehensive information and display facilities will be fully utilised.

Other world trade centres are rising in many countries. In Brussels a 130 acres complex including exhibition halls is scheduled for completion in 1975 and two more centres are planned in Belgium, one in Antwerp and another in Liege. The London World Trade Centre is scheduled for completion in 1978.

The Tokyo world trade centre is being built and three more centres in Japan, four in Germany and two in the Netherlands are in the course of advanced planning.

A three-tower complex is planned as a world trade centre in Pyrmont, New South Wales. The World Trade Centre Association sponsors and co-ordinates the activities of centres, plans data exchanges among centres and the means of trade centre participation in Interfile.

National Trade Centres are usually organised by official, semi-official, or other promotional bodies in domestic or foreign markets. These centres have permanent exhibition facilities which are also utilised for periodically mounted special exhibitions. In foreign locations official sponsorship can add prestige and importance to the displays and special promotions, and it is particularly helpful in issuing invitations and supporting them by receptions and other forms of hospitality.

To executives of potential customer firms a personal invitation issued by a commercial attaché or, perhaps, even by an ambassador usually makes a strong enough impression to secure a good response.

Economic Activity Exhibitions deal with such subjects as export or import trade, insurance, banking, finance, credit, leasing and investment and such other specialised activities which can be interpreted as coming under that heading. These exhibitions are not very numerous and unless a very specific objective is their aim, the same interests are usually more effectively represented at major international exhibitions, where there is a ready made gathering of potential customers.

Touring Exhibitions are itinerant events and their main characteristics are that they come to their visitors' doorstep or as near as it is possible for them to do, and their life span can extend over weeks and months. They can be private ventures organised by one firm, or serve a group of exhibitors of related interests. The dissemination of knowledge of manufacturing techniques and of concepts such as industrial waste recovery, safety, hygiene and welfare are often the subjects of travelling exhibitions organised by official or semi-official bodies. Vans, caravans, trailers, aircraft and cruisers, portable build ings and plastic domes which can be blown up, are some of the exhibition halls of touring exhibitions. The effectiveness of touring exhibitions should be assessed on the basis of their subjective aims. Touring exhibitions often serve as a vehicle for a single or special campaign and their cost effectiveness is then assessed by special criteria.

Mobile exhibition structures can be also incorporated in conventional exhibitions, particularly in open air areas as outdoor stands, or as demonstration facilities supplementing indoor exhibition stands.

Private Exhibitions are held by individual firms in specially hired halls or hotels and are mounted in connection with special campaigns or sales drives or service campaigns. On occasions, when stand space cannot be secured at a current public exhibition, a private exhibition is arranged as a compensation.

Showrooms can be regarded as a form of private permanent exhibition if conceived as such as a matter of a deliberate policy, i.e. a policy of using the showroom as an active marketing medium, which serves sales promotion, public relations and information and educational objectives.

In addition to the display of the range of products manufactured and where appropriate, facilities for demonstrations or performance tests, the history of the company, its research and development capacity, the scope of marketing and service arrangements, perhaps also important achievements and awards, can be displayed.

Works visits by customers and potential customers can be encouraged, professional institutes, schools, colleges and university faculties are invited to

B

visit the works. Some firms have specially trained personnel in attendance at such visits and depending on the standing and qualifications of the visitors appropriately qualified members of the staff assist at conducted tours.

Open days are extensions of random visit arrangements and on such occasions the whole establishment becomes an exhibition for specially invited or selectively admitted guests.

Firms with training schools for operators of their products can make very good use of showrooms with ingenious displays, sectionalised equipment, models of operating principles, slides, films and other audio-visual aids. It can be argued that such arrangements cannot be classed as exhibitions, but it is a fact that the displays and exhibits used, provide an excellent inspiration, if not the actual items for, what might be called, true exhibitions.

The effectiveness of showrooms depends to some extent on the location of the main establishment and on whether they are directly connected with the main establishment or are separate from it. Works in regions remote from centres of commerce or difficult to reach may require separate showrooms in cities of national or regional importance, whilst works easy to reach from main business centres can have showrooms attached to their headquarters. The main difference between public exhibitions and these private quasi-exhibitions is the absence of competitors and of uninvited visitors and the absence of restraints of location and time. The choice of exhibits, the manner of displaying and the choice of visitors are all matters of internal decisions.

A showroom can be an excellent private exhibition only if the space allocated is suitable for effective presentation of exhibits, if information elements such as films, transparencies, multilingual audio-visual aids, etc., are in working order and are up-to-date. Most important of all, competent personnel must be available, to show, demonstrate, explain and conduct visitors, all this without being a burden to normal day-to-day activities.

Occasionally one encounters showrooms which by their decor and show-pieces proclaim past glories instead of current activities, and which somehow manage to produce an aura of obsolescence. Highly polished brass doorknobs bear witness that cleaners are probably the only visitors. When there is a sudden influx of visitors and the showroom has to be used as a waiting room, there are apologetic remarks by executives-hosts and mental notes to do something about it. Perhaps.

The views on the merits, demerits, costs and nuisance value of these quasi-exhibitions activities vary considerably. However if the objectives of the exercise are clearly defined in terms of aims, means and resources and if they are then effectively pursued on that basis, it soon becomes apparent whether the purpose is being achieved.

Exhibitions without Exhibition Halls are sales promotion ventures for consumer goods lasting from one to several weeks and arranged with local or regional sales outlets shops, stores and accompanied by cultural events, arts exhibitions, theatre and film performances. These ventures are usually supported or assisted by official bodies or government departments. Book weeks and similar product oriented ventures are sponsored by interested trade associations, e.g. wine testing days, national food product sponsorship, folk-art or national speciality displays. Stall holders who graduated from their booths and stalls mounted in medieval thoroughfares, squares and market places, to lock-up shops in later times, now return to some extent to these streets. Festive seasons, celebrations of historic or pseudo-historic events, anniversaries of all kinds, serve as motive or pretext for elaborate decorative schemes and illuminations. Shopkeepers who would normally remain behind their imposing façades relying mainly on their shopwindows to attract customers, now again move out into the street like their slightly less respectable brethren in less sophisticated places, and by personal appearance ensure that by-passers are suitably invited and persuaded to enter their establishments.

One often wishes that exhibition stand personnel would serve a short apprenticeship with such traders just to learn the rudiments of the art.

On some occasions the favourable atmosphere created by these special promotions is exploited and used as a background for a sales drive for industrial products.

Exhibitions in the USA
In the USA the exhibition scene is characterised by the importance of conventions and conferences many exhibitions being regarded only as supporting events rather than of primary importance in their own right.

A list of 173 conventions, exhibitions and trade shows in the 1971/1972 calendar issued by the US Department of Commerce states that 'conventions and trade show managements listed welcome attendance at their meetings from abroad'.

The 173 events listed can be arranged under three collective headings of conventions, exhibitions, and combined conventions and exhibitions.

The different descriptions given to events under these main headings are shown in the table below which also indicates the numerical relations:

CONVENTIONS	64	37%
(Conventions, Congresses, Conferences, Forums, Meetings, Scientific Meetings and Sessions)		
EXHIBITIONS	48	28%
(Expositions, Shows, Trade Shows, Fairs, Displays, Bourses)		
CONVENTIONS AND EXHIBITIONS	61	35%
(Combined events of convention items with exhibition items)		
Total	173	100%

In the brief description of the aims and scope of the events listed, the discussion of *management problems* and the advancement of management interests is specified in eight events and the problems and advancement of marketing is specified in twenty-two events. Thus in contrast to exhibitions in other countries where the emphasis is still only on selling, in the USA the discussion and demonstration of management and marketing techniques is considered as a normal part of exhibition activities.

Some examples of the programme descriptions will illustrate the point:

> An annual 'working convention' of the Bank Marketing Association 'also features exhibit booths containing products and services of interest in marketing bank's services'.

> A meeting of the Livestock Marketing Congress serves the 'advancement of marketing methods and concepts'.

> At a Machine Tool Show 'management conferences for metal working executives will be held'.

These are of course the declared aims and programme intentions, the reality of them would have to be assessed after the event, but it is interesting to note the previously quoted invitation for attendance from abroad to meetings and conventions, some of which in other countries would be the closed preserve of trade associations not open to outsiders.

2. Exhibition Titles

The title is a distinctive character feature of an exhibition, particularly if it is an expression of its objectives and scope. The manner in which the title objectives are achieved and the continuity of that achievement in the end determine the character of an exhibition. Long established General Trade Fairs and Exhibitions usually carry in their title the name of their host town or region and some venerable institutions still retain their medieval invocation of patron saints. Their aims and scope are defined by tradition and usage, some have changed their character in keeping with modern trends, some mix trade and popular amusement as of old.

The change in an exhibition title can reflect as much a real change in technological objectives as a superficial following of current fashion or an artificial attempt to elevate the descriptive title from a humble trade level to the lofty heights of science.

The emergence of new technologies, products, processes creates a bandwagon effect which encourages several new exhibition ventures to sprout on the same patch, when one would be sufficient.

After one or two appearances they wither to nothing to link with others in what is claimed to be a logical combination. Maintenance becomes terotechnology, lubrication tribology, and what was once waste disposal graduates through materials reclamation to pollution and environmental control.

Some offsprings of sedate parents become in fact fully fledged and bouncing in their own right, e.g. cryogenics from refrigeration, fluidics from hydraulics and pneumatics. There are exhibition titles, mostly of a 'new' or 'first of its kind' variety, which on closer inspection reveal that the change of title is no more than an attempt to be just that much different from an established competitor.

However there are also titles which are so definite and expressive that no doubt can be entertained as to the aim of an exhibition, even if at some of them marketing eyebrows may be raised in wonder. Here are some examples: Aerosols exhibited in Nice, Montreux and Amsterdam, bathrooms and kitchens in Stockholm, border commerce in Ljubljana and Subotica, springs and spring making machinery in Manchester, corsets and ladies underwear in Paris, urban equipment in Nancy, disposables in London. A sociologist may be interested in an exhibition on matrimony, parenthood and adolescence in Essen and on childhood, youth and family in Paris. Sometimes 'new' or 'first of its kind' exhibitions assume alluring titles which to visitors from near and distant shores, uninitiated into the semantics of a newly invented title, hold the promise of interesting and revealing events and useful contacts. Not all of these expectations come true.

Thus for instance a press release announced that a forthcoming

'INTERNATIONAL RESEARCH AND DEVELOPMENT EXHIBITION & CONFERENCE in London has attracted attention from all over the world, and the exhibits already booked range from: New Materials in the Engineering field; Food Technology; Electronics; Ceramics; and numerous new ideas and inventions'.

A leaflet giving details of the exhibition and conference programme stated:

'International Research and Development Exhibition & Conference will stimulate awareness and appreciation of the commercial scope awaiting exploitation of the world's wealth of know-how in scientific and techno-logical research.

'Whereas the achievements of scientists and research groups have received due recognition, many acclaimed as representing a major break-through, their spin-off in terms of full scale application still has vast unrealised potential.

'At this Exhibition there will be demonstrated the products, processes and apparatus offered by exhibiting firms and organisations for sale, licensing, adaptation, development to meet specific requirements or negotiation of agency, franchise and other forms of joint venture agreements.'

Two technologists from a Common Market country decided to visit the exhibition. They were impressed by the promising statements of the aims and of 'the world wide interest' and were eager to glean something of the 'world's wealth of know-how' from a country due soon to make its technological contribution to the Common Market. As a request for an advanced copy of the exhibition catalogue remained without response, they made discreet enquiries. The replies prompted their decision to cancel their visit. They requested a consulting engineer of their acquaintance, a Londoner and interested in R & D problems, to inform them whether they had perhaps missed an important event. His actual report is not suitable for reproduction except for the factual description of the stands and participants. This reads:

'There were twenty-seven stands in the exhibition. The National Research Development Corporation stand showed ten items of inventions and projects developed in partnership with, or with the support of the NRDC.

'Three Universities had stands, and were offering their R & D services. The UK Atomic Energy Authority, The Marine Industries Centre and the Fulmer Research Institute were represented. The Patents Office and the Science Museum (not listed) had stands. One manufacturing company exhibited items of their R & D activity and offered their services.

'One computerised licensing information service and one engineering data service were represented.

'Three professional institutions participated (Physics, Measurement and Control, Independent Laboratories).

'Ten companies offered: Indian telephone equipment, process plant fabrications, testing and measuring instruments, polishing and lapping equipment, a fork lift truck, a concrete repair service and a document

copying service announcing in the catalogue that "attractive hostesses
will be available to help visitors with all copying problems".
'Four stands were occupied by publishing companies.'

Objective information about exhibitions is not easily obtainable without
special effort on the part of the information seeker. The scarcity, paucity and
ambiguity of the information readily accessible, is surprising for a product
so widely sold at such high prices. Detailed information can only be obtained
by approaching promoters, organisers or representatives of exhibitions, but
that procedure in itself requires considerable effort. Thus, the ground is laid
for hasty decisions, cancellations, or simply giving up in despair.

Most lists of exhibitions which are generally available are compiled in a
way which suggests that those compiling them assume that the user knows
enough about exhibitions to find what he needs even if the presentation is not
very effective.

Group headings taken over from traditional industrial classifications compiled for entirely different purposes often lead to misunderstandings or even
absurd arrangements.

When new titles appear they are included in a product group formally
justified, but closer scrutiny often reveals that the basis for such an inclusion
is a misunderstanding of the technological meaning of an exhibition title or
perhaps a bad translation of that title from a foreign language.

The arrangement under product group headings has also the disadvantage
that the titles of exhibitions include items which could legitimately appear
under several other headings, so that several entries would be required. The
appearance of new titles leads to the need for creating new group titles or to
the inclusion of the new exhibition title in groups so remote, that only the
compiler understands the connection. There is no doubt that the variety and
complexity of exhibition titles contributes to the difficulty of arranging them
under meaningful group headings, but the obvious remedy for such a difficulty, namely the provision of an exhaustive index including also subtitles
seems to escape the great majority of compilers of exhibition lists.

There are many reasons for such a state of affairs; one of them could well
be that the process of classifying exhibition information is left to clerical
staff without sufficient discriminatory abilities, so that incoming information
is interpreted on the basis of direct dictionary translations. These sometimes
produce curious titles such as an exhibition of 'blind and revolving shutter
products' and the classifying of 'alimentary equipment' under 'other engineering' instead of under 'food machinery'. These are complaints of minor importance; the problem becomes more serious when an attempt is made to
assess the scope of general titles like 'engineering' or 'technical and industrial',
'trade and commerce', 'world wares', 'crafts and industries'. The vagueness of
these titles is only matched by the vagueness of the decision making process
which uninitiated newcomers to the exhibition scene are advised to adopt in

making the choice on the basis of 'excellent attendances from many different countries.' Assuming that the data currently available would allow us to classify, if not all, at least a great number of the exhibitions in accordance with a system built on the requirements of exhibitors and visitors, there remains the aspect of the quality of the classified exhibitions.

An exhibition may claim by its title, by its programme and by the number of domestic and foreign exhibitors and visitors to exert an international influence and in the formal numerical sense that may be true. Whether the quality of these visitors is of interest to the prospective exhibitor or vice versa is another matter.

There are many exhibition organisers (in the UK about 260), and advisory organisations who can assist but to an outside observer it is a matter of surprise that the exhibition industry which provides as a product such an excellent medium of marketing communications, should be satisfied to use for its own marketing effort a manner of communications so much less than the best available.

3. History of Exhibition

The history and life span of an exhibition is one of its character features and although old age does not necessarily mean decay, youth does not guarantee progress either. What matters most is the maturity of an exhibition as a marketing medium. If a certain exuberance, not quite matched by organisational skill can be excused in a well conceived new venture, one must also make allowances for some measure of organisational stiffness in old established events which have been on the scene for a long time.

Exhibitions can be old, established, recently established and new ventures, but these terms are of necessity of relative significance. The Leipzig Fair celebrated its 800th anniversary in 1965, industrial exhibitions have been in existence for 200 years, the Hanover Fair rose to international eminence within the last 24 years. New highly specialised events need no tradition, if they really fill a marketing need, well established exhibitions can show clear signs of stagnation or decline if they are of the 'we have always done it that way' school.

A well documented review of *historical progress* supported by factual proof can assist in long term planning considerations, as it eliminates doubts about the future viability of an exhibition.

The history of an exhibition provides valuable background information within the frame of the assessment of its general and individual marketing merits.

4. Promoters, Sponsors, Supporters, Organisers

An exhibition can be promoted and organised by the same body, it can be promoted by one organisation, supported or sponsored by another, organised by a third and mounted in the exhibition hall of a fourth. It can of course be initiated, promoted, organised and mounted by the same organisation in its own exhibition facilities. The opportunities for an exemplary display of co-operation, high organisational skill and diplomacy are many. And so are the pitfalls of misunderstandings, crossed lines of communication, local or national idiosyncrasies, plain inefficiency and helpless muddle.

There is no general remedy except to apply best management criteria and techniques in assessing the quality of the exhibition organisation, to exert control from the highest level in the matter of final choice and to institute a method of reporting and assessment which will at least prevent repetitions of past failures, at best ensure success of future efforts.

The *sponsorship and support of exhibitions* can range from a formal eulogy on the first pages of the exhibition catalogue followed by a speech at the opening ceremony, to full active and organisational assistance. It can also imply the protection of specialised interests.

The sponsorship by a trade or other association may have considerable influence on the number and quality of exhibitors, depending in turn on the strength and character of the membership of the association. Such sponsorship can also have a negative influence, e.g. preferential treatment of association members and restrictions or exclusions of non-members, discrimination in stand allocation, etc.

The reputation, standing and organisational skill of an *exhibition organiser* is a contributory merit rating factor, but its influence is mainly felt when it reaches negative values. The business of exhibitions, and a very big business it is, is subject to the same marketing criteria which apply to other goods or services. In this case the product offered is a medium of communications between exhibitors and visitors. Both exhibitors and visitors are customers who constitute the market. The most beautiful exhibition hall without exhibitors would attract no visitors, the most impressive collection of exhibits would have no purpose unless it was seen by visitors. Successful exhibitions are the result of a good marketing concept, of good management and of an understanding for the business needs and human comforts of all customers.

Badly conceived exhibitions have the unfortunate propensity to distribute loss and disappointment impartially to both exhibitors and visitors. An exhibition with badly conceived aims or objectives will not become a good marketing medium only by virtue of being excellently organised in the technical sense of the operation. But the effects of inadequate preparation and organisation can seriously lower the marketing merit of the best conception. The operating capacity of exhibitors and the absorption capacity of visitors is affected, and in extreme cases the reputation of the exhibition suffers despite its inherent marketing values.

And yet some exhibition organisers see their aim only as selling as much floor space at as high a price as the market will stand, at as low a rate of investment in facilities as they can get away with. They are no doubt confirming their historical fairground and side shows lineage, by being very good short term showmen, providing primitive services in not very congenial surroundings, but accompanying the effort by much self-satisfied, self-advertising and self-congratulating noises. There are of course many well organised and well attended exhibitions, which is as it should be, but, even so, strange and paradoxical contrasts can occasionally be observed between the main theme of an exhibition and its services and facilities. Here are some examples:

> A shortage of exhibition catalogues on the second day of an Information Fair, in which the latest achievements in data processing were shown.

> You were invited at the entrance at another exhibition to have a plastic visiting card embossed 'to help you make the most of your time at this exhibition. . . . quick, simple and sure way of obtaining the information you require', in effect you had to queue for 10 minutes to obtain the card.

> At a waste disposal exhibition, the floor was littered with empty plastic cups and papers, refuse bins were overflowing.

> At a food industry exhibition there was bad restaurant service, stale sandwiches, appalling litter of used serviettes and of empty sample containers, etc.

The unfortunate corollary of the situation is that bad organisers seem reluctant to learn from their mistakes, whilst good ones seem to improve their successful ventures all the time.

Part of the problem lies in the fact that only one class of customer—exhibitors—have direct access to organisers, and even that access varies considerably in the degree of influence it exerts, whilst the other class—visitors—have no way to express their views except by being absent, or complaining *post factum*.

The elements affecting the organisation merit of an exhibition are usually listed in the prospectus of organisers with varying amounts of detailed descriptions. It must also be said that there are occasions when the provision of services is more an expression of optimistic intentions than of actual arrangements. Many a disappointment of a delayed completion of the stand, its unsatisfactory furnishing and other shortages result not so much from lack of preparation on the part of the exhibitor as from too much faith in the promises of the exhibition prospectus.

The check lists of the organisational and administrative elements are intended as an indication of the points to watch. They may prove too elaborate for one event or not detailed enough for another. Their purpose is not to say that every time you participate in an exhibition or visit an exhibition your task is to check all the points. An established and well organised exhibition will provide most of the data on its own initiative or on request. If you had an opportunity to verify their claims of services on one or more previous occasions you will have already established a merit rating for that exhibition. They are check lists as much for your preparation as for an assessment of that aspect of the structure of an exhibition. But what to the experienced exhibitor is clear at a glance, is not so apparent to a newcomer or to stand personnel first time abroad.

As a result of superficial impressions during a short visit, visitors from your own or other organisations may blame you for shortcomings which should be really laid at the door of exhibition organisers. Conversely, the lack of knowledge of all exhibition facilities may result in neglecting opportunities for valuable contacts and openings, thus reducing the effectiveness of a costly exercise.

The 'quality' of the technical and personal comfort facilities of an exhibition affects the capacity of stand personnel to perform their tasks and the capacity of visitors to absorb the offerings.

The check lists are also important aids for re-assessing your original exhibiting aims and objectives in the light of the reality of a selected exhibition. It may be that you can expand your aims because a particular exhibition offers more scope for your activities than originally required, or perhaps you have to restrict your objectives because to try to achieve them in an exhibition of low quality would put too much of a strain on your staff.

The realisation of the facilities for potential contacts will also indicate preparatory actions such as the issue of invitations to visit your stand, and most important, it may affect the selection and numbers of stand personnel.

5. Location of Exhibitions

The *geographic location* can be a significant factor of importance to the exhibitor:

The distance of the location from the exhibitor's base determines the cost of resources in terms of time, travel and transport for stand personnel, exhibits and equipment.

Climatic conditions can affect the selection of the stand personnel and may impose restrictions from a health and endurance point of view. The preparation and selection of exhibits may also be affected.

The geographic location is important in relation to competing exhibitions and other marketing activities. These can take place in times before and after the exhibition, and in places en route to and further afield from the exhibition.

For an exhibitor participating in one or two exhibitions, the geographic location is a technical detail. For exhibitors with widespread market interests, the geographic location of all the events in the programme and the incidence of marketing visits to several countries poses serious problems of co-ordination. A distant geographic location can become a decisive factor which can endanger the participation in an otherwise attractive exhibition.

In such cases this participation can be combined with sales promotion visits to the host country of the exhibition and to neighbouring territories. A logistic approach to such multiple marketing activities can make an impressive contribution to operation and cost effectiveness. The actual location site of an exhibition can be *permanent*, i.e. at the established frequency cycle the exhibition returns to the same exhibition site or locality. The location can be *mobile-peripatetic*, i.e. the locations are changed within a defined choice of different locations in an established sequence. Finally the location can be *mobile-free*, i.e. the location is changed without any predetermined rules.

All types of mobility can apply to exhibitions in one country as well as to international changes of location.

The mobility aspect of exhibitions is important from the point of view of long range planning of participation and requires careful scrutiny of venues and their sequences in case there are significant differences in facilities, organisational skill and environmental factors between one event and another.

6. Exhibition Administration and Services

The quality of an exhibition and its effectiveness as a marketing tool for the declared area of interest depends not only on the soundness of its conception, but also on the services, facilities and amenities which it offers to the exhibitor and to the visitor. The organisation of an international exhibition demands the application of varied administrative skills of a high standard combined with a knowledge and understanding similar to that required for a complex business undertaking dealing with customers (i.e. exhibitors and visitors) from all walks of industrial and commercial life.

The *administrative and organisational structure* of an exhibition in most cases reflects the organisational standards of the promoters or sponsors of the exhibition. There are occasions when the administrative skill of an exhibition organiser is superior to that of the promoters or sponsors. In that case exhibitors and visitors are offered a marketing tool of greater effectiveness than they normally employ—providing they take full advantage of it. There are other occasions when the organiser of an exhibition does not, for one reason or another, achieve the standards which would be in keeping with the standing or importance of the subject matter of the exhibition.

In that case customers are offered a marketing tool inferior to their usual standards of effectiveness. Exhibitors and visitors are disappointed and the blame is laid at the door of the easiest target—the exhibition. The scrutiny of the available *facilities, services* and *amenities* of an exhibition is a basic preliminary assessment of its suitability for the purposes of exhibiting and of visiting. For an exhibitor this scrutiny should be not only a formal check of the facilities and services listed in the exhibition promotion literature, but a thorough investigation by a visit before the final decision, or by a review of available reliable reports and interviews with participants. A visitor takes less risks than an exhibitor and in this case discrepancies between promises and reality usually result in no more than personal discomfort and some loss of time.

7. Time Classification Elements of Exhibitions

The three time classification elements of *frequency*, *date* and *duration* of an exhibition must be carefully considered from the point of view of their relation to:

marketing programme and activities (e.g. special sales campaigns, publicity campaigns, production schedules, shortages, delivery difficulties, etc.)

seasonal marketing factors (e.g. harvest, building season, hot or cold season, stock replenishing cycles, product life cycles, etc.)

participation or visiting of other exhibitions:

    serving the same market sector or product group
    serving related market sectors
    serving other market sectors
    other interfering or competing events
    relation to personnel availability

The event frequency of the exhibition is significant for the long term planning of exhibition activities and also when related to the time characteristics of the marketing strategy of an exhibitor.

Some General Trade Fairs are staged twice each year mostly in spring and autumn, some exhibitions combining industrial and consumer goods are staged annually and rarely biennially. The effectiveness of industrial exhibitions staged at annual intervals for industrial activities with longer periods of gestation of new ideas or of significant improvements, is constantly discussed by participating exhibitors. One of the conflicts of ideas is caused by the fact of life that although a gestation period of three years may apply to a particular type of industrial equipment, not all firms start the development at the same time. The question of showing your new development too early, of giving your competitors a chance to evaluate, copy and perhaps even improve on your concept, must be weighed against the advantages of being the first in the field and related to the copying time and effort which your competitors would have to devote to following your lead.

The advocates of longer time interval events maintain that such intervals would contribute to a better maturing chance for new developments and these could be then geared to the exhibition events. Firms with projects not sufficiently advanced would, according to these theorists, be deterred from a premature display. To which others reply, that there always will be firms inclined to steal a march on competitors, no matter in what state of development their project is. The most persuasive argument is one of cost. The attendance at biennial events permits a better application of resources and a better preparation of display and manning. Biennial or longer frequency events may require some other form of display activity between main events. If the marketing objectives require more frequent exposure than a specialised exhibition can provide, private exhibitions or works exhibitions can be used to fill the gap. Participation as 'the odd man out' in other related exhibitions is occasionally used and the display of new products can be harmonised with the rarer exhibitions of sufficiently high marketing merit. From a visitor's point of view the event frequency is not so important as he can mostly substitute other means of achieving his objectives.

The *date of an exhibition* has to be related to the time scale of marketing activities, particularly if they are of seasonal character. A badly timed exhibition participation is not only costly in terms of the expenditure of human and material resources, but can also harm other activities by untimely demands on production schedules, delivery times, development programmes. The concentrated incidence of events in spring and autumn is probably due to the inheritance from the time when fairs held for trade purposes were combined with religious festivals and also to the influence of agricultural fairs held after the harvest was gathered or early in spring.

During the crowded spring and autumn seasons, the proliferation of exhibitions competing with each other for exhibitors and visitors is the source of conflicts and sometimes of despair for prospective exhibitors. Even the most experienced, seasoned and convinced supporters of exhibitions wince at the prospect of making a rational selection of suitable venues during these two seasons.

If several exhibitions serve your market sector in a close time proximity, the marketing merit factors will play an important part in your decision. If the competing exhibitions serve related market sectors, or non-related sectors which are of interest to your customers, you have to assess the relative merits of these competing exhibitions and their ability to attract some, most or all of your customers.

Personnel availability is probably already considered in your marketing programme and activities, and so are the additional factors of holiday schedules, training programmes, special functions and perhaps the seasonal incidence of illness.

The attendance at an exhibition can be affected by non-commercial events taking place at the same time either in the location of the exhibition or in a location of important customers.

Political events, elections, state visits, congresses, both in the host country of the exhibition and in neighbouring and other countries can influence the number of visitors to an exhibition.

The duration of the exhibition is significant for the exhibitor because the number of days and the opening hours of the exhibition determine the exhibition time available and thus influence the choice and number of stand personnel and the stand design strategy. Events of three to four days' duration with high marketing merits may require provisions for receiving large numbers of visitors in a short space of time. At such events it is easy to lose visitors who are also under pressure to accomplish their tasks in a short time and cannot afford to wait for attention or discuss problems in overcrowded conditions. The total number of days of the duration of an exhibition indicates the inclusion of Saturdays and Sundays, which can be important when travel arrangements and visits before and after the exhibition are taken into account.

The variations in the duration days of exhibitions are no doubt influenced by national, commercial and social customs and traditions.

These variations can be quite disconcerting to exhibitors and visitors entering the international exhibition scene and assuming that customs and usages of their home ground will apply elsewhere as well. Some exhibitions have duration periods extended so as to include a Saturday or Sunday or both and are open on these days for the public, reserving weekdays to trade and professional visitors.

The advantages and disadvantages of short versus long periods are very difficult to evaluate. For exhibitors, duration periods of more than five to six days are certainly very tiring and for medium and small firms they present a serious personnel problem.

The quality of stand personnel performance suffers during long duration exhibitions either because the same personnel finds it difficult to maintain enthusiasm throughout the period or because there are changes in the quality when relief arrangements are made.

An advantage of short duration periods of three to four days is that arrangements for the attendance of chief executives can be made with more certainty, and so visitors can also rely on meeting them.

Events of more than five days duration would have to claim a very high marketing merit to justify such an attendance for the whole time of the exhibition. An exhibition lasting three days calls for a short but very intensive effort on the part of exhibitors, but limits the choice of days for visitors who can have conflicting engagements. An exhibition lasting ten days calls for an untiring and sustained effort of the exhibitor, but gives visitors a much better chance of selecting the most convenient time for their visit. The implications of the 'total exhibition time' factor is also discussed in the paragraphs dealing with the tasks of stand personnel and visitors.

A visitor benefits from events of long duration as he has a wider choice of days on which to visit an exhibition, he can sometimes combine two or three events in one trip, or he can utilise the time between two events for other activities if they lie in the path leading to or from the exhibition.

An analysis of the time classification elements of two groups of exhibitions was made from the point of view of the month in which exhibitions are held and of the duration of these exhibitions.

One group is based on the list of 173 USA exhibitions, also discussed on page 65. The second group is based on a list of overseas exhibitions published in the UK. This list contained 610 exhibitions scheduled to take place during the twelve months June 1971 to 1972. The criteria qualifying exhibitions for inclusion in the list were not stated but their importance was implied by the 'international' label carried by the majority of the exhibitions.

It was also evident that many exhibitions which are events of biennial or longer frequency were not included. The list also included a number of consumer goods exhibitions and fashion shows with twice yearly or more frequent appearances, so that numerically their importance was exaggerated in relation to other groups.

An elaborate analysis and weighting procedure would be required to establish the relative importance or merits of the listed exhibitions, but this would not alter the fact that these exhibitions would take place in their allocated time and duration.

A total number of 610 exhibitions to be held in about 44 countries outside the UK was subjected to a time element analysis.

The location of the exhibitions was as follows:

Country	Number of Exhibitions	Subtotals	Percent of total
USA	80		
Canada	34	114	18·5%
Germany	96		
France	56		
Italy	55		
Holland	35		
Belgium	25	263	43·0%
Other European Countries (exc. UK)	161	161	26·5%
Other countries	72	72	12·0%
Totals	610	610	100·0%

TABLE 4. LOCATION OF 610 EXHIBITIONS

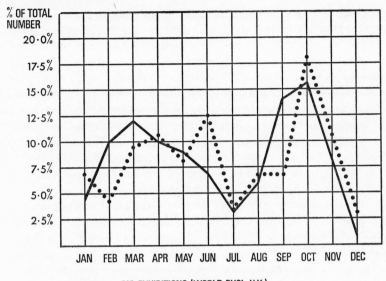

FIGURE 2. MONTHLY INCIDENCE OF EXHIBITIONS

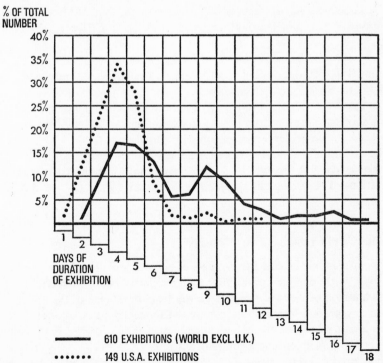

FIGURE 3. DURATION TIMES OF EXHIBITIONS

The result of the *analysis of the incidence* of the group of 173 USA exhibitions during the twelve months of the year is shown in Figure 2. October, June and November are peak months accounting together for 41.5 per cent of the total of 173 exhibitions. February, July and December are months of low activity accounting for not more than 10.5 per cent of the total.

In this list of 173 USA exhibitions, *duration periods* of 149 events could be identified and the results of the analysis are shown in Figure 3. Events of four days' duration showed the highest incidence accounting for 34 per cent of the analysed total of 149 exhibitions.

Exhibitions with three, four and five days' duration accounted for 81 per cent of the total, the group with a range of durations from three days to six days accounted for 91 per cent of all exhibitions.

The total cumulative number of days of duration of the 149 exhibitions was 672 days resulting in an average of 4.5 days per exhibition. The results of the *analysis of the monthly incidence* of the group of 610 overseas exhibitions is shown in Figure 2. September and October are peak months accounting together for 29.5 per cent of the total of 610 exhibitions, February, March and April accounted together for 32 per cent of the total. December and July are months of minimum exhibition activity, accounting for only 4 per cent of the total of 610 exhibitions. The results of the *analysis of duration times* of exhibitions is shown in Figure 3. Events of four and five days show the highest incidence accounting together for 33.5 per cent of the total of 610 exhibitions, durations of nine and ten days accounted together for 21 per cent of the total.

The total cumulative number of days of duration of the 610 exhibitions amounted to 4303 days—equivalent to almost twelve years—and the average duration time was 7 days per exhibition.

The list of 610 exhibitions included 114 exhibitions in the USA and Canada. These showed short duration times and exhibitions with three, four and five days accounted together for 83 per cent of the total.

The exclusion of these 114 North American exhibitions from the total of 610 events did not change the pattern significantly for the remaining 496 exhibitions. The average duration time rose from 7 days to 7.35 days per exhibition.

8. Schedule of Exhibition Time Elements

The assessment of the cost effectiveness of visits to and attendance at exhibitions is a fairly complex procedure, the complexity being characteristic for any evaluation of visits of personnel away from base. One of the difficulties is that any general formulation in terms of monetary values would depend for its interpretation on the cost accountancy method practised in individual firms and so defy independent comparisons.

There are however *person-time factors* which are generally valid, and their measurable values can be subjected to cost or expense allocations in accord with individual practice.

These person-time factors are elements of the time management concept and the purpose of a detailed schedule of time elements is the application of time budgeting principles to exhibition activities to enable a time-cost analysis of personnel resources deployed at exhibitions.

The *time management concept* requires not only a systematic analysis of all time elements involved in reaching your objectives but also a realistic time budgeting for such elements as waiting time, wasted time, normal rest and extra fatigue time, and a reserve time for unforeseen contingencies. In some situations a single task or a limited number of tasks can leave spare time on hand for which subsidiary or fringe interests tasks can be scheduled.

In the exhibition situation the events are of known duration and of pre-determined date and geographical location. The feasibility of accomplishing one or more exhibition taks depends on factors which are partly or wholly *controllable*, or *uncontrollable*. The location, date and duration of an exhibition is outside the control of an intending exhibitor or visitor.

For an exhibitor the preparation of participation in an exhibition is partly controllable as it depends on the time of his application and on the availability of stands.

For a visitor the preparation of a visit to an exhibition is entirely controllable. The time for travel is partly controllable as there is a minimum time governed by the fastest means of travel, whilst the choice of slower media will only result in an extension of that minimum time.

The number of hours which can be allocated as an 'exhibition working day' is partly controllable because it is governed by the exhibition opening hours.

For the exhibitor these opening hours are a required minimum as they represent stand attendance hours—which he may have to increase by providing relief personnel or by performing auxiliary tasks. For the visitor they represent a theoretical maximum which he can not extend, which he can however arbitrarily reduce.

The schedule of time elements listed in Check list 6 represents general headings which cover a majority of activities of persons attending an exhibition in the roles of exhibition stand personnel, of other persons visiting an exhibition in which their company participates and of visitors to the exhibition.

The topographical representation of the locations in which these activities take place is shown in Figure 1 (*See page* 22.) Stand design, construction, erection, dismantling, etc., is not included in the time schedule as it is often a subcontracted activity costed as a whole or dealt with separately. All activities connected with the stand construction combine time and material content so intimately, that a generally valid elimination of the time element would be very difficult.

The productive preparation time for exhibition stand personne list he time spent on briefing sessions, on the preparation of details of customers and potential customers, on listing any other contacts which have to be made, it may require liaison with other departments or divisions of the company and the co-ordination of different exhibitions interests. Technical preparations include such items as stand duty aids, technical data, price lists, discount schedules, etc.

Personal preparations would deal with such details as special clothing, spare spectacles, tape recorders, cameras, medicaments. The preparation for attending new ventures will normally take more time than that required for repeat participation, although even routine participation may require a new approach, or the extension of the scope of the exhibition effort.

For visitors to exhibitions the productive preparation time is spent on preparing the visiting task programme and on the technical preparation for the visit, e.g. schemes, installation drawings, material specifications, delivery schedules, etc.

When the visiting task includes contacts with new or potential suppliers or when it involves prior discussions with several departments, the productive preparation time can reach substantial values. On the other hand when the task is only an extension or continuation of existing supplier relationships, or a review of activities in progress, the time can be of minimum value.

Personal preparations of visitors will be similar to those of stand personnel.

The unproductive preparation time is spent on travel technicalities, i.e. reservations, tickets, internal transport arrangements, etc. It is usually absorbed as an administrative function, except perhaps in cases of intercontinental travel or large numbers of personnel, when the time factor can be allocated to specific attendances or visits.

Internal travel time is time spent on travel from base to the exhibition within a moderate radius, mostly in one region or one country, it would be a minimum for exhibitions located in the vicinity of the base. Alternatively internal travel is the time spent on travelling from a temporary base such as a hotel to the exhibition site.

External travel time is spent on international travel or on long distance travel between different locations in one country. Internal and external travel time definitions should not be regarded as rigid, they can overlap and change meaning, e.g. when international connections between two countries are simpler and faster than are nominally internal connections in others. In some cases internal travel time may be required either to reach an airport or sea port, or between two modes of travel.

The exhibition time is the total time available within the confines of an exhibition. For the exhibition stand personnel it is the time required to prepare the stand, the time of stand attendance and the time required to close the stand.

It includes rest and refreshment periods at the exhibition site.

For the visitor it is the number of hours spent at the exhibition or at several locations of an exhibition, the time spent on internal exhibition movements, and where appropriate the time spent on travel between exhibition locations; it also includes rest and refreshment periods.

The *exhibition task time* is the actual time spent on performing the allocated or programmed main and subsidiary tasks. For the stand personnel it consists of the stand attendance time and the time spent on such other exhibition contacts and activities which were specifically programmed. For the visitor it is the time spent on his scheduled visiting tasks.

The reaction which this exposé of time elements sometimes provokes is: 'Well, if it's all that complicated and uncontrollable, why bother—let's just go and see what happens'.

The reply given to opponents of time budgeting concepts is the same as that given to opponents of other management concepts: it may not always be possible to proceed as planned, it seldom is, but it will be possible to assess at each stage what has been achieved, what remains to be done and what must be left out.

Attending and visiting exhibitions is a discipline with its own technique, but once it has been mastered and systematically applied, all tasks become easier to accomplish, more productive and satisfying in results.

9. Exhibition Catalogues

The exhibition catalogue is a vital element of the exhibition effort and the actions concerned with it should be governed by the objectives motivating the participation in the particular exhibition and by general corporate image precepts. The exhibition catalogue is not only a guide for visitors to a particular exhibition, but in the case of important exhibitions also a reference book with an effective life span of one or more years.

Exhibition catalogue elements which concern an exhibitor are listed in Check list 7, p. 69. The table makes no claim to completeness, some readers will find omissions, others a surfeit of items. The intention is to draw attention to a number of elements which can be overlooked under the pressure of tight time schedules, because of too long delayed decisions, or simply because of lack of experience. The primary aim of your entries and advertisements in an exhibition catalogue is to attract, invite, induce visitors to come to your stand and to establish personal contact with your stand personnel. The term visitors, and not customers, is used advisedly for reasons argued in the discussion of exhibiting motives and objectives. It embraces customers as well as other persons with direct or indirect buying influences, or persons for whose needs you claim to cater, or whom you want to convince of your standing and capabilities.

A reader of the catalogue entry should be informed of what you exhibit, of what, if anything, you do in addition to that, and whether there are any special reasons why that particular reader should visit your particular stand.

When composing the entry, you must also consider that the reader of the catalogue may or may not be familiar with your name. Even if you know that it is a household name, he can be a newcomer to your market, or this could be his first visit abroad, or perhaps he is too young to have heard of your name.

What you exhibit and what you offer must be clearly defined and simply stated, so that it can be easily pinpointed by an interested visitor, by a minor clerk in an information centre, or by a glamorous, allegedly multilingual, but not very bright, receptionist at the exhibition entrance or foreign visitors reception.

The outlines and formal details of editorial catalogue entries are usually suggested or insisted on by the organisers, and last year's catalogue is a good guide to these details.

The lay-outs and arrangements of catalogues of different exhibitions vary greatly and no generally valid recommendations can be made. The description of your exhibits is the most important entry and the arrangement of the catalogue in question will determine the most effective way of presenting it. Next in importance are the address and style of your company and the names and addresses of your local representation and such other outposts which are relevant to the influence sphere of the exhibition.

The entry should also provide, as far as its limitations permit, an indication of your compass of business and capability. Some catalogues provide special sections for exhibitors business entries, in addition to the section listing only the exhibitor's name and his exhibits. When editorial limitations prevent comprehensive entries, and if the marketing merit of the exhibition and of its catalogue justifies it, an advertisement may provide the required space.

New products, new offerings or new benefits should be emphasised and invitations to demonstrations should be included. Special capabilities such as design or consultancy should be mentioned.

If your interests are spread over more than one section of the exhibition you should explore the opportunities for multi-entries, but then the inclusion of all products in the product index requires special attention. It is always advisable not to rely on the compilers of the catalogue to extract all relevant headings from your entry text, but to ensure inclusion and to ease their job by providing a separate list of relevant headings.

For some industries such as chemicals and plastics, an index of trade marks and trade names is of considerable importance. When last year's catalogue had no such index, it may be worth while to use your influence to ensure that it should be included in future. Attending personnel can be listed in the entry, the stand executive or manager by name, attending specialists by function only or by function and name, and the languages spoken on the stand should be indicated.

Special exhibiting objectives, e.g. a search for agents or an invitation to discuss franchise or licence arrangements should be included in the entry, as this may attract visitors who normally would not visit your stand.

Entries in foreign language catalogues should be checked by people competent to assess both the quality of the translation and of the expressions used, and their relevance to your business and to your products.

If you are new to the exhibition host country or if you are introducing new trade marks, trade names, brand names or slogans, check whether they do not conflict with regulations or offend local susceptibilities of custom, taste or even religion.

Designs, three-dimensional shapes, colours, artificial word formation, slogans can be separate or cumulative offenders. An additional pitfall is ridicule or a distortion of meaning in relation to the product, and evocative brand name formations are particularly vulnerable. To offer 'strutting cranes' may not be too bad, but 'laughing sewage pumps' seems slightly inappropriate.

The effectiveness of the exhibition catalogue as a reference book and as an advertising medium, depends to a large extent on the marketing merit of the exhibition and in some cases on the catalogue make-up and arrangement. A catalogue without a product index is useless as a reference book.

Some exhibition catalogues are compiled in a manner which makes the locating of a product of interest such a laborious procedure, that it is easier to go through all the advertisement pages than to follow the different product, stand, name, number, letter, section and page references, in a tiresome sequence. In such cases an advertisement serves partly the interest of the exhibitor and partly the dubious purpose of compensating for the shortcomings of the catalogue.

The remarks made earlier concerning foreign language entries and translations, apply to advertisements as well. In advertisements the language content can be reduced to a minimum by the use of drawings, sketches and photographs which in turn must be vetted, to avoid conflicts. The preparation and timing of all elements involved in exhibition catalogue entries and publicity should be scheduled so as to reach the exhibition organisers in time for the issue of their advance catalogue or similar advance publication. These are usually abridged versions of the catalogue, and it may be sufficient to supply provisional entry details and to amend or revise the full entries for inclusion in the final version of the exhibition catalogue at a later date.

The following entry in the catalogue of a recent international instruments and electronics exhibition is an example of a complete misunderstanding of the purpose of an exhibition catalogue.

'All instruments on display are grouped by function and each group has secondary illumination in addition to the normal stand lighting. The groups of instruments, e.g. pressure flow, temperature, etc., are coupled symbolically by a central motif consisting of several largetransparent edge-lit sheets, one for each function, each sheet carrying legends describing the function and any variant—the sheets are lit in sequence and in synchronism with the secondary illumination groups referred to above—the centre of the motif depicts the X Y Z new product, symbolising its data collection and interface function.'

Let us examine this entry from the point of view of an interested foreign visitor. All he can learn about the exhibits is that amongst them will be 'pressure, flow, temperature, etc.' instruments. He obviously wonders why the 'etc.' are exhibited if they deserve no better description. He is mystified by 'legend-carrying sheets' and wonders whether he will be able to understand these legends 'lit in sequence'. He concludes that the main purpose of the stand is to display edge-lit transparent sheets in which he is not really interested.

Considered more seriously, the entry is an antithesis of any marketing purpose of exhibiting, unless it is a sales plug for the stand designer. The entry does not inform a visitor to the exhibition of *what* is displayed, but only of *how* it is done. It has no post-exhibition value at all.

Another entry in the same catalogue is an example of how it should be done. After enumerating the range of instruments displayed and their applications, the entry concludes:

'Our capability to assume total responsibility in the food and brewing, oil and gas, pulp and paper, and marine industries is emphasized.'

In the technical press pleas are often made for an earlier publication of exhibition catalogues to enable visitors to plan their visits and to use their time economically. There are exhibitions, mostly abroad, which provide catalogues one or two months before the event. There are other exhibitions at which catalogues are only obtainable on entry, on occasions the stock is exhausted after about five hours, the next batch becoming available next day.

Some exhibition organisers show a strange disregard for visitors—who after all are also their customers—because they seem to imply that most visitors know all there is to know about exhibitors, and need no further help from an exhibition catalogue. The omission of a product index from an exhibition catalogue is not only a manifestation of such a disregard, but also of a most 'non-marketing' behaviour. In recent years at an international container exhibition, an international power transmission engineering exhibition, an international power transmission engineering exhibition, an environmental pollution control exhibition and a laboratory wares exhibition, exhibition catalogues had no product index.

A business efficiency exhibition held in 1971 had no catalogue, but only a guide in which several hundred products were arranged under thirty-three headings. When enquiries were made at the information desk, the receptionist had to refer to a 1969 catalogue, which had a product index containing

248 items. There was of course no certainty that all the same exhibitors were participating in both events. In order to find one particular product which was in fact displayed only on three stands, one had to visit 18 stands listed under the collective heading. To make the task even more difficult, the stands on the exhibition plan were printed in full black, so that any attempt at marking the shortest route was foiled. And this was a business efficiency exhibition.

In contrast, an exhibition of measuring instruments provided a separate and very clearly printed plan of stands, including the names of the exhibitors and their country of origin. It requested the visitor in French, English and German 'to mark the stands which he intends to visit, and to trace the shortest route, thus ensuring that no stand of interest will be omitted, and valuable time will be saved'.

Check List 1. *CLASSIFICATION OF EXHIBITIONS*

Whether you are an exhibitor with an established exhibition programme or a newcomer to exhibitions, you will be interested in the classification of the venues of particular interest to you, as in most media the information about them will appear under one or more classification headings. You may be interested in new ventures in your sphere of activities, you may find that general headings are not specific enough for your purpose or that some general trade fairs contain specialised sections which are much larger than some exhibitions devoted entirely to that speciality. When you have established your classification interest you will turn to check list 2 to see whether the titles of the class of interest to you, really cover your requirement or whether you have to consider more than one classification or more than one title, as relevant.

Check List 2. *TITLES, HISTORY, SPONSORSHIP AND LOCATION OF EXHIBITIONS* (page 60)

Following the review of the classification of exhibitions of interest to you (*check list 1*) you proceed to the scrutiny of their titles and their relevance to the widest definition of your interests. You then assess the past and current record of the listed exhibitions and also the quality of their promoters and organisers. The definition of the location of the exhibition will have an important bearing both on their marketing merit and the cost of participating or visiting.

World Fairs—Great International Exhibitions	
Great National Fairs and Exhibitions	
General Trade Fairs and Exhibitions	
international	
national	
regional	
samples fairs	
local	
Agricultural Fairs and Exhibitions	
international	
national	
regional	
specialised	
forestry	
horticulture	
fisheries	
Consumer Goods Exhibitions	
Industrial Goods Exhibitions	
Combined Consumer and Industrial Goods Exhibitions	
Combined Agricultural and Industrial Goods Exhibitions	
General Industrial Exhibitions	
Specialised Industrial Exhibitions	
Exhibitions within exhibitions	
Congresses, Conferences, Conventions, Symposia	
Special Type Exhibitions	
world trade centres	
national trade centres	
economic activity exhibitions	
touring exhibitions	
private exhibitions	
showrooms	
exhibitions without exhibition halls	

Check List 1. *CLASSIFICATION OF EXHIBITIONS*

	EXHIBITION TITLES	
	General	
	Group	
	industries, technologies	
	Specific	
	product, product group	
	discipline, technique	
	service	
	HISTORY OF EXHIBITION	
	history and progress of exhibition	
	character, tradition, reputation	
	statistical survey data	
	PROMOTERS, SPONSORS, SUPPORTERS, ORGANIZERS	
	government or other authority	
	independent, commercial	
	industrial or trade associations	
	professional institutions, societies	
	chambers of commerce	
	press or publishers	
	non-profit-making body	
	others	
	LOCATION OF EXHIBITION	
	geographic location	
	permanent	
	mobile—peripatetic	
	mobile—free	
	distance from exhibitor's base	
	distance from transport terminus	
	location environment	
	metropolitan	
	provincial	
	industrial	
	agricultural	
	mining	
	marine	

Check List 2. *TITLES, HISTORY, SPONSORSHIP AND LOCATION OF EXHIBITIONS*

	ADMINISTRATION	
	executive	
	secretariat	
	foreign relations	
	halls, buildings, open areas	
	technical services	
	financial	
	inland and foreign exhibitors reception	
	inland and foreign visitors reception	
	information bureaux, kiosks, desks	
	EXHIBITION PUBLICITY	
	pre-exhibition publicity, in host country, in other countries.	
	during exhibition (important in metropolitan locations)	
	publicity material for media	
	live radio, television, newsreel facilities	
	new products publicity	
	posters, leaflets	
	labels stickers, printing blocks, badges	
	press information office, regular press conferences	
	invitation cards, complimentary tickets	
	RESTRAINTS AND RESTRICTIONS	
	limitations on stand design, exhibits	
	publicity, sound, light, moving elements	
	limitations and discrimination in allocation of stands	
	formal difficulties and delays, e.g. visas, permits	
	restrictions on personnel (nationality, political)	
	restrictions on imported labour force	
	high cost of local labour and/or materials	
	lack of skilled local labour and/or materials	
	strikes, delays, postponements, cancellations	
	inadequate security, pilfering, damage	

Check List 3. *EXHIBITION ADMINISTRATION*

This check list is concerned with the administrative features of an exhibition and the implications of their strictness, liberality or laxity as they affect your own exhibiting efforts, stand design, selection of exhibits, publicity and perhaps even selection of personnel. The quality and character of the administration may be directly influenced by promoters or sponsors (*check list 2*) in some cases, or not at all, or only to some extent in others.

	EXHIBITION HALLS AND DISPLAY AREAS	
	exhibition grounds	
	exhibition halls	
	open exhibition areas	
	test and demonstration areas	
	new products section	
	SPECIAL FACILITIES FOR:	
	congresses, conferences, symposia	
	lectures, film shows	
	EXHIBITION HALLS AND DISPLAY AREAS SERVICES	
	security	
	lighting	
	heating, ventilation, air conditioning	
	public address system	
	storage facilities	
	W.C. and washing facilities	
	first aid facilities	
	STAND SERVICES	
	electricity, gas, water	
	telephones	
	compressed air, vacuum, steam	
	waste disposal, stand cleaning	
	stand erection and dismantling	
	stand decoration and repairs	
	fire protection	
	HIRE FACILITIES	
	furniture, typewriters, calculating machines, office equipment	
	refrigerators, cookers, percolators, electric kettles	
	crockery, tableware, glassware	
	fire extinguishers	

Check List 4. *EXHIBITION FACILITIES, SERVICES AND AMENITIES*

The physical facilities, services and amenities of exhibitions can vary considerably from venue to venue and are best assessed on the basis of personal experience. If your exhibiting programme includes regular participation in an exhibition, this check list can be used as a questionnaire for stand personnel or visitors, so that changes in quality or services or improvements can be noted. A dossier of services and facilities will also assist in assessing the merits of the exhibition environments and of the exhibition complex. (*check lists 12, 13*).

	SPECIAL SERVICES	
	customs clearance arrangements	
	patents protection	
	exhibitors club	
	interpreters, guides	
	travel and airline bureaux	
	hotel and accommodation reservation office	
	theatre and entertainment booking office	
	COMMUNICATIONS	
	post office, telex, international telephone service	
	public address system	
	messengers	
	AMENITIES	
	restaurants, snack bars, refreshment trolleys	
	cloak rooms, left luggage rooms, lost property office	
	baths, showers, hairdressers, massage, swimming pool	
	rest rooms, meeting rooms, shelters	
	first aid, chemists	
	shops, newspapers and magazines kiosks	
	TRANSPORT	
	parking arrangements	
	car hire facilities	
	taxi stand	
	public transport arrangements (frequency, season tickets)	
	internal exhibition transport	

Check List 4. (*continued*)

	Event frequency of Exhibition	
	single	
	seasonal	
	semi-annual	
	annual	
	biennial	
	multiennial	
	other frequency	
	Date of Exhibition	
	fixed	
	movable	
	Duration of Exhibition	
	1 day	
	2–3 days	
	4–5 days	
	6–7 days	
	8–9 days	
	other	
	Time competing events	
	other exhibitions	
	political events	
	non-commercial events	

Check List 5. *TIME CLASSIFICATION ELEMENTS OF EXHIBITIONS*

The classification check lists 1 and 2 helped you to identify exhibitions nominally of interest to your marketing effort. This check list will enable you to add the time elements of frequency, actual dates and length of duration to the record of these exhibitions. The frequency and dates will influence your overall programme and pinpoint conflicting venues. The location (*check list 2*) and duration will influence costs, time competing events can have a bearing on the attendance.

Check List 6. *EXHIBITION TIME ELEMENTS* (page 66)

This activity check list should be applied to individual exhibitions selected for participation or visiting. At first sight it may appear that it should not be used until the selection process is completed, but the listed time elements can have a decisive influence on personnel requirements and availability of several competing events, so that a preliminary review is important. The scope of the tasks which can be performed and their cost in time will be other factors affecting the merits or demerits of an exhibition.

C

	Preparation time (exhibitor or visitor)	
	productive	
	definition of objectives	
	programme of tasks	
	documentation	
	task aids	
	unproductive	
	travel arrangements	
	hotel reservations	
	formalities	
	Internal travel time (exhibitor or visitor)	
	from base to destination	
	between termini	
	between hotel and exhibition	
	External travel time (exhibitor or visitor)	
	long distance or international	
	between mixed task destinations	
	Exhibition time (exhibitor)	
	duration of exhibition	
	daily opening hours	
	stand duties	
	preparation	
	attendance	
	closing	
	extra-stand duties	
	visiting other stands	
	exhibition authority	
	conferences, symposia	
	personal contacts	
	intelligence tasks	
	fringe interests	
	rest and refreshment periods	
	internal exhibition movements	

Check List 6. *EXHIBITION TIME ELEMENTS*

	Exhibition time (visitor)		~
	number of visiting days		
	daily visiting times		
	internal exhibition movements		
	rest and refreshment periods		
	Exhibition task time (visitor)		
	direct visiting tasks		
	stands		
	contacts		
	information centres		
	intelligence tasks		
	subsidiary tasks		

Check List 6. (*continued*)

Check List 7. *EXHIBITION CATALOGUE*

The exhibition catalogue check list serves two purposes. One is to provide a guide to the benefits which can be obtained from an exhibitor's entry, the other is to assist in the evaluation of the merits of the exhibition and its administration. The failings or shortcomings of an exhibition catalogue are usually pointers to a weak administration or to a lack of co-ordination between sponsors and organizers.

	Exhibitor's individual entry	
	name, address, telephone, cable, telex	
	branches, agencies, connections	
	exhibition stand	
	exhibits	
	other products and capabilities	
	new products, new benefits	
	special items, star features	
	demonstrations, tests, lectures	
	stand executive, specialists, languages	
	invitation to discuss	
	agencies, representations	
	licensing	
	franchises	
	joint venture arrangements	
	subject index entries	
	trade name/mark entries	
	advertisements	
	in text	
	in special section	
	covers, section dividers	
	spine	
	inserts, markers	
	translations	
	entries	
	advertisements	
	slogans	
	timing	
	provisional entry	
	final full entry	
	Exhibition Catalogue quality and utility	
	exhibitors interest utility	
	visitors interest utility	
	directory value	
	pre-exhibition availability	

Check List 7. *EXHIBITION CATALOGUE*

PART TWO

Motives, Visits, Merits, Selection

The survey and appraisal of structural and organisational elements of exhibitions dealt with in chapter one provided the basis for discussing marketing *motives for exhibiting, visiting* of exhibitions, marketing *merits of exhibitions* and *final selection* of exhibitions, which are the subject of four sections of this chapter. In the first and second section the motives for exhibiting and visiting exhibitions are examined against the background of observed attitudes and the marketing motive of maintaining the share of the market is illustrated by a case study. The marketing merits of exhibitions and the influence of the different exhibition environments are the subject of the third section. The fourth section deals with the technicalities of the final selection of exhibitions for stated motives or objectives and includes comments on notional market merits and risk elements the consideration of which can assist in the decision making process.

In this chapter the check lists are placed at the end of each section.

10. Motives for Exhibiting

Attitudes to Exhibitions

A rational decision whether to participate in exhibitions and, if so, in which exhibitions must be based on a definition of your marketing motives, on an assessment of the merits of suitable exhibitions and on a selection of exhibitions compatible with your motives and your resources. Experience and continuous observation leads to the conclusion that in many cases such a rational approach to an exhibition effort is, if not completely lacking, only seldom consciously applied.

A summary of 110 interviews conducted over a period of two years will best illustrate the attitudes to exhibitions. The interviews were conducted with executives of firms regularly participating in national and international exhibitions.

The spectrum of attitudes to exhibitions, expressed by interviewed decision-making executives ranged from one extreme of absolute rejection, through indifference, passive acceptance of the inevitable, and reasoned approval, to the other extreme of uncritical enthusiasm.

A disconcerting absence of rationale was noted in a majority of strong negative statements. Persons professing to 'hate' or even 'loathe' exhibitions, or to find them 'corrosive' and 'repulsive' regarded their position and rank as sufficient proof of competence to make such pronouncements, without having to justify them. The statements made in relation to exhibitions generally were further probed to establish the degree of discrimination between 'participating' and 'visiting' activities.

Most of the shallow negative attitudes were confirmed by generalizing statements that 'it's all the same', i.e. participating and visiting activities are equally unpleasant. Executives who passively accepted the need to exhibit 'because our competitors do' did not see the need to visit exhibitions in which they did not participate. 'It would be a waste of time' or 'our salesmen are better employed in the field' and similar pronouncements disposed of the question. Positive attitudes to exhibitions were found to apply to participation as much as to visiting, with perhaps some reservations which are best characterized by one statement 'we visit as many exhibitions as we can, but we participate in as few as we can get away with'. Decisions to participate were attributed to a combination of pressures exerted by trade associations, official bodies, persuasive exhibition organisers and sponsors, who provided proof of 'all the important firms in our sector taking part'. Ever increasing demands placed on human and material resources led to decisions based on doubtful motives. In some large organisations with elaborate publicity and exhibition departments, the instinct of departmental self-preservation acted as an encouraging selection factor and the criteria applied were very far removed from sober marketing considerations.

Familiarity with an exhibition in which 'we have always taken part', the availability of elaborately prepared exhibits and stand fixtures, the preservation of a budget allocation and similar argments decided the participation in an exhibition.

Conversely in times of tight budgets it appeared easier and safer to summarily curtail exhibition activities on the ground of their excessive budgetary and manpower demands, than to undertake an elaborate and tiresome selection of the few exhibitions which deserved participation, from the many which clamoured for it.

Negative attitudes to visiting exhibitions were traced to: disappointments with obtained results, high cost for meagre returns, lack of suitable personnel, depletion of base office personnel. The sources of the disappointments proved to be: inadequate definition of aims, assigning of unsuitable personnel, selection of wrong exhibition, poor preparation of visit, lack of visiting strategy, or a combination of some or all of these avoidable shortcomings.

Badly organized exhibitions deepened these self-inflicted disappointments. Only in three of 110 cases investigated were disappointing results turned later into positive benefits by a systematic assessment of what was in fact achieved in relation to what could have been achieved, and what therefore should be done next time.

11.   Participating in Exhibitions

In greatly simplified terms the intention to participate in an exhibition requires answers to the following questions:

Why do we want to exhibit?

What do we want to exhibit?

Where do we want to exhibit?

In terms of the marketing concept the reply to the first question requires a definition of your business, of your markets, of your position in them, of your marketing mix and of the range of marketing media you employ.

The reply to the second question requires a selection of offerings (products, services, etc.) which you have chosen in the context of the objectives defined in the reply to the first question. The reply to the third question requires a review of exhibitions serving your markets and your objectives as defined in the replies to the first two questions.

Organisations with a full awareness of their corporate marketing aims and of their position in the market in which they operate will find no difficulty in replying to the first and second question. This may apply equally well to large corporations as to medium and small companies, even if the latter do not always express their marketing orientation in a currently fashionable jargon. But there are exceptions in both camps. It may seem presumptious to demand a corporate heart searching exercise before embarking on such a simple undertaking as participating in an exhibition, but the demand becomes fully justified if only some thought is given to the potential marketing impact of exhibitions, to the great rewards which can be gained, to the danger of substantial losses which can be sustained, and most of all to the opportunities which are missed.

The selection of exhibitions suitable for a particular set of marketing objectives is a matter of individual assessments, of a search for optimum solutions and of judgment.

In the following paragraphs an attempt is made to define the motives for exhibiting and to present a method of selection in terms as widely applicable as possible and on the basis of a systematic procedure.

The essence of that method is that it consists of three steps of assessment. The first step is the *definition of the marketing motives for exhibiting*. The second is the *location of exhibitions* which, on the basis of existing knowledge, could serve these motives. The third step is the *selection of exhibitions* in which participation can be implemented.

Ideally the three steps would follow each other in orderly fashion, but in the real world neither motives, nor existing knowledge of exhibitions or even the allocation of resources are so well defined and measurable as to allow such an orderly sequence. In reality the three steps will interact, motives will be modified, objectives narrowed or extended and budgets cut back or enlarged, before a final balance is struck.

12. Marketing Motives for Exhibiting

The motives for exhibiting take their clue from marketing objectives and strategies and thus, in turn, become marketing motives. The principal activity motives are of a conceptual character and are concerned with different forms of conduct in the market and can be reduced to the three principal motives of *increasing*, *maintaining* or *recovering* a share of the market.

They suffer to some extent from the width of their definitions and unless we also define subordinate motives of a fundamental nature and establish for them a system of ranking, or priorities, the object of the exercise, that is a systematic and rational approach to exhibiting would be defeated.

The ranking of subordinate motives must be flexible enough to allow any of them, in certain circumstances, to be elevated to principal motives or at least to top rank subordinates.

Whilst the desire to increase your market share provides an obvious progressive motive for exhibiting, merely *maintaining a market share* may appear at first sight to be a regressive motive, but there are situations in which such a policy seems appropriate.

The example of imports of motor cars being restricted to a 'safe percentage of the market' so as not to upset indigenous manufacturers is well known. Another example is given in more detail in case study 1 page 78.

Market penetration motives are frequently generated by acquisitions and mergers, by diversification activities, as protective measures to counteract shrinking markets, or competitive threats to market sectors, or more constructively by an energetic and outward looking marketing policy. If the market penetration target is a planned economy market the most favourable timing of the participation in an exhibition could be determined by the incidence and length of the planning period and the ordering and negotiating periods applicable to the particular goods. You can aim at maximum impact and prepare to apply that impact in time before the next full planning period.

Alternatively, and if justified by the situation, you can attempt a market penetration exercise in the middle of the planning period, your aim being to fill gaps created by unfulfilled promises of other suppliers or, more rarely, by supplementary budget allocations.

Market development motives are more suitably evolved for new products, equipment, processes, concepts. The character of a new market sector may require a probing exercise because marketing research investigations, whilst establishing the existence of a substantial potential also found that reactions to the exhibitors attack on that sector can not be predicted with sufficient certainty to justify the cost of a full scale launch. The participation in an exhibition of known impact is considered as the best means of probing into the market at reasonable expense.

Market exploration can be a valid motive for exhibiting, if market research investigations indicate that an exhibition is the only viable marketing medium or the best practical means of exploring the potential of that market.

The infiltration into a new market can be greatly assisted by participating in exhibitions, if such participation is planned and executed as an integral part of the overall marketing strategy and if it is co-ordinated with other media and activities. It can be just as costly and damaging to rely on an exhibition to take the whole burden of a marketing campaign as to neglect that most versatile of marketing tools.

Sales promotion is one of the most frequently quoted motives for exhibiting. More than that, people who still regard marketing as no more than a fanciful name for selling also define exhibitions as sales promotion functions. If the difference in interpretation were confined to semantics no great harm would result. The fact that more often than not the same people interpret sales promotion as sending our three sales representatives where previously two operated and consider the manning of an exhibition stand tantamount to temporarily suspending operations in the field. They also naively proclaim that the best way to obtain good results from an exhibition is to secure a stand near an entrance or on a main gangway.

If sales promotion is an exhibiting motive, it must be assumed that the exhibition effort is one of the elements of a planned sales campaign. It is therefore no more than sound logic that the selection of exhibitions suitable for participation and the manner in which to participate, should be based on and be in harmony with the intended exhibitors general marketing and sales promotion strategy.

The elements of that strategy which will most decisively affect the initiative and decision to participate in an exhibition are:

The promotion planning period
Sales objectives
Market penetration targets
Promotion budget
Promotion continuity and flexibility.

The time element of the promotion planning period is important, because exhibitions by their nature, require long term planning. Most exhibitions with a high marketing merit are heavily booked. Some may be biennial events, several may overlap or have very close venue dates. This means that new entrants to the exhibition scene would require advance planning periods of at least two to three years before they can participate.

Companies already participating in exhibitions have an easier task, unless of course the campaign is a venture into a new market sector and thus becomes a newcomer to the relevant exhibitions.

The definition of *market penetration targets* will determine the title and timing of exhibitions suitable for the declared sales objectives. An overall promotion budget which includes a provision for exhibitions will enable the selection of exhibitions with the highest merit within the limitations of the budget. Promotion continuity plans and provisions for flexibility will indicate long term sales promotion objectives, targets for the next planning period, possibly the widening of the market penetration targets and thus of the exhibition effort.

For some products the effects of exhibiting may not become apparent for several months after the exhibition, for others only the second or third appearance at a particular exhibition, will produce a significant response. This means that planned exhibition activities must have a built-in flexibility to meet foreseen variations of response as well as totally unexpected reactions. A negative response to a new development requires prepared counteraction, an overwhelming response can be embarrassing if no provisions are in hand to cope with it.

Marketing of innovations and improvements. When this is an exhibiting motive, their inevitable exposure to the strong and penetrating light of an exhibition requires a frank and critical questioning of the elements of newness.

Is the improvement the result of progress or is it only an improvement of a hitherto inadequate feature?

Is a new development just catching up with competitors or is it overtaking the field?

Is there an improvement in design or only a change in appearance?

Is it an innovation or merely a novelty?

Does it offer new benefits or does it only remove existing shortcomings?

Genuine newness deserves maximum exposure, spurious newness requires muted treatment lest it draw attention to a previous failure or deficiency.

Some exhibitions provide special *facilities for new products* such as separate display areas, competitions, awards, separate catalogue entries. Where these facilities are not available it is up to the exhibitor to emphasize the subject by display signs, posters, special entries in catalogues.

Some improvements for which exhibitions are good marketing media are of the kind which might be called '*anodyne improvements*'. They are concerned with noise reduction, elimination of vibration, reduction of toxicity, stress and strain reduction, waste prevention, reduction and elimination, and similar efforts. Although socially and economically very laudable, such improvements often encounter the resistance of customers-manufacturers, the inertia of intermediary customers and the lack of knowledge of ultimate users.

An exhibition provides the opportunity to demonstrate the improvements to a cross section of the market, to encourage the more progressive manufacturers, to enlighten the end users and to put pressure on intermediary customers. A good, even if somewhat dated, example is the case of a tractor engine with a considerably reduced noise level. The majority of first equipment manufacturers showed little interest in paying extra for this improvement and environmental considerations were not as yet fashionable at the time.

At an agricultrual exhibition in Switzerland this 'noiseless' engine was exhibited and demonstrated because, as chance had it, no other 'exhibition finish engine', was at the time available. A very wealthy farmer witnessed the demonstration and immediately ordered several tractors with such engines. This, for a Swiss farmer a very rash procedure, naturally puzzled the exhibitor, as the robust customer and his even more robust farmworkers were not particularly known for their sensitivity to engine noise. As can be guessed the motive when disclosed was a commercial one. The excellently situated farm had a great number of tourists staying in many of its chalets, and they did not like to be wakened at 6 o'clock in the morning. Noisy tractors meant either losing valuable working hours, or not less valuable tourists.

The marketing of pioneering concepts or products as a motive for exhibiting goes one step further than the motive for innovations and improvements. It is fraught with pitfalls and dangers the gravest of which is that pioneering concepts often induce a product orientation even into the decision-making process of organisations which are normally market oriented. Publicity executives and stand designers find pioneering products much more interesting than existing ones and they are fascinated by the opprotunity to extol their virtues in a new idiom of display and superlatives. Only companies practicing management-by-objectives techniques will have no difficulty in applying them to motives of marketing a pioneer concept or product.

Before a truly pioneering concept is to be exhibited, the most important question to be asked is, what can be achieved as a result of showing this pioeering effort at a particular exhibition and at a particular time. Complex and speculative time-acceptance factors need to be evaluated—a procedure difficult enough for a new exhibit, let alone a pioneering one—technological, market, possibly even social and economic repercussions must be foreseen, reactions of competition anticipated. It is not enough to extrapolate past experience and to hope that events will follow the established pattern. If the display of the pioneering exhibit involves functional or operational elements the reliance on a single prototype can be fatal. The single prototype syndrome is critical enough in the development state when rogue components, accidents, failures or freak conditions of a single unit can cause long and costly delays.

In the environment of an exhibition such failures have as devastatingly negative an effect, as have badly finished or inadequately functioning units requiring constant adjustments and demonstrated to the accompaniment of profuse apologies and explanations, particularly if they are a central element of the exhibition effort. A pioneering exhibit presented in a form and method as near to its future normal use as possible, functioning properly and finishep to a reasonable standard will demonstrate the feasibility of the concept and its reliability.

'Ahead of time' *exhibits* which are even more advanced than pioneering ones require special consideration. Paradoxically their utopian character imposes less restraints on their exhibition treatment than that of merely new or pioneering exhibits.

The display of 'ahead of time' exhibits usually benefits from a certain duality of purpose. The underlying conceptual and functional principles should be explained in scientifically valid, but simplified, terms and also in generally understandable popular terms. The actual exhibits should demonstrate an area of immediate practical applications and also the scope for future, perhaps even visionary, developments and possibilities.

The remarks concerning the display aspects of exhibiting pioneering and 'ahead of time' exhibits are to some extent anticipating the discussion of stand design and of exhibits dealt with in detail in the following chapter, but in the case of these exceptional exhibits it is important to subject the motives for exhibiting to a critical feasibility test of the necessary display techniques.

Marketing strategy. Opprotunities for making otherwise *elusive contacts* can be a strong subsidiary motive for exhibiting and is best illustrated by a few quotations from press reports of exhibitors' statements:

'We make chemical processing equipment consisting of a combination of semi- and fully automatic units. The nature of some products processed by our equipment is of a nature discouraging free access to the plant in which it is installed. The result is that in such applications we are only called in when serious trouble develops. The equipment is almost completely trouble free when we can instruct and keep up to date process engineers, maintenance men, electrical engineers and instrument setters'.

'By participating in suitable exhibitions in markets with critical applications, we invariably find that our stand is visited by the otherwise elusive technicians. We find that we can solve many worrying, but from our point of view, easily corrected malfunctions and that we collect extremely valuable fault locating information'.

'Our customers can talk freely to our management'.

'Customers with production problems can talk to our engineers'.

'The people operating our equipment are usually so far removed from us, that misuse and underexploitation of potential performance is a disturbing occurrence. We participate in strategically located public exhibitions and also stage private and mobile exhibitions to overcome this problem'.

A marketing strategy of *challenging entrenched positions* of competitors deserves, in abstract marketing terms, a better position than that of a subordinate function, but in the environment of the exhibition, the challenging exhibits must be assured of a high marketing impact before they can serve such a strategy. Irrespective of whether the challenge is fought as a test of strength between rival giants, as a David-Goliath contest or as an exercise to eliminate small fry—the motives for exhibiting should be subjected to a scrutiny of their validity on the basis both of the absolute marketing impact of the exhibits and of the special impact required for a successful challenge.

Marketing techniques. Participation in an exhibition as a means of initiating implementing or sustaining marketing techniques and functions is usually motivated by special conditions in the exhibition host country, or in the case of large international companies by their marketing policies. The motives for such participation are seldom strong enough in their own right and are more likely to share their influence on the final decision with public relations motives and external activity motives.

Public relations. Conventional public relation activities of presenting the corporate image of an exhibitor are a natural subsidiary motive for exhibiting. In exceptional situations an exhibition can provide the only acceptable means for an expression of gratitude or for extending hospitality to special customers or influential bodies.

External market influences such as the advent of or the changes in the political and economic grouping of markets, the conclusion of trade agreements, the granting of development and reconstruction aid and loans provide valid motives for participating in exhibitions, particularly if encouraged by official bodies and perhaps supported by cost participation.

Marketing Motives—Case Study 1.

A manufacturing company participating regularly in major exhibitions, relevant to their international marketing of industrial catering equipment, attained a position in the market which form an overall strategy point of view was quite satisfactory, and which was gained against a very strong and sometimes vicious opposition of competitors. After the battle, all competitors settled down to an uneasy sharing of the market. The systematic and continuous observation of the market by the company's marketing researchers indicated that due to their superior marketing techniques, a further substantial increase of their market share would be quite feasible. But it was also established that such an expansion would provoke a very strong reaction of competitors. All the products competing for the market, although well established in their current form, were in a declining phase of their technological life cycle. The company had at that time developed a new range of products, strongly protected by patents and due for launching two years hence. They were faced with the problem of the manner of exhibiting, i.e. with defining the objectives of the forthcoming series of participations in exhibitions which were scheduled in their long term exhibition programme. The question of not exhibiting at all was broached theoretically, but rejected for a number of reasons, of which the decisive was the almost certain loss of stand space in a number of very heavily booked exhibitions.

The main policy consideration was not to provoke a price cutting war which would affect the price policy of the new range, when it became available. The danger was seen in the mounting of an intensive exhibition effort, in keeping with past practice, which had made a substantial contribution to their success in the market. Such an effort was bound to be interpreted by competitors as a further incursion into the settled pattern of market shares.

The marketing motives for exhibiting (Check list 8, p. 80) were defined as:

 principal activity motive:
  maintaining existing market share
 subordinate functional motive:
  sales promotion of established products.

The exhibiting activity techniques (Check list 18, p. 174) were defined as:
 appealing to:
  customers
  end users
 display and demonstration of features of exhibits
  performance
  economy
  operation
 display of service and spares capabilities
  service availability
  spares availability.

As can be seen from the definitions of motives, design and appearance features were not included as display elements. Normally at a biennial event at least a new colour scheme would have been introduced, together with improvements in shape and probably in performance.

The stand personnel was very thoroughly briefed about the policy on which the objectives were based and all executives visiting the exhibition were also explicitly informed about the policy and the exhibiting technique. This briefing was particularly important as enthusiastic sales personnel and sales executives could have easily misunderstood the mild tone of the exhibition efforts and perhaps tried to compensate for it by unwittingly disclosing future plans.

	Principal Activity Motives	
	market share	
	increasing	
	maintaining	
	recovering	
	market penetration	
	horizontal	
	vertical	
	lateral	
	redirected	
	market development	
	market probing/exploration	
	market infiltration	
	Subordinate Functional Motives	
	sales promotion	
	exhibits, (products, processes, services)	
	established	
	modified	
	improved	
	marketing of innovations and improvements	
	exhibits in new application	
	exhibits with new features	
	offering new benefits	
	solving new problems	
	test exposure of exhibits with	
	new qualities	
	new versatility	
	new method of operation	
	new design, shape, colour	
	new exhibits	
	new to industry	
	new to market	
	new to market sector	
	introduction of:	
	new trade marks	
	new brand names	

Check List 8. *PRINCIPAL AND SUBORDINATE MARKETING MOTIVES FOR EXHIBITING*

	marketing of pioneering	
	prototype exhibits	
	pioneering exhibits	
	exhibits in pioneering technologies	
	intertechnology combinations	
	interdisciplinary combinations	
	'ahead of time' exhibits	
	marketing strategy	
	elusive contacts	
	operators	
	installators	
	maintenance	
	users	
	challenging	
	supplier monopoly	
	supplier oligopoly	
	competitor's product arrogance	
	exploiting	
	customer monopoly	
	customer oligopsony	

Check List 8. (*continued*)

		Marketing Technique Motives	
		inviting interest in:	
		agency, distributorship	
		wholesaler arrangements	
		exploring opportunities for arrangements of:	
		franchises, licences	
		assembly	
		manufacturing	
		joint ventures	
		support of parent company for:	
		home or foreign branch	
		agent, distributor	
		co-operation of parent company with:	
		foreign subsidiary	
		associate company	
		autonomous member of group	
	Public Relations Activity Motives		
	presenting corporate image of:		
	internationalisation of activities		
	capability of new groupings		
	total scope of:		
	activities		
	outposts		
	facilities		
	capabilities		
	reputation		
	establishing in new market		
	redeeming tarnished image		
	counteracting prejudices, antagonisms, hostility		
	indirect promotion, exhibiting as:		
	'thank you' gesture for		
	large contracts		
	official assistance		
	only means of extending hospitality to:		
	institutional customers		
	authorities		

Check List 9. *MARKETING TECHNIQUES AND PUBLIC RELATIONS MOTIVES FOR EXHIBITING*

Check lists 8, 9, 10 deal with a range of marketing motives arranged in three groups. One or two of the principal marketing motives (*check list 8*) may be sufficiently important for one exhibitor who will consider some public relations motives (*check list 9*) as optional activities of no particular significance for a particular exhibition. Another exhibitor will see the motive of challenging a monopoly situation (*check list 8*) not as a subordinate, but as a main motive for exhibiting. The check lists could point to motives, not considered in the normal course of an exhibition effort, they could also disclose gaps in marketing techniques employed at exhibitions. For the purposes of one exhibitor they could be reduced to a few items, for another they may have to be extended to cover exhibition activities of the various companies of a large group. The definition and ranking of motives for exhibiting will determine the merits of exhibitions in relation to these marketing motives and it will also point to the techniques of exhibiting (*check list 16*) and appeal targets (*check list 18*) compatible with these motives.

	External Market Influence Motives	
	grouping of markets	
	political blocks	
	economic communities	
	customs unions	
	trade agreements	
	liberalisation	
	special privileges	
	trade booms	
	discoveries of natural wealth	
	economic changes	
	political changes	
	development and reconstruction	
	development plans	
	national	
	regional	
	local	
	development aid	
	tied	
	free	
	reconstruction	
	planned	
	special	
	financial incentives	
	credits	
	loans	
	investment privileges	
	currency advantages	
	participation in exhibitions combined with:	
	trade missions	
	special promotions	
	congresses	
	conventions	
	symposia	

Check List 10. *EXTERNAL INFLUENCE MOTIVES FOR EXHIBITING*

	invitation, encouragement, participation in cost by:	
	home government ⎤	
	official body ⎱ to exhibit abroad ———————	
	trade association ⎰	
	marketing grouping ⎦	
	foreign government ⎤	
	foreign regional authority ⎱ to exhibit in their country	
	foreign importers grouping ⎦	

Check List 10. (*continued*)

INDUSTRIAL	OTHER	CONCEPTS
Buyers	Economists	Management
Sellers	Statisticians	Marketing
Users	Sociologists	Technology
Operators	Academics	STATUS
Engineering	Consultants	Chief executive
Production	Technologists	Senior executive
Maintenance	Students	Executive
Services	Apprentices	Staff
Research &	Visitors' companions	VISIT TO COUNTRY
Development	Parties	VISIT TO EXHIBITION
Design	Excursions	First
Projects	Sightseers	Frequent
Process	LEGAL	Regular
Laboratory	INSPECTORATES	Last
Testing	STANDARDS	Planned
Despatch	APPROVALS	Ad hoc
Packaging	OFFICIAL	PERSONALITY
Storage	Government	Enthusiastic
Transport	Local Government	Balanced
Administration	Municipal	Apathetic
Clerical	Trade Missions	Hedonistic
Publicity	Associations	Puritan
Public Relations	trade	Hypochondriacs
Market Research	professional	ATTITUDE
COMMERCIAL	Trade Unions	Positive
Banks	Consumer Protection	Neutral
Investment	Military	Negative
Finance	Civil Defence	Objective
Insurance	Police	Prejudiced
Surveying	Security	

TABLE 5. CATEGORIES AND TRAITS OF EXHIBITION VISITORS

13. Visiting Exhibitions

This section is concerned with visiting exhibitions, an activity pursued by a great variety of persons for a wide range of purposes. In social hierarchy visitors range from heads of state, royalty, ministers, chief executives of international corporations and financial institutions, to humble buyers, users, consumers, apprentices, students, schoolboys. The decision to visit an exhibition can be prompted by a casual sightseeing interest, by an optimistic hope that something useful will be located or by a well founded assessment of what the exhibition can offer. One government official will do no more than ceremoniously open an exhibition another will show a genuine interest and knowledge of its objectives and aims. Some visitors paying the price for the laxity of their preparation will conclude at the end of their visit that they had wasted their time, others will find that they benefited in time, expense, acquired information and contacts, even more than their systematic preparation led them to expect.

Visitors of different provenance, occupation, rank, also differ in social behaviour, attitudes, temperament and other personality traits. Some of the categories of visitors encountered at exhibitions and some of their traits are listed in Table 5.

The motives for visiting and the visiting tasks are discussed in detail and the implications of visiting time management are illustrated by a case study.

Visitors
This section is concerned with visitors with definite marketing interests and these can be: visitors, visitors who are also exhibitors (but not at the exhibition visited) and exhibitors who visit other sections or other stands of the exhibition.

There is no substantial difference in the requirements for preparation, definition of objectives and tasks as far as the three categories of visitors are concerned, except that the performance of the tasks will be technically easier for exhibitors acting as visitors. They have a base from which to work and make arrangements, they can reciprocate hospitality, they have access to internal exhibition information and services. On the other hand, unless they are specifically assigned to visiting tasks, their stand duties take preference and their time is not so easily managed as that of other visitors.

Preparation and Motives
The identification and definition of *visiting motives and interests* and the preparation of the visit are the two main activities preceding a visit to an exhibition. Both these activities are time consuming elements but within reasonable limits, they are not subject to date or time span constraints. On the other hand the actual exhibition visit is strictly circumscribed by the

venue, the date and the time span available. The details of the definition of interests and the preparation of the visit can be modified and corrected in the light of changing circumstances. The task activities of the actual visit can be modified and corrected only to a very limited extent because they are usually performed on the basis of a tight schedule. If special provisions can be made for such corrective actions, they should be included in the actual brief and as such become part of the main task, eliminating the need for *post factum* adjustments. The statement of objectives and tasks, the auxiliary documentation and other task aids, the time allocation and schedule of contacts, in short all that is contained in the preparation of the visit, exerts its influence on then person assigned for the visit and becomes subject to his interpretation and personality responses. First before the visitor reaches the exhibition and then during the visit, when the exhibition environment exerts its own cross-influence. The exhibition environment can affect the exhibition task time which can be comfortably sustained. This applies particularly to conditions such as open air stands at exhibitions which take place early in spring, when unexpected frost and snow or persistent rain can occur, or exhibition halls with overheated and/or dust laden atmospheres, or with unheated and/or draughty halls. Unsatisfactory catering arrangements, lack of cloak rooms and rest facilities also affect the time span, which is bearable.

Good exhibition ground facilities such as efficient post office services, banks, interpreters, snack bars, refreshment trolleys, rest facilities, enable a better use of the time available. The opening hours of the exhibition, distances between different locations of exhibition halls or areas, exhibition ground transport, ease of orientation, etc., are other important time factors.

Exhibition opening times vary within comparatively narrow limits of six to nine hours, the majority being in the eight to eight and a half hours range. To what extent these opening hours can be exploited by a visitor depends on such a diverse collection of influences that it is not only hard to generalise on the best way to achieve maximum exploitation, but not advisable to do so, lest the application of such generalisations generate more sources of conflicts than precepts for effective action.

The need for the systematic planning of the participation in exhibitions is generally recognised, even if not fully implemented, but the visiting of exhibitions is unfortunately often left to *ad hoc* arrangements. The securing of an air ticket and of hotel reservation is regarded as a sufficiently important organisational achievement needing no further elaboration.

The topography of an exhibition (*Figure 1*) and the review of exhibition time elements discussed in the previous chapter (*pages 45, 50 and Check lists 5 and 6, pp. 64, 66*) demonstrate the need for advanced planning of exhibition visits both in the interest of an economic use of human and material resources and of an effective accomplishment of tasks.

The planning of a visit to an exhibition should be based on a statement of aims and objectives, the character of which will depend on individual needs.

The effectiveness with which these objectives are reached, can be measured only if they are clearly defined in qualitative and quantitative terms.

Exhibitions catering for your product, your market, your customers or for industries connected with, or influencing your market are natural targets for your visit. Your visiting strategy will be governed by the merits of the exhibition *per se*, by its merits for your particular need or objective and by the reconciliation of your aim with your resources.

The motives for visiting exhibitions usually fall into three main interest categories: *buying, customers, intelligence.* Depending on the scope of the exhibition the main interest categories can be supplemented by optional fringe interests. A special motive is the visiting of exhibitions in combination with other visiting activities.

The time restraints affecting exhibition visiting activities suggest that in addition to a statement of objectives, the different tasks which must be performed to achieve these objectives, need some qualification of relative importance. Intending visitors who by their status or function are intimately involved in the motivation process of visiting, will be naturally conscious of these qualifications, but when the visiting task is delegated to other persons a more formal procedure must be adopted.

Buying Interests

Buying interests can be considered within fairly flexible limits as mainly resale oriented, product oriented or plant oriented. Materials, components, complete products can be purchased for resale. Basic materials, half products, components and finishing materials bought for incorporation into your own products are product oriented purchases, and so are auxiliaries, accessories and some complete products. The same items when sold as spares or replacements can be purchases for resale.

Machine tools, processing equipment, materials handling and storage equipment are typical plant oriented purchases.

The different buying interests may require special expertise, they may be channelled through central buying functions, they can be subject to an established routine or a matter of *ad hoc* decisions. The co-ordination of the different buying interests, the importance and urgency of individual tasks and the merits of exhibitions relevant to these tasks will determine the choice of events most suitable for visiting. The analysis of timing, cost and resources will narrow that choice to an optimum selection.

If buying interests are the main motive for visiting an exhibition, the stands to be visited and the contacts to be made can be pre-selected before the visit. The majority of tasks performed should be active and the preparation for the visit should include specifications, drawings, delivery schedules, price margins, credit requirements and other elements of the purchasing activity relevant to the particular products, processes or services which are of interest to the visitor-buyer. At the exhibition the visitor can encounter any one of the three basic groups of suppliers: present suppliers, potential suppliers and lapsed suppliers. The suppliers in each group require a different approach.

The exploration of opportunities for agency or distributor arrangements, manufacturing licences, franchises and joint venture arrangements can be considered as resale or product oriented interests, depending on your organisational structure and the character of the arrangement aimed at.

Present Suppliers

All contacts with current suppliers should be active. It would be a strange relationship indeed if there was no reason at all to praise or to blame, to promise more orders, or to warn of cut-backs, to talk as well as to listen. At the very least, there is the reason to pay a courtesy visit to the stand of a supplier so as not to give offence by ignoring him.

Benefits can be derived from contacts with otherwise elusive executives and technical personnel, information can be gathered about future developments, about competitors' activities, about large orders placed by competitors which may affect deliveries of your own not so impressive orders. If your supplier is a smaller company than yours, you will show an appreciation of their good service, give re-assurance about the future, impart reasoned and well substantiated reprimands about shortcomings and generate a modicum of general goodwill.

If your supplier is a much larger company than yours, he should, by virtue of his marketing expertise, appreciate your reliance on his supplies and your importance as a customer. If that is not the case, you may have to probe a bit deeper to find more weighty influences than the ones encountered.

On the other hand, your own advanced methods or farsighted planning will encourage him to give you some preference in the supply of new or improved products. An important supplier may be able to impart interesting information about the use of his products by your competitors, information not necessarily secret, but normally not broadcast beforehand.

The size of his stand and his largesse in hospitality will encourage many visitors, providing you with opportunities for contacts with interesting people and probably with competitors with whom an exchange of views would be otherwise unlikely. Many a market conflict and impending price war was thus avoided.

Potential or New Suppliers

Contacts with potential suppliers can range from a passive collection of information through placing of well defined inquiries to placing of definite trial or quantity orders. The visitor, as buyer or potential buyer, is in the most favoured position for receiving full attention. Caution is sometimes required so as not to allow a tentative inquiry to be taken or deliberately interpreted as a serious intent to change sources and then being flaunted as such to the discomfort of the present supplier. An exhibition is an easy field for such manoeuvres which have been known to upset relations with well established suppliers, to harden their attitude when granting discounts and to cause other upsetting reactions. The fact that from a marketing point of view this is the wrong way to react, makes little difference to the actual outcome. Large suppliers with a near monopoly position or with a very strong hold on the market are particularly susceptible to take unreasonable umbrage at the daring of a smaller customer, to seek new sources of supply.

Lapsed Suppliers

You may have severed relations with an otherwise good supplier because of his failing in one aspect, e.g. deliveries, or price, or a technical detail. There may have been personal reasons for the severance, a clash of personalities, delicate questions of fringe benefits or a change in buying policy. You have reason to believe that the sources of the conflict have been corrected. In all such and similar cases, it may be difficult to re-establish normal contacts without some real or imagined loss of prestige or pride. The hospitable background of an exhibition offers an excellent opportunity for both parties to come together again, neither losing face in the process.

Customer Interests

Customer interests are mainly concerned with contacts with direct and indirect customers and users. If such contacts are the main motive for visiting an exhibition, then its merits in that respect must be fairly substantial to justify such a visit. If that is so then, regulations permitting, serious thought should be given to participation in the exhibition, because all marketing interest tasks can be performed more effectively by an exhibitor than by a visitor.

If your customers know that you are usually in the habit of visiting a particular exhibition in which they participate, or if they have invited you, they will expect your routine or special visit to their stand. A number of situations can develop.

Depending on your relations with them, their importance to you, and their standing in their industry, your customers may have some ideas of the rank of the visitor whom they expect. They may think that the person delegated is lower in your hierarchy, than their expectation. If the exhibition is an important one for the industry concerned, your customers are perhaps surprised that you are not exhibiting, whilst your competitors are. Several of your customers are exhibiting and they may be sensitive about the order in which they are visited, the length of the visit, the importance of the visitor. All these attitudes may seem trivial, but they remain trivial only as long as you, as a visitor, representing your company, are aware of them and are prepared to deal with them in a serious or lighthearted way, whichever fits the situation better. You must be ready with a plausible explanation, why your company is not exhibiting, and if you are not as 'important' as they expect and if it shows in their reception you will take it in good grace and prove by your preparation for the visit, how seriously their problems are taken. Preparation and tact will establish your position and pave the ground for your follow-up visit.

If you are a senior executive, make a special effort to visit customers-companies smaller than yours, particularly if you discern in them signs of future growth. Visits to your customers' stands can provide opportunities to hear comments of users and in critical situations, e.g. of service or spares complaints, it may be advisable to offer your customers assistance in dealing with users. Such an offer implies that you were aware, when planning your visit, that such contingencies may arise, and that you made an appropriate time allowance in your visiting schedule.

An indirect customer interest task is the support given by visitors from an organisation to the stand personnel of its subsidiary, branch, agent or distributor participating in an exhibition. In this case however the visitor assumes the role of an exhibitor.

Intelligence Interests
Intelligence is usually an integral part of buying, customer and marketing interests, even if not declared as such. The visiting of information centres, trade associations, official or semi-official representations or bureaux can be part of a specific interest task or an intelligence task.

The attendance at conferences, symposia and lectures is mostly a passive information gathering task subsidiary to a main interest task. Active participation by a visitor who is not an exhibitor is usually an information imparting exercise with a content of marketing elements, whilst a resulting discussion can be of intelligence value. In some situations, one or more of the visiting interests are declared as requiring only observation and gathering of information and they then become intelligence tasks. On rare occasions personal contacts are expressly excluded from these tasks. This is not a very effective way of performing intelligence tasks and the results are usually as poor in quality as the concept. There is also the danger, in some countries, of contravening laws of industrial espionage. Genuine intelligence interests are usually generated by market and marketing research activities and the tasks are sometimes entrusted to visitors to exhibitions engaged in other tasks. In such cases there is a great risk that unless the intelligence task briefing is very explicit and an adequate time allocation is made for it, a systematic intelligence task can degenerate into a superficial *reconnaissance exercise*. A special intelligence task is the evaluation of the merits of an exhibition. This can be a general assessment made for record purposes, or an investigation for a specific objective of marketing or future exhibiting.

Fringe Interests

In addition to the specialised tasks defined by the main visiting objectives an exhibition is a good occasion, if time permits, to review product design, display techniques, selling methods in your own field as well as in others related to, or even remote from your main interest.

Your main tasks may be of a product oriented interest but depending on your knowledge and experience you may notice resale opportunities. The review of products for resale may be your main task, but new developments in storage and handling techniques relevant to your business, if exhibited, may prove of additional interest.

For one category of visitors works canteen equipment can be a plant oriented interest for another only a fringe interest. The review of fringe interest provides not only useful information for your own sphere of activities, but can also serve as a refreshing interlude to your main task and it can help to gain a new perspective on your own activities. You may find that others do things in a way which could be applied with benefit to your own activities, you may also note with satisfaction that your own way is the best, or at least as good as that of others.

Combined Visits Interests

When the marketing functions of a company contain a substantial element of visits to international markets, the visiting programme will in most cases include some or all of the following elements:

Visits to subsidiaries, branches, agents, distributors.
Visits to customers.
Visits to users.
Visits to exhibitions, congresses, symposia.
Special sales campaigns.

The frequency of the visits will vary depending on the market structure, the product, the replacement cycle, service requirements, and on the resources available. In the interest of economy the visiting of exhibitions should be integrated, whenever possible, with other external visits. The economies which can be achieved by including exhibitions in the visiting programme will depend on the number of exhibitions relevant to the marketing strategy and whether active participation, visting only or a combination of participation and visiting is required. The further away from base such visits take place the greater is the influence of integration on the cost effectiveness of the human and material resources employed for the purpose.

Visiting Tasks

The tasks required to deal with defined visiting interests can be active, passive or combined active-passive.

Active tasks are usually concerned with establishing personal contacts, which can be pre-selected if the persons are known, they can be defined by company, or product or industry with an indication of the rank or function to be aimed at. Active tasks can be also concerned with negotiations, with receiving information as well as giving it.

Passive tasks are mainly concerned with gathering non-personal information and data, with making observations, witnessing tests, demonstrations, etc.

In the course of performing passive tasks, non-scheduled personal contacts are occasionally made, and then pursued as active tasks to a degree depending on their importance. The *combination of active and passive tasks* is the most flexible technique for achieving visiting results, but this flexibility calls for a considerable amount of preparation, self-discipline and time control.

Each of the three types of tasks are in turn subject to a further qualification. They can be of intrinsic or extrinsic character. The terms intrinsic and extrinsic are used to emphasise the flexibility which is essential in performing exhibition tasks—the terms essential and non-essential would be much too strong and absolute.

Intrinsic tasks are tasks of primary importance to the achievement of the stated objectives. These tasks are the subjects of specific instructions, require a systematic execution and should be specifically reported on.

Extrinsic tasks are of secondary importance. They can be observations of general attitudes, noting of opinions and rumours, making incidental and social contacts, gathering information on subsidiary or fringe interests.

The classification of tasks, as so much else in the exhibition scene, should not be regarded as requiring rigid divisions which must be adhered to. The underlying purpose of the definitions is to analyse as far as possible the elements which constitute a complex whole and thus to assist in the assessment of their relative values in relation to the main objectives.

Visting Contacts

The establishing of personal contacts is so obviously a natural aim of all exhibition activities, that it may become a self-sufficient objective leading to a neglect of other assigned tasks. It is therefore of interest to examine the character of such contacts and to attempt to grade them in order of import-

TYPE OF CONTACT	CONTACT TECHNIQUE	CONTACT TIME	CONTACT FREQUENCY
special interest	by appointment	short (5–10 min)	first
general interest	planned	medium (15–30 min)	single
auxiliary interest	ad hoc	long (1–2 hours)	repeat
fringe interest			multiple
routine			
courtesy			

TABLE 6. VISITING CONTACTS

ance. Contacts made by a visitor have the following type, time, technique and frequency characteristics:

Contacts made by special appointment can be assessed in respect of their duration, although this assessment would be subject to considerable correction factors, depending on the location of the exhibition. A special appointment made at an exhibition in Scandinavian countries can be timed as to its start and finish to within 5 minutes in South American countries the limits would be more in the region of one to two hours. Special interest contacts which yield no immediate results, in one country need no more than one repeat visit, once your requirements are stated, in another country three to four return visits are required to achieve results.

A qualitative and quantitative assessment of the planned contacts, corrected by local attitude factors and related to a particular exhibition, will provide an indication of:

time and personnel requirements,
feasibility of fulfilling the task,
expense and cost values.

On the basis of these indicators decisions can be made whether visiting an exhibition is the best way of achieving the expected results or whether alternative means are available and if so, at what expense and cost.

Authority of Visitor
Persons assigned to visit an exhibition should be given a detailed definition of their tasks and of the ramifications of their authority to act on behalf of their organisation. This applies particularly to the following activities:

supplier contacts: placing formal inquiries
    requesting tenders and/or quotations
    discussing orders
    promising orders
    placing orders

customers contacts: soliciting orders
    discussing, dealing with and/or settling warranty and service claims
    discussing and/or accepting requests for modifications of products, conditions, prices, etc.
    accepting and/or approving product modifications, price alterations, changes in delivery schedules, credit arrangements, cancellations.

other contacts:
    social activities, entertaining, invitations to visit home base, participating in official functions, political events, publicity, public relations.

At first sight it may appear that awareness of company policy and of marketing directives should provide sufficient safeguards for the proper execution of visiting tasks. However, even in the best of marketing oriented companies the rate of penetration of its policy into different strata of the organisation can vary considerably. These variations, which affect the appreciation and response to policy precepts, can have several sources. The most obvious one is that of natural variations experienced in human communications channels stemming from the differences in the qualities of senders and receivers.

Then there are differences in interpretation due to disparities and conflicts of divisional, departmental and personal interests, both real and imagined.

From the point of view of the activity of visiting exhibitions, a very significant factor is the change of roles. A visitor to an exhibition is often cast in an external role which is different—and mostly extended in scope—from his internal role as defined by his position in the organisation he serves. Some enjoy the new role, on others it imposes a severe strain, some use it to pay off old scores, some disclose capabilities far beyond their current internal position. The majority of tasks which a visitor-presumptive performs in his internal role, are of a well defined and mostly instrinsic character and are carried out under supervision and in an environment with built-in controls, and opportunities for correction. Extrinsic tasks are usually in the minority and subject to various restraints. In his external role as visitor to an exhibition some of the extrinsic, mostly social, tasks are new or assume greater importance than they had internally. The restraints are different and in the case of foreign exhibitions the added complication of a strange environment is perhaps further confused by an unknown language. If several persons from the same organisation are visiting an exhibition, the need for a definition of tasks and authority becomes the more important, the larger the organisation.

If there are taboos in some areas or carte blanche permissiveness in others, these should be clearly stated. There is hardly a more disconcerting experience than for two persons from the same organisation to meet unexpectedly on the same stand yet pursuing different enquiries, or for one visitor to follow unknowingly in the footsteps of another and to be unaware of what information was sought or imparted by his predecessor.

Exhibition Visting Time Elements—Case Study 2.

This case study relates the story of one visit to an exhibition of mechanical handling equipment abroad. The story started in an uneventful way and was related by a consultant who was visiting a company in connection with a diversification problem and incidentally became involved in planning a visit to an exhibition. The company manufactures special-purpose attachments and Mr. Smith, an engineering executive of the company, was interested in finding an alternative source of supply for a built-in component unit. In the past the company had participated in an important biennial exhibition abroad but in the wake of an economy drive the participation in exhibitions abroad was severely curtailed 'because exhibiting abroad is more expensive'. The company exported 36 per cent of its output and as several overseas customers were overdue for a visit, the opportunity of seeing them at the forthcoming exhibition and locating a supplier of the required unit, was an obvious solution. Mr. Smith decided to send his assistant for a one-and-a-half-day visit to the exhibition and arrangements for travel and hotel were put in hand. This decision was taken in January, the exhibition was scheduled for March of the same year.

The subject was casually mentioned to the consultant at lunch for no other reason but that he was known 'to be interested in exhibitions'. His reaction was that the visiting time seemed rather short and he suggested that the occasion should be used for an exercise in the systematic planning of an exhibition visit. The suggestion was accepted with slightly indulgent smiles. The first step in the exercise was to define the motives for visiting. These were stated as:

> to contact several customers
> to locate one or two potential suppliers of the built-in unit.

It was pointed out that as a matter of principle this definition was too vague as it relied on the fact that the person delegated for the visit knew all about the unit and the customers.

The definition of motives was revised and emerged as:

> visits to customers at exhibition:
> > at least four customers are known to exhibit
> > another three are very likely to exhibit
> built-in unit must comply with company's specification, delivery schedules and price range
> supplier to provide satisfactory evidence of service and spares facilities in seven countries with particular emphasis on three territories
> eight to ten potential suppliers of the required unit are likely to exhibit
> sixteen to eighteen users of such units of different makes are likely to exhibit
> user opinions should be obtained on finally selected suppliers.

The numbers of likely customers, suppliers and users were deduced from an examination of the available catalogue of the exhibition of two years ago.

In the time budget of the visit the following considerations were taken into account: the time allocation was based on informative short contacts of 20 minutes duration, on probing contacts of 30 minutes duration and on negotiating contacts of 60 minutes duration. The allocation of the three types of contacts to customers, suppliers and users was tabulated as shown in Fig. 4.

It was anticipated that three customers, three suppliers and four users would require repeat contacts. According to this schedule 15 hours and 50 minutes of net exhibition time would be required to accomplish the task.

D

Interviews with:	Customers							Suppliers										Users																
	1	2	3	4	5	6	7	1	2	3	4	5	6	7	8	9	10	1	2	3	4	5	6	7	8	9	10	11	12	13	14	15	16
first contacts short 20 min	●	●				●	●	●			●	●	●	●	●	●	●	●	●	●	●	●	●		●		●	●		●	●	●	●
medium 30 min			●		●				●	●														●		●			●				
long 60 min																																	
repeat contacts short 20 min			●	●	●							●												●		●				●		●	
medium 30 min				●					●	●																							
long 60 min																																	

	Interviews	
Customers	8 × 20 min =	160 min
	2 × 30 min =	60 min
Suppliers	9 × 20 min =	180 min
	4 × 30 min =	120 min
Users	17 × 20 min =	340 min
	3 × 30 min =	90 min
	43 interviews = 950 min = 15 hours 50 minutes	

FIGURE 4. TIME BUDGET FOR A FOUR-DAYS' VISIT TO AN EXHIBITION

A time budget for three types of contacts for interviews with seven customers, ten suppliers and sixteen users. A total of forty-three interviews consisting of thirty-three first contacts and ten repeat contacts.

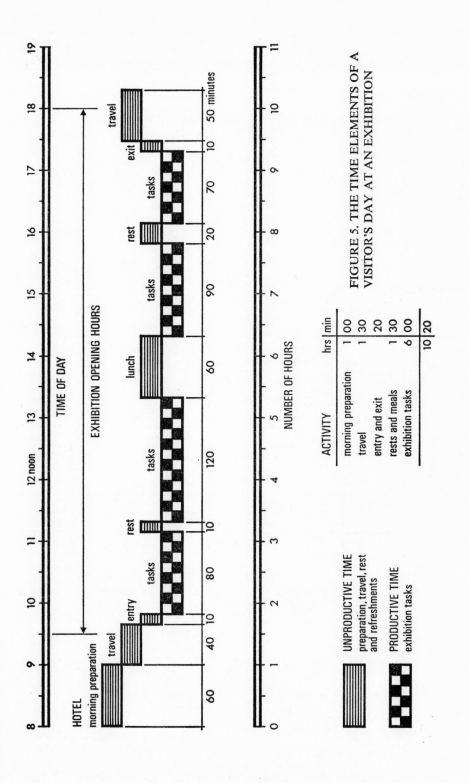

FIGURE 5. THE TIME ELEMENTS OF A
VISITOR'S DAY AT AN EXHIBITION

ACTIVITY	hrs	min
morning preparation	1	00
travel	1	30
entry and exit		20
rests and meals	1	30
exhibition tasks	6	00
	10	20

UNPRODUCTIVE TIME
preparation, travel, rest
and refreshments

PRODUCTIVE TIME
exhibition tasks

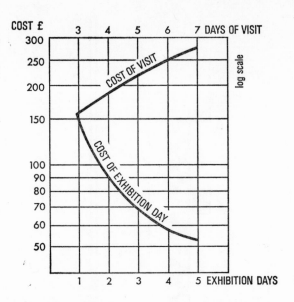

Cost of external travel per return flight	£70·00
Salary of visiting executive per day	£13·00
Expenses per day	£15·00

Total number of days of visit	3	4	5	6	7
Number of days at exhibition	1	2	3	4	5
Travel out and return	70·00	70·00	70·00	70·00	70·00
Salary	39·00	52·00	65·00	78·00	91·00
Expenses	45·00	60·00	75·00	90·00	105·00
Nominal cost of visit	£154·00	£182·00	£210·00	£238·00	£266·00
Nominal cost of exhibition day	£154·00	£91·00	£70·00	£59·50	£53·20

FIGURE 6. NOMINAL COSTS OF VISITING AN EXHIBITION

An example of the cost effectiveness of a time management approach to visiting exhibitions for a range of one to five exhibition days.

The time elements of the exhibition were:

daily opening hours: 9.30 to 18.00 hours
travel time hotel to exhibition: 40 minutes
travel time from exhibition to town: 50 minutes

The catering facilities at the exhibition are good, but a sit-down meal takes at least one hour.

On the basis of these data it was found that the available daily exhibition task time would amount to six hours (*see Figure 5*). Taking all these factors into account, the theoretical minimum time for the visit would be three exhibition visiting days. This would not allow for any excess waiting time or for wasted interviews, nor for any contingencies such as delays in the open air area due to bad weather and the like. No time would be available for visits to more than five customers, for visiting non-scheduled stands, nor for any fringe interest visits. It was clear that in reality four days at the exhibition would be required to achieve the set objectives.

The one and half day visit originally proposed would allow contacts with not more than two customers, four potential suppliers and six users. The operational advantages of a four days visit became apparent. Such a visit would provide the flexibility in making contacts, a minimum of irritation resulting from unavoidable time wasting, and the probability of completing the task early on the fourth day of the visit, enabling the return by an earlier flight. This last possibility opened the question of any contacts en route the return flight. In fact, a visit to a prospective customer located on the path of the return flight was overdue and tentative arrangements for that visit were made.

It was suggested that in addition to the time budget investigation a purely nominal cost analysis should be carried out to place the alternative visiting times on a comparable basis and to provide a formula for future use.

For the purpose of the exercise the following nominal values were taken as a basis for calculations: the salary of the person assigned for the task was taken as £3042 p.a. (cost to the company) equivalent to a daily rate of £13 (234 working days p.a.). Out-of-pocket expenses were assumed at £15 per day, and the cost of air travel as £70 for a return flight. The original proposal of a one-and-half-day visit and alterative three and four-days visits were subjected to a time and cost analysis taking into account the nominal values agreed and the fact that the total internal and external travel time would take one day each way. The comparison of the cost for different periods of the exhibition visit is illustrated in Figure 6. The total cost for a two-days visit is £182 resulting in cost per exhibition day of £91. The total cost for the four-days visit is £238 resulting in a cost per exhibition day of £59.50. The cost per contact time hour would be £15.15 for the two-days visit and £9.90 for the four-days visit.

CARL A. RUDISILL LIBRARY
LENOIR RHYNE COLLEGE

Preparations for the visit included:

> specifications and installation details of the built-in units and a question-
> naire concerning service and spares facilities
> brief dossiers on ten customers
> a simple, duplicated form in A.5 format listing critical points of built-in
> units and providing space for noting users' opinions in code

Travel and hotel arrangements were made by the company's travel agent.
Three of the company's overseas agents were notified of the visit by telex, two
confirmed their own visit and in turn gave details xxxxxx of how they can be
contacted.

The end result of the visit was summarised as follows:

Visits to customers' stands:
> in fact seven customers exhibited, all were visited, five repeat visits
> were paid.

Contacts with visiting customers:
> four customers from three countries were contacted through the
> foreign visitors reception bureau and discussions with them were
> held at the exhibition and in the hotel.

Suppliers of built-in unit:
> the stands of twelve potential suppliers were briefly surveyed and
> their literature collected during the first day of visit; short dis-
> cussions were held with four and subsequent negotiations with
> two of the last four suppliers.

Users of built-in units:
> twenty users exhibited, fifteen of them were users of units made
> by four most promising suppliers; these fifteen were visited each
> once, and three twice.

Company's overseas agents:
> two agents were contacted and the standing and service facilities
> in their territories of the two short listed potential suppliers were
> discussed.

Trial orders for three units each were placed with two suppliers for compatibility tests and technical evaluation.

The exhibition task was completed at noon of the fourth day and several
fringe interest stands were visited. Contacts made by telephone and telex with
potential customers located in the path of the return flight resulted in meetings
with two potential customers and a trial order from one of them who incidentally specified the make of one of the built-in units which were the subject
of final negotiations.

A total of eleven customer contacts and two potential customer contacts
were made, fifteen users were interviewed, two overseas agents were contacted.

In a final review and discussion of the exhibition visit a question was asked about the significance, if any, of a cost per contact figure, as used in assessing a salesman's efforts. The answer was that in a mixed task situation like the one encountered even the total cost effectiveness can be assessed only after a considerable time has elapsed and when the results can be evaluated. A cost per contact assessment would have to provide some weighting of contacts as obviously two thirty-minutes' contacts with customers cannot be directly compared with three twenty-minutes' contacts with users. The contacts with customers could result in orders, the contacts with users could be abortive. Vice versa, the contacts with customers could produce no more than some goodwill but the contacts with users could prevent a serious mistake in the selection of suppliers.

The exercise has to be seen as a whole and the time-money implication should be related to the overall magnitude of the issues involved. The eleven customer contacts represented a yearly turnover of £137,500, the two new contacts a potential of £12,500 p.a. The purchase value of the built-in units would be £37,400 p.a. Thus the total sum of the transaction involved could be presented as £187,400 and a total nominal cost of the excursion as £238. At a 100 per cent overheads rate this cost would be £476 representing about 0.25 per cent of the total sum involved. If this seemed a reasonable ratio then all is well but if it were considered excessive, then it must clearly be stated why that is so, and what other basis for budgeting is acceptable.

Alternative the cost per contact can be considered. A one-and-a-half-day visit would have yielded a total of twelve contacts at a nominal cost of £182 which at a 100 per cent overheads rate would amount to £364 and thus to £30 per contact. The four-days visit yielded a nominal total of 38 contacts at a total cost of £476 amounting to £12.50 per contact. One can also look at the issue from the point of view of marginal yields. If there was an initial justification for a short visit costing £364 then the probability of achieving much better results at an extra cost of £112 (i.e. the difference between £476 and £364) would surely justify the longer visit. Yet another point of view can be taken on the basis of the probability that the meagre results obtained from a short visit would have required at least one other short visit. On the basis of time budgeting alone this means that two short visits result in a productive to unproductive time ratio of 2:4, i.e. two exhibition days to four travelling days, whereas a four-days visit has a productive to unproductive ratio of 4:2. The cost for two exhibition days resulting from two short visits would be £364 per exhibition day, for the four-days visit the cost is £119 per day.

This rudimentary example of time budgeting for exhibition visiting not only shows the benefits of such an approach but also highlights a phenomenon met again and again in large organisations and small. Engineers breathing mathematics, eating calculus for breakfast and modifying several PERT diagrams out of recognition between lunch and tea, treat a visit to an exhibition with less mathematical forethought than they would a family picnic.

	Visitors	
	Visitors—exhibitors	
	Motives for visiting	
	buying interests	
	purpose	
	resale	
	product	
	plant	
	suppliers	
	present	
	new/potential	
	lapsed	
	customer interests	
	intelligence interests	
	fringe interests	
	combined visits interests	
	Visiting tasks	
	active	
	passive	
	active–passive (combined)	
	Visiting contacts	
	type	
	technique	
	time	
	frequency	
	Authority of visitor	
	supplier contacts	
	customer contacts	
	other	

Check List 11. *VISITING EXHIBITIONS*

This check list deals with visiting tasks, their motivation, definition of interests and personal contact techniques. The review of visiting tasks should be made with the help of the topography (*Fig. 1*) of the particular exhibition which is visited, the exhibition time elements (*check lists 5, 6*) and if appropriate with exhibitions intelligence check lists 32, 33. If the authority of a visitor requires clarification, the discussion of this subject in the text (*page 95*) will indicate the specific areas of responsibility which need definition and checking. Case study 2 (exhibition visiting time elements) and Fig. 4, 5, 6 provide a good background for a review of visiting tasks.

14. Marketing Merits of Exhibition

In general terms the *marketing merit of an exhibition* is determined by the marketing acumen with which the organisers have conceived and defined its aims and scope, and by the organisational skill and proficiency with which the aims are implemented.

An assessment of the *general marketing merit* can be made by a scrutiny of the following merit elements:

The validity, from a marketing point of view, of its title and declared aims and scope (*see page 37*)

The competence of the organisation and the efficiency of technical arrangements (*see page 40*)

The quality and quantity of visitors attracted to the exhibition in relation to the stated aims and scope.

The quality and quantity of exhibitors in relation to the declared scope and aims.

The geographic location of the exhibition (*see page 43*)
The environment of the exhibition.

The geographic sphere of influence of the exhibition.

An evaluation of the general marketing merit elements in relation to the particular objectives and tasks of exhibitors and visitors, will produce individual *subjective marketing merits*.

The general marketing merit of an exhibition is of interest to exhibitors and to visitors as a first indication that the exhibition is serving their area of marketing.

The subjective marketing merit of an exhibition from the point of view of exhibitors and visitors is determined by the effectiveness with which their own marketing tasks are served by the exhibition. Exhibitors will be particularly interested in the quality and quantity of visitors and in the sphere of influence of the exhibition and its outward strength.

Visitors will be interested in the first place in the quality and quantity of exhibitors.

The assessment of some of the merit elements must be based of necessity on past performance. Exhibition of long standing can be relied upon to maintain or improve the standards of their technical organisation. Long term stand contracts enable an assessment within fairly safe limits of exhibitor participation and quality. The assessment of the quality and quantity of visitors is subject to some uncertainty, as in the event considerable variations can occur particularly due to unforeseen circumstances. Even new exhibitors must declare their intention at least twelve months in advance, whilst visitors can decide at the very last moment not to attend. The merits of an exhibition can be distorted by a change in trading patterns in that particular market, by a decline of attendance or by overcrowding, by the emergence of competitive ventures, by labour difficulties, by changes in the political or economic climate. To some extent the merits can be assessed to a degree on the basis of information supplied by the organisers, providing it is supported by evidence of reliability and meaningful analysis.

The assessment can be supplemented and verified by a close scrutiny of exhibition catalogues for one or more previous years, by questioning relevant trade associations, customers, friendly competitors and consular posts in the case of foreign exhibitions.

Trade journals usually review important exhibitions in their field, however their reports in many cases are no more than summaries of press hand-outs with a few highlights of interest. On several occasions personal interviews which the author held with the reporter responsible for a review yielded very enlightening additional information. The merit rating of exhibitions for which participation is planned for several events ahead should be constantly reviewed and brought up to date. The exhibitions' general rating and even more important its subjective rating related to your own marketing objectives should be assessed as to improvement and decline, and also in comparison with other existing or newly arrived competitive exhibitions. In short you should treat an exhibition as a discriminating buyer would treat a highly priced product or service.

An exploratory visit is the best way to assess the marketing merits of an exhibition. Even after all the pertinent documentary information is obtained and analysed, there are always intangible impressions which cannot be conveyed by a report and which to an individual prospective exhibitor could be of considerable importance. Exhibitors participating in an exhibition have of course an excellent opportunity to assess its subjective marketing merit, providing that their own marketing objectives and exhibiting motives are clearly defined and used as bench marks and that the assessment procedure is made a subject of explicit instructions (*see also exhibition intelligence, page 208*).

Exhibition Environments

The general and subjective merits of exhibitions are further influenced by the environment in which they are held. The space-time characteristics of exhibitions place them in a unique position in the environment. They are of it, yet only for a short space of time. Their impact may or may not continue after they have closed down. Depending on the strength of that impact they can alter the environment, or at least substantially contribute to changes in it, or alternatively they may leave hardly any trace. Some exhibitions with long years of tradition behind them, enhance their importance and influence as time goes on, others have not much more to offer than a slowly dying memory of old glories. However the better defined their purpose, the more purposeful their aims, the more they become within their environment a microcosm with a separate identity. Because of that insularity of their short existence it seems that exhibitions have *two environments*. An *external* one, i.e. the environment in which the exhibition is held, and an *internal* one, i.e. that created by the exhibition as a self-contained unit. The frontiers between the two environments are not always clearly defined, some elements operate in both, some only in one or the other.

A perceptive and imaginative marketing attitude will indicate to exhibition organisers, how best to take advantage of a favourable external environment and how to overcome, counteract or compensate for an unfavourable one.

Exhibition organisers with no such perception and no imagination, manage to waste the opportunities which a cosmopolitan or metropolitan environment offers them, by mounting in it catchpenny events of parochial unimportance.

Visitor Environment

In the environment of an international exhibition, of high marketing and organizational merit, the exhibitors' stand personnel can encounter a vast range of visitor categories. These categories are listed in Table 5, p. 86. The fact that they contain so many individual functions does not necessarily mean that all would appear as single and separate persons. In a large organisation the 'buyer' may be in fact a person delegated by a purchasing department which in turn is subject to the control or directives of technical or commercial decision influences.

In a small organisation a purchasing function involving complex technical and commercial decisions may be concentrated in one person. A visitor could combine several roles because his organisation could not, or would not, delegate more than one person to visit the exhibition. A well selected, trained and prepared stand team will be able to cope with all technical and commercial problems, but it can exert only a small degree of influence over the incidence of occasions on which they are confronted by the different categories. The time factor becomes very important and the only way to control it is to discriminate in the time allocated to the different visitor categories, and to use as many non-personal aids as is compatible with an effective exhibition performance. Such aids must be seen to be used only in support of personal attention, or as temporary expedient to relieve the tedium of waiting of a visitor, but never as substitutes of the person to person contact. The identification of the quality of the visitor, of his interest, his status and his buying influence becomes a vital, initial approach function as it will determine the character of the action to be taken. This identification is also an essential element of post-exhibition analysis and follow up actions.

The influence categories of an industrial product, later discussed in more detail, are illustrated in Figure 9, p. 156. In normal trading conditions the inner circle confrontation is the end result of the peripheral influences exerted in both semi-circular sectors. An assessment of the influence category and of the proximity factor of the visitor's interest, during the opening stages of the interview is important in any situation. For industrial products incorporated in one or more assemblies before they reach the final product and its user, the influence and proximity factors determine the approach to the visitor and the need if any, of calling in specialists, e.g. application engineers, designers, chemists, etc.

An important marketing factor is the number of new visitors, particularly if they can be identified as to their status and interest. The opinion that it is a great merit if an exhibition admits only trade buyers and trade visitors, needs serious investigation. Some exhibition organisers boast about the exclusion of the general public from their events and some exhibitors clamour for such exclusion. It is by no means certain that such an exclusion generally contributes to the marketing quality of an exhibition. Many industrial products are so remote from the ultimate user that they could only benefit in the markets from a nearer acquaintance and better understanding among the general public. Separate days or special hours of attendance are a compromise arranged where too great an influx of the general public is anticipated, although this in itself should be a sign that the public is interested, and if so it should be not only admitted but invited.

In general trade fairs with sections covering a number of different industries, the total number of visitors is an indication of limited value to the exhibitor, unless his exhibits are represented in several sections. For exhibitors with one stand, the position of the hall in which the stand is located, the position of the stand in that hall, and the influence of these positions on the likely flow of visitors is more important than the total number of visitors passing the turnstiles.

Exhibitor Environment

The quality and quantity of exhibitors participating in an exhibition is a cardinal merit factor and its correct assessment can, and should influence your decision whether to participate in an exhibition and if so in what manner.

The exhibitor environment requires evaluation of three main groups of exhibitors: customers, competitors and suppliers.

Not all three groups would be necessarily represented at the particular exhibition you are investigating but perhaps at another exhibition serving the same market this could be the case.

The customer environment can include current, new, potential and lapsed customers and an evaluation of the potential purchasing power is one way of establishing the merit of that group of exhibitors. On the other hand your exhibiting objectives may aim at a different goal such as the introduction of a new product or the demonstration of your service capabilities, in which case you will survey the group of customers from the point of view of their susceptibility as targets for your tasks.

If your products are of the component, auxiliary or accessory type, the willingness of your customers to acknowledge their incorporation, or to display them on their stands or both, has an important bearing on the merit rating of the exhibition.

The term exhibitors-customers extends also to indirect customers and users. The evaluation of their quality will be based on other criteria, but always related to your marketing strategy and to your exhibiting objectives. The assessment of their exhibition effort is interesting as a matter of background information and possibly from the point of view of an identification of your products in their exhibits if the case applies.

The importance of the competitor environment of the exhibition needs no special emphasis. The national and international standing of your competitors in relation to your position, their marketing skills and resources compared with yours, their importance in your particular market sector—perhaps the absence from the exhibition of market leaders, or their attendance in strength, all these factors noted and evaluated by marketing research will influence your decision, your budget allocation, your selection of exhibits—and your exhibition strategy.

During the exhibition you will supplement your information by up-to-date observations. Particular attention should be paid to your competitors' exhibition efforts, and to their comparison with your own effort.

The supplier environment is of secondary interest unless your exhibiting objectives include buying interests, or changes of sources of supply. The merit of the suppliers' environment will then depend on the capacity of exhibitors as actual or potential suppliers. An analytical review of the main groups of exhibitors will also enable you to form a picture of the corporate environment in which your own exhibition effort will operate and contribute to the assessment of the internal technological environment of the exhibition. It will reveal whether you will be in the company of leaders, improvers or followers in your particular market.

The national provenance of the exhibitors is significant for the assessment of geographical markets and of import-export patterns. The examination of the exhibition catalogues of two or three preceding exhibitions will disclose the changes in participation, the development or decline of the exhibition, the relative importance of lapsed or new participants.

The analysis can be carried out by methods ranging from simple ranking and weighting to sophisticated data processing, the criteria applied depending on the basic data available and on the complexity of the situation.

The rank could indicate the objective importance of the exhibitor as an organisation and the weight his subjective standing in the market. For well established exhibitions the changes in participation of important exhibitors may be a sufficiently good indicator of the up-to-date merit of the exhibition.

The continuous systematic observation of the exhibitor environment is of particular value when you are participating in exhibitions in different countries serving the same market, or when you are participating in annual or other sequences of the same exhibition.

Exhibitions of high marketing merit are very good indicators of the mood of the market, but a deliberate and systematic effort must be made to read the signs. Supplementary merit factors of the exhibitor environment could be added by reviewing the participation of exhibitors outside the three main groups.

Participation of official bodies, government, local government, municipal and institutional can open opportunities for personal contacts which normally would be difficult to establish. An invitation to visit your stand is the most natural request at an exhibition whilst in other circumstances it may not be welcome or advisable. Exhibitors of products of indirect marketing interests, but of direct plant or office interest such as instrumentation, materials handling, safety, office equipment, can provide you with an opportunity to see new developments in these fields.

The presence of several banks, investment institutions and insurance companies is a sign that serious business transactions are usually conducted during the exhibition. It must of course be established whether more than simple foreign currency exchange facilities are provided.

Banks with offices at an exhibition usually issue reports about their activities at these events which may provide comments on your competitors and customers. International exhibitions of repute are often visited by official trade missions and in the case of planned economy markets, contacts with such missions can be of important marketing value.

For some products or markets the indirect merit indicators can do no more than strengthen a decision taken on other merits, for others they could be factors of considerable importance.

Marketing Environment

The marketing environment of the exhibition may affect your decision to participate in an exhibition. If the motive for exhibiting is a market penetration or market entry objective, a careful analysis of the marketing environment, of the sophistication of the means of distribution and media is essential for a successful exhibition effort. Your competitor-exhibitors can back up their stand activities by effective marketing facilities, whilst the more response there is to your stand, the more your own modest resources will be strained. An investigation of the marketing environment may thus lead you to a different emphasis of your exhibition objectives. Your exhibits could be chosen with a view to attract the attention of potential agents rather than direct customers.

The availability in the market of container terminals, free ports, free trade zones or free transit zones are important marketing environment elements, particularly for market entering and market penetration objectives. Associations of import agents, consumer protection societies, government or official test and approval agencies must be considered as influencing the overall market environment.

The external marketing environment of the exhibition is significant for territorially defined markets, as the majority of visitors to an exhibition will come from the exhibition host country. The actual percentage of inland to foreign visitors varies considerably but it is safe to assume a figure of not less than about 70 per cent of inland visitors and in most cases the same minimum proportion of inland exhibitors.

Demographic Environment

For the exhibitor the demographic merit of the location of the exhibition is its relation to his marketing activities both in the narrow context of the exhibition in which he participates and in the wider sense of his general marketing policy. The locale of the exhibition, i.e. the town, region, province, country in which it takes place endows it with a sphere of influence created by the importance and demographic character of the location. Thus for example exhibitions held in or near London, Paris or New York will benefit from the metropolitan and cosmopolitan character of these cities, exerting a *centrifugal* outward penetrating *marketing force*, whereas local exhibitions held in Elda or Colmar will benefit from the *centripetal* inward saturation *marketing force* of these locations.

The centrifugal marketing force in metropolitan locations will extend the influence of the exhibitor to government offices, corporation headquarters, financial and investment institutions, foreign government and trade representations, trade missions and trade centres and to contacts with people visiting the metropolis on other than exhibition business.

The centripetal marketing force in enclave locations exerts its influence on a concentration of specialised industrial or commercial activities giving opportunities for a strong impact on a narrow sector. Large scale exhibitions serving internationally significant industries will derive maximum benefits from cosmopolitan locations, highly specialised regional or single industry oriented exhibitions will benefit most from local exhibitions. However there is no inherent advantage in the locale except in relation to the marketing merit of the exhibition taking place. The merit of a well organised international exhibition with an established reputation is in no way affected by its location in a provincial town, a badly organised and badly housed exhibition will not redeem its failings by being held in a cosmopolitan capital city.

A critical assessment of the demographic environment of the exhibition will influence decisions concerning the manning of stands, the inclusion of special exhibits, the visits of executives not directly connected with the exhibition effort (financial, legal, patent specialists, licence negotiators) or the attendance of technicians expert in particular fields of the market.

Technological and Industrial Environment

A sober and dispassionate assessment of the technological position of your products in their markets is a basic requirement of marketing. It may have to be adjusted from the general to the particular market in which the products are exhibited. If such an assessment is not available, the advent of an exhibition effort provides a good opportunity to highlight the need for it.

The technical simplicity or complexity of the product, its up-to-date, advanced or perhaps obsolete design features, its pedestrian, sophisticated or exaggerated appearance, its adequate, excellent or poor performance—all these factors add up to its technological position in relation to a particular exhibition and to the market it is intended to serve. An evaluation of the technological position should be made in relation to the state of art in that market and against the background of competitive products exhibited and otherwise available in the market. This evaluation will show which product advantages can be emphasised, which shortcomings should be subdued and in some situations the decision may be reached to postpone participation or not to participate at all.

The circumscribed markets for industrial components, elements and auxiliary equipment are particularly sensitive to technological position factors, whilst complete products operate in more open markets, where their overall marketability has a decisive influence. An exhibition held in a highly industrialised country or in a region specialising in the particular industry it serves is located in a technological environment of predominantly external character It remains an environment of merit irrespectively of the quality and quantity of exhibitors participating in the exhibition.

Let us for example assume that the exhibition is not very well organised and only one technologically prominent exhibitor stands out among competitors of lesser quality. This exhibitor could gain a considerable advantage from his exceptional status. That is, if he makes sure that his presence is known to potential customers who otherwise would not bother to visit an exhibition, which from their point of view, has a low marketing merit.

The exhibition can be located in an *external industrial environment* which is expanding, stagnating or regressing, be it because the industries are in one of these states of their life cycle, or because external circumstances exert an encouraging, maintaining or restricting influence.

The exhibition can have an *internal industrial environment* which is in a state of stagnation whilst the external environment is expanding or vice versa. The evaluation of these factors will assist you in arriving at a merit rating of the exhibition from this technological and industrial point of view.

Symposia and conferences combined with an exhibition also contribute to the shaping of the internal technological environment of the exhibition. The merit rating of such events is not an easy matter and must be related with care to your exhibiting objectives. A symposium of high technological merit does not necessarily elevate a low merit exhibition to a higher level, nor does an exhibition of high marketing value necessarily ensure a high technological merit of a symposium combined with it.

Usually there is a connection between the industrial and technological environment of the host country and the merit of an exhibition-symposium combination. Occasionally such combined events of high technological merit are held in, what might be called, an industrially incongruous environment.

Exhibitions-symposia on automation, instrumentation and cybernetics held in Yugoslavia and Hungary are examples.

Scientific Environment

The presence or proximity of universities, technical colleges, scientific institutes, research laboratories can influence the marketing merit of an exhibition located within their radius of influence or access.

The buying expertise of customers can be augmented by calling on the services of members of faculties or specialists. Testing and experimental facilities of institutes can be used for assessment purposes, both by the customer and by the exhibitor. The claims made for advanced designs or progressive concepts are subject to scrutiny by people with up-to-date knowledge— even if often only theoretical—of the latest achievements.

You have to assess how such an environment will affect your exhibits, how it will help or hinder your marketing strategy.

On the whole one can say that a sophisticated scientific environment will be favourable for progressive equipment or for products based on sound design and operational principles, and unfavourable to products with overt or hidden characteristics of design or operational obsolescence.

Exhibition Hall Environment

The environment of the exhibition hall or area in which your stand is located is not crucially important as long as the facilities are adequate. When this environment is exceptionally favourable as it could be with airy, well-proportioned air-conditioned halls, or exceptionally unfavourable as it would be with a crowded maze of upper floor galleries neither properly lit, nor adequately ventilated, then the hall environment becomes a merit factor. In some exhibitions you may find some old halls and some new ones and from your point of view as an exhibitor it may be important in which of these your stand is located and in which the stands of your competitors. The quality of the hall environment is certainly perceived by visitors and they are influenced by it. Their inclination to linger just that much longer in a favourable environment has been frequently observed.

The range of moods created by exhibition halls, consciously or by default, is very wide indeed. You have the busy atmosphere of the woodworking section of an exhibition, with the high-pitched whine of saws and the inviting aroma of sawn timber.

You may witness the grotesque spectacle of giant plastic moulding machinery spewing out half useless components with faults which would not even pass the eyes of an inspector looking the other way, and the sight of endless queues of visitors of assorted sexes and ages spending up to 10 minutes of waiting time to secure the free gift of a plastic bucket of sickly yellow colour and probably with a weak spot somewhere in its bottom. You can enjoy the aesthetic pleasure of darkened stands with cunningly lit display cases of precision instruments or electronic components, vieing for your attention as much as would jewels or crystalware.

But you have also the spectacle of unbelievably crowded stands, which seem to have come straight from the street market, in which suppliers of motor car and boating accessories so lavishly indulge.

The general quality of the exhibition hall will also affect your stand position. Not all exhibitors can have first class positions, and the better the hall layout and design, the less chances of dead corners, obscured views, obstructing columns and draughty gangways.

There are exhibition halls which by their poor quality seem to belie their purpose. An old building is usually blamed for all shortcomings, but it is not a very valid excuse. Promoters of exhibitions have by the nature of their business access to the best and most ingenious designers. Why they do not inspire them to take the same advantage of an existing structure as stage designers do for their daily bread within the limitations of an old theatre building, is a matter of surprise or, perhaps more aptly, another example of marketing myopia so well documented for other products.

In the case of multifloor exhibition buildings, the environments of different floor locations assume added significance. If you can only secure a stand on a first floor which in fact is no more than an overflow area, the potential flow of visitors may be seriously affected. You may have to compensate for such a disadvantage by issuing special invitations and additional publicity, in other words incur extra cost. If your exhibiting objective is to attract a great number of new contacts even such extra efforts may not produce the required result. A multifloor building designed for exhibition purposes poses other problems. The efficiency of lifts and escalators, effective signposting, access and exit locations, become important factors. You may be reluctant to accept a top floor location, because top floor attendances are reputed to be lower than average, but the availability of direct express lifts may counteract that assumption effectively. The top floor may contain a restaurant or another special feature and your stand will benefit by its proximity to the resulting flow of visitors. Regrettably, once more it is difficult to give a general ruling on the merits or demerits of such locations. An assessment of the situation can be made by judicious questioning of actual exhibitors and best of all by personal reconnaissance.

Stands and Exhibits Environment
The aesthetic and functional quality of exhibition stands and of displays of exhibits is usually a reflection of the exhibitors' attitudes to design.

Fashion in stand design and display techniques come and go as they do in other spheres of life. In an exhibition environment they will be mostly the reflection of styles prevailing in the exhibition host country, which will account for the majority of the exhibitors. A prospective foreign exhibitor needs to take note of that environment and relate it to his intended participation and to stand designs so far adopted by him. What appeared more than adequate in one location, may prove disastrous in another. The bold and daring stand suitable for a cosmopolitan setting, can appear pretentious and exaggerated in more modest provincial surroundings.

Your observations of stand design and display techniques of exhibits should be related to the general standard of exhibition stands, to the standard of stands in your sector of industry, in your exhibition hall or other relevant groupings, with particular attention to the stands of competitors. If previous experience is not available and if repeat participation is contemplated, a systematic survey conducted by your stand designer accompanied by your stand manager, usually handsomely repays the trouble taken.

Stand Manning Environment
The problems of stand personnel are fully discussed later on, but the stand manning environment of an exhibition deserves a note of its own. The expertise and professionalism of personnel manning the stands at an exhibition has a high marketing merit content. Your own stand personnel will be subject to comparison with those of your competitors and the comparison will be made by very influential judges—your customers or potential customers.

At international exhibitions your neighbours may be international companies with multilingual experts. Conversely, at another exhibition and despite your more modest stand, you are the exhibitor who paid the exhibition host country the compliment of stand personnel speaking the language of the country, even if it is a rare language, whilst your big neighbours did not bother.

The quality of the manning of stands can set the 'tone' of an exhibition and contribute to its reputation. The assessment of the quality of stand manning can be made on the basis of recent past experience and observation, of exhibition intelligence, press reports of interviews and when conferences or technical discussions are part of the exhibition programme, on the basis of a scrutiny of speakers and participants.

National Environment
Economic environment factors have the most direct influence on the marketing environment, and generally they are also best documented and widely communicated. Information about changes in internal credit conditions, investment policies, politico-economic conditions, industrial groupings and similar factors is less readily available and in markets inclined to reticence in publishing such information deeper probing is required. Impending changes

in import quotas, tariffs, custom duties are obvious factors requiring timely observations. The prevailing trading pattern in market sectors which are of particular interest, the ratio of private to public trading, the importance of government trading agencies should be reviewed. Existing or projected agri- cultural or industrial development schemes, investment subsidies or aid grants, tax concessions, international loans should be related to your marketing objectives.

Political environment factors can affect the decision to exhibit and the scope and mode of participation. An unfriendly political climate could indicate that it would be wiser to use alternative means of marketing, an exceptionally friendly one could encourage a more sumptuous participation than would be normally considered. In an unstable situation a diplomatic absence may prove less embarrassing at a later date than participation during a time of impending change. Products of direct or indirect strategic character are particularly affected by this factor.

Discrimination by the public sector against suppliers on the basis of their national origin, or prejudices of the private sector can adversely affect the marketing merit of an exhibition. A friendly political environment, the estab- lishing or renewing of political associations can affect it favourably.

Legal environment factors. Legislation can affect the choice of exhibits and under certain circumstances the marketing techniques and price policies which have to be adopted, e.g. monopolies and antitrust legislation, standards requirements, price regulation, distributors and agents legal protection, exclusive market arrangements, franchises, unfair competition legislation, advertising restraints.

Social environment factors may favour low priced mass consumption goods in one situation or luxury and leisure goods in another. Changes in social habits, in incomes, in housing programmes, in health services, would indicate, depending on the direction of the change, a favourable or a discouraging situation for the products affected, e.g. building, hospital, public works equipment.

Aesthetic Environment
The assessment of the esoteric values of aesthetics generally and of appear- ances and taste particularly is full of pitfalls, but in the environment of international exhibitions it deserves serious consideration.

The exhibition offers an opportunity for direct comparison at close quar- ters of styles, shapes and colours of displayed exhibits, of the stand and of its elements. To disregard that aspect of your exhibition effort is as inadvisable as to disregard the now acknowledged emotional involvement of industrial buyers making purchases of industrial equipment.

The aesthetic environment of your exhibits and of your stand will be dif- ferent in Denmark and Portugal, in Hong-Kong and Rio de Janeiro, in Mexico and Bombay. Although a badly designed stand can spoil the effect of well designed exhibits, exhibits not acceptable on aesthetic grounds will not be made more acceptable by the best stand design. The question of what is bad, acceptable or best design must be left to the beholder.

The Cultural Environment can have an indirect influence on the merit of an exhibition. It can enhance the understanding of visitors for sophisticated or science based products, it can also cause very critical attitudes to inadequate products or presentation. Theatres, concert halls, art collections and other cultural events can provide opportunities for extramural contacts and entertaining, which in carefully selected cases can be of great value.

Geographic Spheres of Influence

The description of the geographic sphere of influence of an exhibition is usually based on the national origin of exhibitors and visitors, on their total numbers and on the number of countries they came from.

The sphere of influence of an exhibition is an important marketing merit factor which cannot be determined in an objective way that would be generally valid, but must be assessed in relation to individual marketing objectives.

It may be interesting to note that one exhibition was visited by 22,000 buyers from 22 countries and another by 110,000 buyers from 55 countries, but much more information would be required to be able to relate these figures to the marketing strategy of an individual exhibitor.

Whatever the definition and character of a market is, all marketing activities will have a *space element*. There are definable territories or geographic areas of past, current and planned future activities. It is from this point of view that the geographic influence range of an exhibition is important. The definitions of spheres of influence are of necessity fairly open. Thus *local* may mean a sizable town, an industrial or urban conglomeration or a market town and its agricultural hinterland. A *national* sphere of influence needs no comment, but an *international* sphere of influence can range from two small neighbouring countries to many large ones. A sphere of influence which, due to special circumstances extends over the whole of the North American continent could be classed as *continental*, such a sphere extending to both Americas as *intercontinental*. For some marketing objectives the general economic structure of an area can be a decisive factor and for some world wide operations the United Nations designations of Economic Class I, II and III areas could be significant.

From the point of view of Alpha Company, conventional geographic areas may be of no more than formal conceptual value and the company would have to construct its own categories strictly related to its marketing strategy.

From the point of view of Beta Company one or more, or a combination of several geographic categories, could provide the required basis for selection and decision.

General Merits	
Subjective Merits	
Exhibition Environments	
internal	external
visitors	
exhibitors	
marketing	
	demographic
technological	
industrial	
	scientific
exhibition hall	
stand	
stand manning	
national	
aesthetic	
cultural	
Geographic Spheres of Influence	

Check List 12. *MARKETING AND ENVIRONMENT MERITS OF EXHIBI-TIONS*

This check list is compiled in general terms to provide a guide to a qualitative assessment of an exhibition, of its marketing merits and of its environments. The check lists dealing with the classification of exhibitions, their administration, services and facilities (*check lists 1, 2, 3, 4, 5, 6, 7*) indicate the material and quantitative elements involved. These may be a matter of available records or may need checking. Their merits for specific exhibiting or visiting motives and aims must now be subjected to evaluations by judgment and discrimination. Check lists 13 and 14 should assist in the difficult task of evaluating the relative merits of several exhibitions which could serve your marketing aims.

Check List 13. *MERITS OF THE EXHIBITION COMPLEX*

This check list deals with the internal exhibition environment elements which affect the merit of an exhibition. Some of the items listed may be of no importance to your current aims, but may be well worth noting for future reference. There may be items not listed which need adding to the list.   In any case the exhibition complex and its merits for your particular marketing effort are critical factors which not only influence your decision to participate but can also determine the effectiveness of your exhibition effort.

	Exhibit display groupings	
	markets, market sectors	
	industries, processes, services	
	Exhibitors	
	total number of exhibitors	
	frequency of participation in last three events	
	numbers and quality of exhibitors	
	main display groups	
	customers and potential customers	
	primary, intermediate, end users	
	market or market sector competitors	
	product or product range competitors	
	suppliers, direct, indirect	
	group exhibits (national or other)	
	foreign exhibitors (countries)	
	Official participants—(inland and foreign)	
	government, local government, municipalities	
	institutions, chambers of commerce	
	trade promotion offices	
	international development and co-operation agencies	
	trade associations	
	professional institutions and associations	
	Exhibitors or participants—indirect	
	banking, credit, investment, leasing	
	insurance, transport, shipping, packing	
	publicity media	
	radio and television	
	publishers	
	technical and trade journals	
	technical and trade books and handbooks	
	trade directories	
	exhibition bulletins, directories	
	research institutes	
	market and marketing	
	opinion polls	
	economic	
	sociological	
	other	

Check List 13. *MERITS OF THE EXHIBITION COMPLEX*

15. Selection of Exhibitions

The intention to participate in an exhibition was expressed in a previous phase of the decision-making process by defining the motives for participation. The next step was the listing of exhibitions nominally compatible with the defined motives. As we approach the final stage of decision making, that is the selection of exhibitions in which participation will be implemented, a critical scrutiny of the preceding steps is required.

It may be argued that the previous selections, if made rationally and on the basis of valid aims should not require any further review. Theoretically this may be true, even if inadvisable, and in practice it sometimes is so because strong departmental or executive influences, or in smaller firms, personal convictions or prejudices preclude a revision of declared motives.

But neither the data generally available about exhibitions, nor the nature of a realistic and flexible marketing strategy warrant a headstrong attitude. Having made this apology to formalists, we can proceed to review and probe the motives for participation and the motivations which led to the definition of the marketing motives for exhibiting. The depth and extent of that probing will depend on the role and hierarchical position of the person wielding the probe. A simple scrutiny of the marketing rationale of the motives may suffice in one case, a dismissal of motives based on parochial or vested interests could be necessary in another. The approval and reinforcement of strong functional motives and their evaluation to a higher rank of importance can contrast with an enquiry into the omission of valid motives because of ignorance or fictional obstacles. The results of this review and filtering of motives will establish a final range of motives and their order of importance.

Merit Rating

The check lists dealing with marketing motives for exhibiting, motives for visiting and marketing merits of exhibitions, enumerated the factors relevant to the selection of exhibitions suitable for participation. But decisions cannot be based on a list of factors. A measure of quality and quantity is required so that preferences can be expressed, the expression of preferences being the essence of any decision making process.

Merit rating can be used for measuring quality or performance, but any such rating can be only as good as the judgment of those operating it. If merit rating is regarded merely as a tool and not as a means in itself, and if it is used with circumspection, reasonable results can be ultimately obtained. Even in situations where data and performance assessments are plentiful and reliable and the means of selection as sophisticated as modern science and technology can make them, there comes a point when merits have to be rated and weighted, when judgment has to be used.

In the exhibition situation, complexity variety and interaction of all kinds is abundant, but enough information is simply not obtainable or if eventually it could be obtained, the effort to do so in terms of cost and time would defeat the main object of the exercise which is to make decisions about participating in exhibitions. We must therefore take recourse to *elliptical merit rating* by reducing the factors involved to those considered as key factors, or as otherwise critical.

Elliptical merit rating can be used for its advantages of shortening a merit rating procedure, but its disadvantage must be taken into account—it can obscure the presence of constraints and negative influences, when the judgment of critical factors is at fault. For the selection of exhibitions elliptical merit rating is not a palliative but a dire necessity.

In some situations a systematic merit rating has to be supplemented by the consideration of market features which can be best described as *notional*, *condition* and *attitude* market characteristics. They are seldom susceptible to exact quantitative evaluation, but their qualitative assessment can add another dimension to the merit rating of an exhibition.

The *risk elements* of an exhibition provide another set of factors which can affect the merit rating and therefore the decision to participate in, or visit an exhibition. Examples of market features which can be used as aids for merit rating and selection are arranged in check lists no. 14 and 15. Notional market characteristics are based on territorial, population and economic activity concepts. Market density, freedom and progress constitute the market condition group of factors and attitudes factors are listed under market and official attitudes and market discrimination headings. The list could be extended almost indefinitely. You may find that none of the quoted examples fits your case, or that situations which are presented as risks, to you are no more than routine procedures. The examples are offered in good faith and in a good cause, you are invited to provide more.

Notional Market Characteristics. The exhibitions in which you will participate or which you will be visiting will serve a market. The definition of that market may be sufficiently well expressed in the exhibition title, in its tradition, or its established reputation may be a reliable indication of that market.

When selecting exhibitions you have to reconcile the target-market which you expect to reach by exhibiting, with the market offered by the exhibition and assessed by its marketing merits. However, your target-market may have physical or conceptual boundaries far beyond the reach of the exhibition.

Notional market characteristics attributed to your target-market can help in such cases in the final selection of exhibitions or in shaping your exhibition strategy for the events already selected.

A territorial market concept may indicate that your target-market is continental and you may have the choice between a number of smaller exhibitions covering the continent or one or two large ones attracting exhibitors and visitors from the whole continent. On the other hand your market can have a pronounced regional or local bias and in addition to its territorial aspect you may have to consider its linguistic elements, or potential socio-logical obstacles to your products. At the same time you could encounter an overcrowded market with an antagonistic attitude or a spacious one with a receptive attitude.

The marketing concept of an exhibitor and his range of products may lead him to a *technology definition* of his markets and it is important for him to be able to assess the influence range of an exhibition in relation to the technology or technologies which it serves. It is equally important to ascertain that an exhibition in fact has no such concept or falls between two stools in that res-pect. On the other hand an exhibition may bridge two or more interacting technologies and so give exhibitors and visitors new market insights and opportunities.

If the motives for exhibiting or visiting have a strong technological content the merits of the technological environment of the exhibition assumes a dominant role. In locations of concentrated industrial activity the industrial environment can also contribute to the merit of an exhibition.

The linking of several subjects or concepts in one exhibition can be the result of a number of reasons or initiatives. General trade fairs are *linked subjects exhibitions* as a result of historic development and tradition in the case of old established events, and as a result of deliberate policy in newer events.

The organisational aspect of linked subjects exhibitions can range from a haphazard mixture of stands catering for the different interests to an effective division into different sectors, so that the end result is more in the nature of a series of specialised exhibitions linked only by the common site and organisa-tion. Exhibitions catering for specialised interests can link subjects in logical combinations of two or more items. There are natural affinities, e.g. main-tenance and safety, hygiene and welfare. There are universal affinities when one activity, product range or concept is relevant to almost any other activity, e.g. materials handling, packaging and storage, measuring, inspection and testing, waste disposal and material recovery, leasing, contract hire and ser-vice contracts.

Different technological techniques combine in the solution of newly emerg-ing problems, interaction between technologies and other disciplines results in linked activities, e.g. bio-medical engineering, bio-medical computing, bio-astronautics.

In some cases the linking of different subjects in one exhibition seems to be devoid of any logical or marketing justification. It is usually revealed as a blatent attempt to fill an exhibition hall which would otherwise remain partly empty of stands. To the visitor it is as transparent a device as the provision of lavish rest areas, which are, in effect, empty stand spaces filled by tables and chairs. To all, except perhaps to the most unobservant, such devices demon-strate clearly that had it not been for the failure to sell space, the organisers would not have provided the irrelevant added interest items, nor would they be so concerned with the seating comfort of visitors.

Exhibitors have usually a cogent comment—'never again'.

In the selection for participating, the merits of linked-subjects exhibitions should be related to the dominant marketing motives of the exhibitor and to his subjective merit requirements. In the selection of exhibitions for visiting, *linked subjects exhibitions* based on natural affinities can have a special attraction for visitors with *buying interests* or *intelligence interests*, as it is more than likely that most of the linked subjects will be of primary or subsidiary interest.

The organisational quality of linked-subjects exhibitions has a considerable influence on their marketing merits. A clear separation or grouping of the component subjects helps the visitor to locate the stands of interest and to obtain a general impression of the offerings and it is thus also of benefit to exhibitors.

There are still organisers of smaller exhibitions who believe that mixing the stands of different subjects lures the visitor into areas which he would normally miss. All that such arrangements in fact do is to irritate the serious visitor and burden stand personnel in strategic positions with the task of acting as additional information bureaux.

When selecting *exhibitions* which are *combined with conferences or symposia* one is often faced with an additional selection problem, namely whether to participate actively or passively in these gatherings.

Once more, decisions to participate should be based on the assessment of the events in relation to the defined marketing motives and to the quality of the contribution one could make. The decision then to be taken is whether to participate only in the exhibition, only in the conference, or in both.

The application of marketing criteria to science-based conferences may be anathema to some, but perhaps in time the realisation will grow that spreading knowledge, is even semantically, not so far removed from marketing it. In other words directing and encouraging its flow from those who generate it to those who want to use it. Except that in the case of scientific knowledge it should be done scientifically.

The participation in conferences and symposia is mostly subject to special charges and there are two schools of thought about the beneficial or deterrent influence of such charges. One view is that an exhibition of substantial marketing merit in its own right should be able to afford financially the mounting of a conference. Such an exhibition should be interested not only in the prestige value of an exclusive assembly of prominent names, but also in the widest possible dissemination of the subject matter.

The other view is that only an appropriate fee can provide the means for organising the conference and securing the services of speakers. Fee-paying participants are usually re-imbursed by their company, and for interesting events there may be too many candidates.

Persons interested, but not necessarily in the right department, or perhaps not of sufficient rank, have no access to those making the decision. A selection based on office nepotism is not necessarily the best way to spread the knowledge which the conference can impart to the most deserving recipients. The result is often that the same faces are seen and the same views are heard more than once and in time the social aspect becomes more important than the technical or scientific content.

The Risk Spectrum

When establishing a merit rating for an exhibition it is advisable to locate the critical risk elements involved. The relative importance of the risk spectrum of any particular exhibition and your own attitude to these risks will determine the influence of the risk factor on the final merit rating.

If you are a determined *security seeker* even marginal risks may deter you from exhibiting, but if you are a *risk taker* you will weigh the risks against other merits and so make your final decision. The risk spectrum usually comprises four types of risks or their various combinations:

> controllable
> assessable
> predictable
> unforeseeable

and following are some examples of risks which could affect the decision to participate or visit an exhibition, or sway the decision between choices of near equal merit.

Exceeding the exhibition budget is an *assessable* and *controllable* risk for experienced exhibitors and visitors, it should be *predictable and assessable* for newcomers who do their homework, but becomes unforeseeable for those who plunge into exhibition activities without proper preparation.

Design stealing is a *predictable* risk, damage to exhibits *predictable, assessable and controllable.*

Controllable risks should probably not qualify as risks, because they can be eliminated at extra cost. However, if you are a risk taker you may decide against the extra cost and for the risk. An example is an exhibition location where electricity supplies are subject to disruption due to overloading or natural forces, or where other services like compressed air or steam are likely to be inadequate or erratic. This factor may be critical for exhibits relying on these services for their display technique. Where such risks exist it is better to convert to static displays unless mobility is essential.

In some locations services may be erratic but fuel supplies plentiful. In such cases it may be possible to generate your own services for your stand only or in co-operation with other exhibitors. If your choice is between two or three exhibitions of almost equal merit but one of them has a propensity for disputes, delayed openings and cancellations it becomes the most favoured candidate for elimination. From past experience or information you will deduce that in the best of cases your costs will be higher because of the likelihood of *extra-extra overtime,* your stand may not be finished to its best standard, your stand personnel may become disgruntled, your potential customers may stay away.

If you are involved in a cancelled exhibition and if it is technically feasible you may decide to counteract the loss of marketing opportunities by mounting your private exhibition. This is easier said than done and only a limited number of exhibitors could do it. The disruption, delayed opening, postponement or cancellation of exhibitions is a *predictable* risk at exhibitions known to be prone to labour disputes and strikes and it is also assessable in terms of expenditure, but not in terms of lost opportunities both at the cancelled event and at other events which could have served the same marketing purpose.

Health hazards and climatic hazards are mostly both *predictable and controllable risks*.

An exhibition which is a 'first of its kind' venture, particularly when the organisers are not very well known, constitutes a predictable and assessable risk which can be reduced by limiting the scope of participation providing that such a limitation does not impair the achievement of a reasonable effectiveness of the effort. Alternatively a negative decision is preferable to a half-hearted participation.

Participation in exhibitions as a result of encouragement by governments, official or other bodies, may involve an *assessable* expenditure risk, when these ventures are based not on viable marketing motives but on national or regional prestige or propaganda aims.

A small firm attacking a quantity market runs the *predictable* risk that a very good response to its exhibition effort may overwhelm its production capacity. A premature display of new products can expose even a large firm to the same risk.

The risk of being exposed to staff recruiting manoeuvres is given as an explanation for not manning the stand by specialists.

Apparently some exhibitors turn exhibitions into recruiting centres and a few years ago it was reported that electronics manufacturers in the USA have hesitated to participate in one of the leading exhibitions, or even to send their observers to the show for fear that some of their engineers would be hired away by competitors. For them it was obviously a *predictable* risk.

The incidence of competitive events is an ever-present risk, although in most cases it should be a *predictable* one. The fact that the exhibition organisers seldom mention let alone emphasise such competitive events, maintaining complete silence if they are exhibitions competing for the same customers, should not deter a prospective exhibitor from making his own investigation.

Non-exhibition events such as festivals, sport events, congresses and similar gatherings are often described as an added attraction to an exhibition taking place at the same time. Such claims need careful examination. It may be perfectly true that they will generate an increased flow of visitors, but there is the *predictable* risk that they may also create traffic and accommodaton problems which could more than obliterate any potential benefits.

Legislation which may affect your decision to participate in an exhibition can be a *predictable* risk in countries with a propensity for sudden changes in legal or administrative measures and in some territories these changes may be to an extent *assessable*. Paradoxically or logically, depending which way one looks at it, in countries with a stable legal and administrative structure, changes when they do occur are mostly *unpredictable*. There are of course omens of change which allegedly are very obvious to the initiated, although on closer inspection their foresight is mostly revealed as hindsight. If you come from an established and liberal environment to an exhibition located in a volatile and perhaps at the same time restrictive one, there is a predictable and controllable risk that unless special preparations are made, your instictive reactions when negotiating, your attitudes to demands for special safeguards, your irritation at what to you appear as petty and unnecessary complications, may seriously affect the success of your exhibition effort.

Marketing relevance selection
When the first step in the selection procedure was completed, the motives for exhibiting or visiting were defined, rated and weighted. The second step was the location of suitable exhibitions, the rating and weighting of their structural elements and of their marketing merit factors.

You could have arrived at the merit rating of an exhibition by means of a sophisticated data processing technique or your personal experience told you that one exhibition is excellent for your purposes, another exhibition would be, if it were not held at an awkward time, a third is held in a promising export market. A situation may arise where your merit rating for an exhibition can be set, without further investigation, at maximum value, but others which are new ventures need detailed analysis. Even so, it may be advisable to check a known exhibition for extraneous factors such as special competing events or changes in political or technological environments.

The marketing relevance *selection procedure* is best illustrated by an exercise which is based on real events and locations but with the omission of the actual titles of the exhibitions and of the name of the exhibiting company.

The exhibits were service prone products sold to primary application customers and also to end users. A decline in sales was caused by a spate of failures of a component which had been obtained from a subcontractor. An improved design of that component not only eliminated the source of trouble, but opened opportunities for marketing the main product to a new sector of applications.

Four *main marketing motives* for exhibiting were defined on the basis of Check lists 8 and 9, and their relative importance was expressed by a five points rating scale, the values being 1=not important, 2=desirable, 3=important, 4=very important and 5=essential. The marketing motives were coded for easier matrix use and the result of the rating was:

Marketing Motives for Exhibiting	Code	Rating
Recovery of market share	M 1	5
Sales promotion of improved products	M 2	5
Marketing of products in new applications	M 3	4
Contacts with operators and users	M 4	3

The company had many years of exhibition experience to its credit and it was comparatively easy to select seven exhibitions if four countries which nominally qualified as suitable for the company's general marketing objectives. The general marketing merits of these exhibitions (*Check list 12*) were well known, and their quality was expressed by a five points rating scale, the values being:

1=poor

2=fair

3=good

4=very good

5=excellent.

The exhibitions were coded for matrix use and the result of the rating was as follows:

Exhibitions—General Marketing Merits	Code	Rating
General Trade Fair (W. Germany)	EXH 1	5
Specialised Industrial Exhibition (UK)	EXH 2	2
Specialised Industrial Exhibition (France)	EXH 3	3
General Industrial Exhibition (UK)	EXH 4	2
Industrial Exhibition (Italy)	EXH 5	4
Specialised Industrial Exhibition (W. Germany)	EXH 6	5
Specialised Industrial Exhibition (UK)	EXH 7	4

In addition to their *general marketing merits* the exhibitions were also assessed as to their *subjective merits* in relation to the special international marketing motives of the exhibitor. Three subjective merits were selected as significant and their relative importance was expressed by the same five points rating scale which was used for marketing motives.

The subjective marketing merits were coded for matrix use and the result of the rating was as follows:

Subjective Marketing Merits	Code	Rating
Visitors (quality, international provenance)	SM 1	5
Exhibitors (potential customers) environment	SM 2	4
Geographic sphere of influence	SM 3	3

FIGURE 7. MARKETING RELEVANCE SELECTION OF EXHIBITIONS

The matrix tabulation of motives and exhibitions and of their rating values and the four steps of marking and calculations are discussed in detail on pages 126–130

EXHIBITIONS / GENERAL MARKETING MERITS

MARKETING MOTIVES	RATING OF MOTIVES	EXH 1	EXH 2	EXH 3	EXH 4	EXH 5	EXH 6	EXH 7
		5	2	3	2	4	5	4
M 1	5	2	3	1	2	2	3	2
M 2	5	3	3	2	2	2	3	2
M 3	4	3	1	1	1	1	2	1
M 4	3	2	3	2	3	1	3	3

	EXH 1	EXH 2	EXH 3	EXH 4	EXH 5	EXH 6	EXH 7	
M 1	20	21	8	14	18	30	18	
M 2	30	21	16	14	18	30	18	
M 3	27	6	7	6	8	18	8	
M 4	16	**15**	12	15	7	24	21	
	93	63	43	49	51	102	65	TOTAL GENERAL MERITS OF EXHIBITIONS

SUBJECTIVE MARKETING MOTIVES

EXH 1	EXH 2	EXH 3	EXH 4	EXH 5	EXH 6	EXH 7	RATING OF MOTIVES	
5	2	3	2	4	5	4		
3	1	2	1	2	3	2	5	SM 1
3	3	2	2	3	3	3	4	SM 2
3	2	2	2	2	3	2	3	SM 3

EXH 1	EXH 2	EXH 3	EXH 4	EXH 5	EXH 6	EXH 7	
30	7	16	7	18	30	18	SM 1
27	18	14	12	24	27	24	SM 2
24	10	12	10	14	24	14	SM 3
81	35	42	29	56	81	56	
93	63	43	49	51	102	65	
174	98	85	78	107	183	121	SELECTION MERIT POINTS OF EXHIBITIONS-MARKETING RELEVANCE CRITERION

The selection was made by means of two sets of matrix tables shown in Figure 7, and in a sequence of four steps, as follows:

Step one: The exhibitions which can serve the four marketing motives of the exhibitor are marked with one of three multiplication factors 1, 2, 3, which represent a qualitative assessment of the suitability of each exhibition for these marketing motives. The values can be interpreted thus:

          1=no special impact could be expected from participation,
          2=a fair to good impact can be expected,
          3=very good opportunities for making a noticeable impact can be expected.

Step two: The values resulting from the marking are now computed by adding the exhibition rating and the motive rating and by multiplying that sum by the entered quality factor.

Thus for EXH 1 this would be:
for M 1 $5 + 5 = 10 \times 2 = 20$
for M 2 $5 + 5 = 10 \times 3 = 30$
for M 3 $5 + 4 = 9 \times 3 = 27$
for M 4 $5 + 3 = 8 \times 2 = 16$

Total points 93

The total *general merit* gained by exhibition EXH 1 amounts to 93 points.

If there were no other considerations than the general marketing merits of the seven exhibitions in relation to the main marketing motives the order of selection would be:

Exhibition	Points
EXH 6	102
EXH 1	93
EXH 7	65
EXH 2	63
EXH 5	51
EXH 4	49
EXH 3	43

E

Step three: The seven exhibitions are now subjected to the same procedure as in step one, but in relation to the subjective marketing motives which they can serve. The multiplication factors are entered in the three columns, the general merit ratings of the exhibitions and their subjective marketing ratings are added, the resulting sums are then multiplied by the entered factors. The sums of the ratings thus obtained represent the total subjective merit points gained by each exhibition.

Step four: The total general merit points gained by the exhibitions in step two are now added to the corresponding total subjective merit points and the final sums represent the *selection merit points* for each exhibition.

The order of selection merits is now:

Exhibition	Points
EXH 6	183
EXH 1	173
EXH 7	121
EXH 5	107
EXH 2	98
EXH 3	85
EXH 4	78

Exhibition EXH 5 moved into fourth place changing place with EXH 2, and exhibitions EXH 3 and EXH 4 also changed places. Essentially the order remained roughly the same as at the end of step two, but if only four exhibitions would qualify for final selection, perhaps as a result of budget considerations, then the influence of the subjective merit rating gaines importance from a marketing point of view.

In this example the rating values are restricted to five points and the multiplicators to three values and only addition and multiplication is used for the sake of simplicity. More complex rating values and more sophisticated methods of merit rating can be employed, depending on the means available and on the actual need to use such methods. In fact the seven exhibitions would be subjected to additional selection factors such as expenditure, distance from base, local advantages or obstacles, availability of stand space, etc. The method of weighting can be simpler or one can apply other than numerical criteria, or it can be left out altogether. The presented primitive graphical method can be further developed on a three-dimensional basis or by using circuitry or fluidics or by programming a computer. The main objective is to arrive at a reasonable selection using valid methods and sound judgment. In the context of exhibition activities the information gained by experience of past efforts is an excellent guide and the analysis of such efforts deserves the application of the best methods and best technical means available.

Selection of Exhibitions—Case Study 3.

A company in the field of metals, in the widest sense of the term as basic materials and half products, with international buying and selling interests and operating through agents, wholesalers and distributors underwent a change of the chief executive. The change was initiated following a board decision to change the sales method from indirect to direct selling. It was implemented by premature retirement of the incumbent and the engagement of an executive with proven marketing success in another, somewhat related but narrower field.

Even before the change in office took place a review of exhibitions was initiated, the objectives of which were defined as follows:

Reason for review:

A change of sales method from indirect to direct selling.

Objectives of review:

To locate relevant exhibitions suitable for participation.
To compare the exhibition medium with other direct selling media.

The review of exhibitions was entrusted to the sales department and delegated to the publicity department, normally engaged only in placing technical press advertisements of a general prestige character through agencies which also carried out all graphical work. The review produced a list of nine exhibitions which included in their title the general term metals or named metals. Up to that point neither the term nor the concept of marketing played any part in the procedure and it was at this stage the new chief executive of the company intervened. It became clear that what was intended as a change in overall marketing strategy was interpreted by the sales department (perhaps understandably as a result of long years of habit) only as a change in selling methods and a not very welcome one at that.

It was also established that company personnel had neither the technical resources nor the mental attitudes required to produce such a survey and that re-educating and burdening internal personnel with the task whilst current activities were in a state of change, would adversely affect these activities and create unnecessary frictions. It was decided to enlist outside assistance and to commission a survey on the basis of revised and new objectives which read as follows:

The assessment of exhibitions as marketing media suitable for the implementation of the new marketing policy to be carried out in three phases:

Phase one will be concerned with establishing a list of exhibitions which could be classified as coming within the scope of the defined objectives.

Phase two will be concerned with establishing the merits of the listed exhibitions, the material and human resources involved and the costing of selected exhibition activities.

Phase three would be concerned with a comparison of exhibitions and other marketing media.

The marketing elements to be used as guide lines in listing exhibitions were indicated as:

The needs of primary, intermediate and end categories of actual and potential customers, converters, users.

The implications of working, forming, fabricating, finishing and protecting techniques.

The implications of new developments in extracting, refining, enobling, alloying and of combinations of metals with non-metallic materials.

The implications of substitutes for metals and of metals as substitutes for other materials.

The implications of predictable future working techniques and usages. The task objectives of phase one were defined as:

To survey exhibitions relevant to the company's business and to the above marketing elements and to compile a list of exhibitions suitable for direct and indirect participation and for visiting and intelligence surveys.

At the briefing session it was pointed out by the outside consultant that the revised objectives were so widely drawn that almost the whole spectrum of exhibitions would have to be surveyed and that the brief sounded more like an elaborate marketing research assignment than a review of exhibitions. This was conceded, but it transpired that the review of exhibitions was intended as a preliminary step to later research and that the background to the formulation of the brief was the very successful use of exhibitions by the new chief executive, in his previous position.

If an aside by the author is permitted—this approach seems to be symptomatic of cases when a new chief executive is appointed on the strength of his marketing success in another less all-pervading field. His conceptual interpretation of the marketing task retains full theoretical validity, but its translation into a new reality requires the application of many critical restraints.

But to return to the case study.

The consultant agreed to justify his criticism by preparing an outline of the areas which would be involved in the review. This outline was presented in graphical form reproduced in Table 7, and verbal comments were made at the explanatory meeting. It was pointed out that apart from cost and time considerations the outline had all the hallmarks of a long-range planning exercise rather than a preliminary to an intended marketing research investigation aimed at short and medium term targets. As a result of that presentation it was decided to limit the exhibition survey to five areas of marketing activities. Two were high volume and high turnover but low profit areas and three were areas in which competition had a much larger share of the market.

The selection of exhibitions for participation and visiting was made on the basis of the method of allocating merits and weights described in the relevant chapters, but details of it unfortunately cannot be disclosed. The final selection was made by means of the graphical methods described on page 126 and illustrated in Figure 7.

The marketing motives for exhibiting were identified partly by selection from Check lists 8, 9, pp. 80, 82, and partly by defining special ones; the motives for visiting were defined by selection from Check list 11, p. 104.

TABLE 7. THE MARKETING AREAS OF METALS (pages 134–137)

The elements and concepts involved in the marketing of metals are shown in 22 activity groups ranging from primary extracting and treatment activities through working and fabricating of metals to usage, application and final metal scrap disposal and recovery.

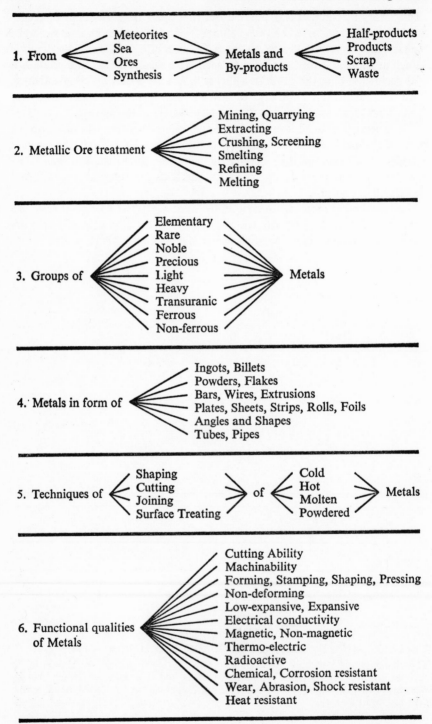

TABLE 7. THE MARKETING AREAS OF METALS (pages 134–137)

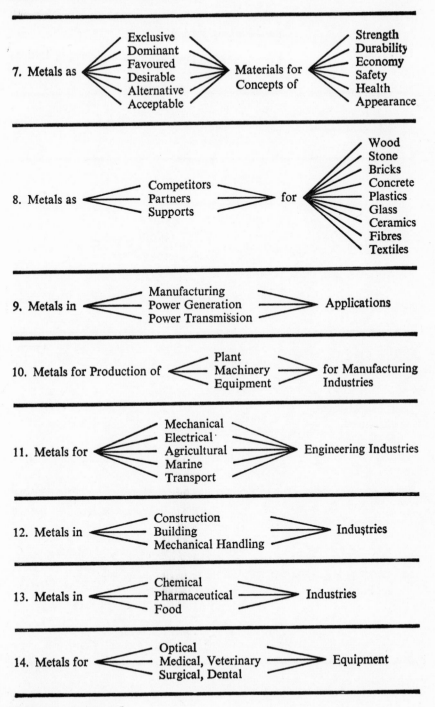

7. Metals as
- Exclusive
- Dominant
- Favoured
- Desirable
- Alternative
- Acceptable

Materials for Concepts of
- Strength
- Durability
- Economy
- Safety
- Health
- Appearance

8. Metals as
- Competitors
- Partners
- Supports

for
- Wood
- Stone
- Bricks
- Concrete
- Plastics
- Glass
- Ceramics
- Fibres
- Textiles

9. Metals in
- Manufacturing
- Power Generation
- Power Transmission

Applications

10. Metals for Production of
- Plant
- Machinery
- Equipment

for Manufacturing Industries

11. Metals for
- Mechanical
- Electrical
- Agricultural
- Marine
- Transport

Engineering Industries

12. Metals in
- Construction
- Building
- Mechanical Handling

Industries

13. Metals in
- Chemical
- Pharmaceutical
- Food

Industries

14. Metals for
- Optical
- Medical, Veterinary
- Surgical, Dental

Equipment

TABLE 7. (*continued*)

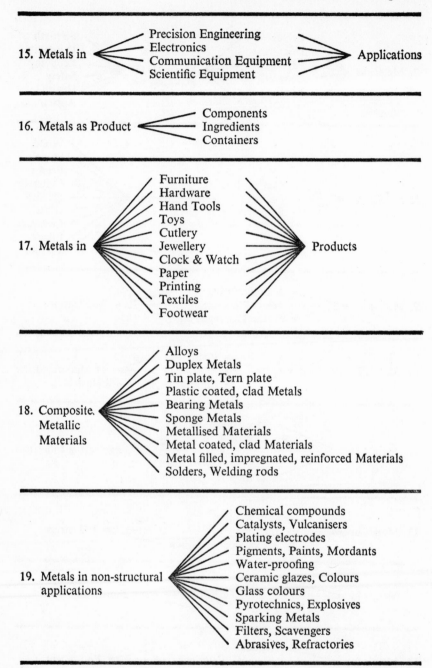

15. Metals in — Precision Engineering / Electronics / Communication Equipment / Scientific Equipment — Applications

16. Metals as Product — Components / Ingredients / Containers

17. Metals in — Furniture / Hardware / Hand Tools / Toys / Cutlery / Jewellery / Clock & Watch / Paper / Printing / Textiles / Footwear — Products

18. Composite. Metallic Materials — Alloys / Duplex Metals / Tin plate, Tern plate / Plastic coated, clad Metals / Bearing Metals / Sponge Metals / Metallised Materials / Metal coated, clad Materials / Metal filled, impregnated, reinforced Materials / Solders, Welding rods

19. Metals in non-structural applications — Chemical compounds / Catalysts, Vulcanisers / Plating electrodes / Pigments, Paints, Mordants / Water-proofing / Ceramic glazes, Colours / Glass colours / Pyrotechnics, Explosives / Sparking Metals / Filters, Scavengers / Abrasives, Refractories

TABLE 7. (*continued*)

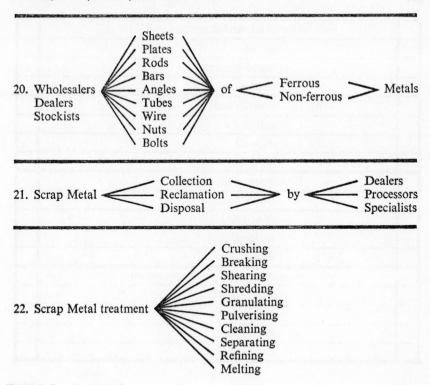

TABLE 7. (*continued*)

	Territorial market concept	
	global	
	intercontinental	
	continental	
	international	
	national	
	regional	
	local	
	Population market concept	
	ethnographic	
	demographic	
	sociological	
	linguistic	
	Economic activity market concept	
	technologies	
	industries	
	disciplines	
	linked subjects	

Check List 14. *NOTIONAL MARKET FEATURES*

Check lists 14 and 15 deal with conceptual market features, market conditions and attitudes. The systematic steps leading to the selection of exhibitions and the assessment of quantitative and qualitative merits can be supplemented by factors listed in check lists 14 and 15. Some of these factors, e.g. declining or static markets, can be assessed objectively, some are more difficult to define, e.g. neutral or friendly official or unofficial attitudes. Where merits of several exhibitions are fairly well balanced, one or more of these supplementary factors can decide the selection.

	Market density	
	empty	
	spacious	
	open	
	crowded	
	overcrowded	
	Market freedom	
	free	
	sheltered	
	restricted	
	closed	
	Market progress	
	leapfrogging	
	developing	
	static	
	declining	
	dead	
	Market attitude	
	enthusiastic	
	receptive	
	indifferent	
	unreceptive	
	antagonistic	
	Official attitudes	
	privileged	
	friendly	
	neutral	
	restrained	
	hostile	
	Market discrimination	
	sophisticated	
	progressive	
	mature	
	mediocre	
	primitive	

Check List 15. *MARKET CONDITION AND ATTITUDE CHARACTERISTICS*

PART THREE

Exhibition Activities

The exhibition effort is a blend of two groups of elements: a group of non-personal material structure elements and a group of personal activity elements which operate within the frame of the material structure. A weakness of the material structure affects the personal performance and inhibits its effectiveness. A weakness of the personal activity element reduces the exhibition effort to a three-dimensional advertisement.

The main components of the material structure are the features exhibitied (i.e. exhibits) the location of these features in the exhibition complex and the technique of exhibiting them.

Stand personnel is the most important personal activity element and its performance is decisive for the effectiveness of the exhibition effort. Publicity public relations and intelligence can be described as hybrid elements; they operate within the material structure, but also outside it. Publicity exerts its influence on the material elements of stand design, on exhibits and on exhibiting techniques and it can contribute to the effective performance of the personal activity elements. The crucial task of personal activities is the encounter with exhibition visitors. The discussion of Transposition and Confrontation deals with the buyer-seller activities and their transposition at an exhibition, with peripheral influences and buying influences of visitors.

16. The Material Structure

The central and most important elements of the material structure are the exhibits, the term being used in its wider sense not restricted to physically identifiable products but also embracing capabilities and concepts.

Exhibits can be products, materials, half products and components in all the diverse forms in which they appear either as units in their own right or as parts of other units, or incorporated in complex assemblies. Depending on their physical and dimensional attributes they can be displayed in their natural state, or represented by substitutes. If their role in life is only fulfilled by incorporation in other products, the applications in which they are contained may constitute the exhibit. Processes, techniques and services can constitute independent offerings, or they can be media for demonstrating materials and products which can display their qualities only in association with, or against the background of, these processes, techniques and services.

Capabilities can be presented to potential customers as saleable contract capacities or alternatively they are exhibited in a combination with products, processes, techniques or services which can become negotiable only when supported by one or more of the capabilities, e.g. special purpose design, research or consultancy.

The exhibiting of esoteric *concepts* by physical societies and government or independent scientific organisations at trade and industrial exhibitions is a comparatively new phenomenon, although there is a long tradition of meetings combined with demonstrations of scientific concepts in the enclaves of learned societies. *Locations* are the different possible habitats of exhibits. Although the *exhibition stand* is the natural location of exhibits and in the majority of cases it is the only one, other locations can also form a part of the material structure.

Large and rich firms able to afford it, have their own building or *pavilion* and guided by long term exhibition policies and the merits of particular exhibition events, may decide that that is the most economical method of participating.

Participation in *collective stand arrangements* is occasionally supplemented by an individual stand if organisational rules permit such procedure. The size or layout of an exhibition stand is on occasions unsuitable for exhibits of large dimensions, and the stand capacity is supplemented by attached or separate projection or cinema facilities. Thus the exhibits, or some of the exhibits, are displayed on these 'projection locations'. Products of component character can be exhibited on the *stands of other exhibitors* who can be primary, intermediate or end users, either in their built-in state by emphasising their presence, or as separate exhibits or both. In some cases no more than a show card can be used to indicate the application.

Open air areas can contain individual stands for exhibits, or they can be reserved for demonstrations and tests for products exhibited elsewhere in the exhibition grounds or halls. The open air aspect of many exhibitions is affected by the climatic conditions prevailing in the exhibition host country, where optimistic expectations of the organisers seem to weigh heavier than the disappointing year to year experience of exhibitors. Considerations of cost obviously play their part. The question how the attraction of a weatherproof arrangement can be made to bring in added revenue required to compensate for that cost, is a marketing problem which most other businesses have to solve almost daily but exhibition organisers seem to shun.

Some exhibition grounds provide facilities for free standing displays of suitable products. In other showcases, columns, pedestals and similar items can be used for displays outside halls or in their precincts. Often these facilities become available as a result of the imagination and initiative of exhibitors. Pumps operating fountains, shelters from plastic, aluminium and stainless steel materials, open air sculptures made from tubes, rods, slabs and even from containers are examples of such 'special' locations for exhibits.

For products such as office and communication equipment, a special location opportunity arises in information centres, official offices and on other exhibitors stands.

The exhibition site and exhibition halls can also provide opportunities of a permanent or transitory nature for exhibits incorporated in the physical structure of the exhibition. Examples of products suitable as such exhibits are: passenger and goods lifts, escalators, catering equipment, public address systems, advanced or spectacular building methods for exhibition halls, tents, marquees, lamps, flooring, paving—the list is almost endless.

The policy of the organisers will determine the acceptibility of such exhibits and the degree of publicity and recognition which they can receive. Once this is established the paramount concern of the exhibitor is to ascertain to his own satisfaction the functional suitability of the exhibits for their purpose and to ensure the highest possible degree of faultless operation, weather stability, appearance and when necessary, refurbishing, renewal or replacement. Permanent exhibits are also seen by visitors to exhibitions mounted on the same site, but not directly connected with the markets for these exhibits. For products with wide horizontal market characteristics such as most material handling equipment or lighting equipment, this permanent exposure can be of great marketing value.

Some exhibitions provide display opportunities in town centres, at railway stations and at air ports. Suitable products such as special purpose vehicles, cranes, automatic vending machines can be displayed on roped off pedestals or similar locations. Smaller products, e.g. cameras, instruments, fastening devices, can be displayed in showcases which some hotels also provide.

The techniques of exhibiting are many and varied and their effectiveness very often depends more on the ingenuity of a simple device than on the amount of elaborate equipment or lavish expenditure.

Technical achievements of one branch of technology help to display the advances of another. The technique of exhibiting is closely connected with stand design and is also influenced by the quality and versatility of the stand personnel, subject discussed in subsequent paragraphs.

The Exhibition Stand

A discussion of exhibition stands leads inevitably to the topic of aesthetics and their influence on the marketing role of the stand and exhibits and on the effectiveness of their contribution to the exhibition effort.

The response to aesthetic and style elements of industrial products is more complex than an appreciation of appearance. The principal visual stimuli of shape and colour can combine with stimuli of noise, smell and touch. Ergonomic factors play their part when human use, handling or operating is involved.

In the appraisal of machines and instruments we react not only to their general shape, but also to the arrangement and touch of handwheels, levers and control knobs, to the clarity of scales and dials.

Depending on our personality and experience these arrangements may please us or displease us, contributing to the general impression. Assessment of the operating efficiency of a piece of equipment can be affected consciously or subconciously by shapes and colours. Our first favourable colour impression of an instrument can be modified by a clumsy arrangement of operating knobs, a well shaped accessory is mentally rejected because of its, to the beholder, awful colour. A streak of oil functionally fully justified, running down a clean light grey surface may suggest some malfunction, the same streak against the background of a narrow black band of paint would not even be noticed.

The aesthetic environment of exhibitions was briefly discussed on page 116. At an exhibition you are in a sense in a theatre except that not one, but many stages compete for your attention. Theoretically, a product of inherent excellence of purpose and function and with good marketing merits to its credit should need no more than a bare stand for its stage to display its quality and the benefits it can bestow on the buyer. The theatre has used that device, if actors will forgive the simile of marketable products. In practice we need a stand design.

Stand Design

Exhibition stand design is the subject of excellent textbooks in many languages and like publicity is the realm of specialists. But specialists have to be briefed and instructed in the wishes and aims of their task givers whether as members of the same organisation or as outsiders.

Aesthetic factors cannot be calculated or specified but the difference between functional excellence and gimmicky fussiness can be recognised, even if it cannot be measured by objective values. Stand design is not a matter of generally valid formulae, but an experimental process of reconciling the marketing aims of the exhibitor, the design aspirations of the stand designer, the restraints of the exhibition site and of the most critical, although not the most important factor—the budget. The great opportunity which an exhibition offers is, that ingenuity very often can accomplish what expense cannot.

Exhibition stands for industrial exhibitions should serve the same marketing motives which decide participation in an exhibition, which govern all exhibition activities and which determine the choice of exhibits and the technique of exhibiting.

In the overwhelming number of cases the exhibits will be industrial products, and if services, capabilities or concepts are featured they will mostly have a substantial engineering or technological content. The exhibition marketeer and the stand designer require technical information to enable them to present to visitors the advantages and benefits of the exhibits.

The stand designer will enact that presentation by providing an exhibition stand and displaying the exhibits in a manner which will enable the marketeer to play his main role of personal contacts and to exploit fully the supporting cast of the exhibits and the background facilities of the stand.

The technical engineer (whose attitude to publicity is discussed on pages 181 and 183) has on the whole a less apathetic and less hostile attitude to exhibitions than he displays towards advertising. Somehow exhibitions seem more respectable, perhaps because they are, like his products, three-dimensional or because they are housed in big buildings. Asked by the stand designer how he should best display that one unique feature of his products which distinguishes it from competitors he will refer him with a superior air to the operating manual, or with a condescending smile to the leaflet concocted by his confederates in publicity. He will also suggest that the apprentice school could make a scale model or section of the products and paint it red and blue. When confronted with the statement that all this was done before and could he perhaps suggest something new, he will reply that he has enough trouble to produce new ideas for products let alone for the stand designer's exhibits. When reminded that they are also his exhibits, he is somewhat surprised. There are of course exceptions.

Engineers with a real understanding of the stand designer's problems, can make practical suggestions which not only overcome difficulties but are an inspiration to the designer. A stand designer grappled for years with the problem of displaying a colossal compressor which could be inspected only by climbing up to a cat-walk. He discussed the problem with an engineer and friend, who recalled his diploma project for which he had to design a similar compressor. He was at the time struck by the contrast between the beauty of the rotor and the ugliness of the housing. That was enough for the stand designer. At the next exhibition, a gleaming, slowly revolving rotor, suspended almost invisibly in midair with changing lights playing on its blades drew great numbers of spectators to an exhibition hall normally only sparsely populated by the few visitors interested in very big machines. The display won an award and the following additional benefits were gained: transport and packing costs reduced by 62 per cent, accessible stand space increased by 31 per cent.

In large halls of international exhibitions abroad some stands are raised to conscpicuously higher than floor level, some are lowered to give the impression of a sunken ampitheatre, but the great majority are at a sober floor level. There are elaborate giant stands in a curious style making somewhat clumsy allusions to what their designers think is modern art. There are stand designs which one sees year in year out and which are obviously dedicated to a constant formula perhaps valid some years ago and retained ever since as safe and workable.

There are also many very good and some excellent stands in styles almost universally acceptable proclaiming very clearly their marketing purpose by functional displays of products, by the regard paid to the flow of visitors and their temporary comforts and by an unobtrusive civility of the stand personnel coupled with determination to deliver their message.

Some stands are very good displays of the designer's ingenuity, well applied when it serves the marketing purpose of the exhibits, misused when it serves no one but the designer's urge to express himself.

Stand Design Intelligence
The important role of publicity tasks throughout the pre-exhibition, exhibition and post-exhibition periods is emphasised in the chapter on publicity. The role of the stand design function ostensibly covers only the pre-exhibition period and perhaps the period just after opening. In fact, if not the function, its intelligence component should be active throughout the exhibition period. This need not necessarily mean the allocation of that particular duty to one person, it is enough if provisions are made to note the operational aspects of the stand, and the effectiveness and impact of any new features or techniques, to observe difficulties experienced or benefits derived from such innovations. At exhibitions of high marketing merit or in an environment of sophisticated stand designs the intelligence task should extend to a survey of other stands with particular attention to those of competitors and customers.

Stand Design and Publicity
The need for good communications and co-operation between stand design and publicity functions is self-evident, but it is not enough to accept the office display of humorous slogans or the conviviality of social encounters as signs that such co-operation exists. It is a management function to ensure that the declaration of close collaboration are checked as to their validity not only in the volatile areas of these two activities but also in the more mundane matters of technical production and organisational effectiveness.

As these two functions operate in very expensive media, a lack of co-ordination obscured by vapours of creativity can be very costly. On occasions when strong personalities despair of getting some inspiration for their creativity from their engineering task masters, co-operation between the two functions can be too close for the good marketing health of the exhibition effort. Publicity and exhibiting become self-contained activities in which the exhibits and stand personnel are only secondary elements manipulated for the attainment of the ultimate goal—a stand design reproduced in glossy magazines and widely discussed—among other stand designers and publicity practitioners.

Exhibits

The choice of exhibits is governed by the marketing motives for exhibiting, by the marketing merits of the exhibition and by the stand and its environment. The different environments of the exhibition were discussed on pages 105-117 and they exert their influence on stand location and design. The location and size of the stand can impose limitations or offer opportunities to stand designers and can also affect the choice of exhibits particularly if they require special services. In your exhibition merit rating procedure you have already checked the availability of these services on the basis of the check list of structural elements and by assessing the environment and organisation merists of the exhibition. Another selection criterium for exhibits is the strategy planned for stand activities, the activity features to be emphasised and those to be toned down or eliminated. General marketing strategies may have to be modified to take account of special market opportunities in the exhibition host country, or perhaps of some local restrictions.

The range of exhibits which will be subject to that selection can vary for individual companies as much as for individual exhibitions. Some internal conflicts or pressures can also exert their influence. Engineers are inclined to insist on too many technical details as essential display items. Sales departments have a tendency to produce long lists of products which must be displayed as representative of the range. If these demands are not filtered through a mesh of marketing criteria the result is often that on the engineering side prominent technical features of an exhibit are obscured by an array of items of minor importance, and on the sales side, exhibits representing products responsible for a very small share of sales occupy a very large part of the display area, relegating those with a much bigger share to a smaller stand space. This is, of course, a very crude generalisation of observed phenomena, but it is quite revealing to find—by personifying the character of engineering products—how many elderly, big and clumsy characters who take up a great volume of manufacturing resources have a low market impact, whilst smaller, more compact, better built, one could almost say, nicer members of the family, not only sail through their production lines, but also make a very good impression on the market.

Materials and half-products are often prominently displayed in other exhibitors' products and in the attempt to emphasise their versatility, elaborate and ingenious devices are used to demonstrate their adaptability to shapes and contours, their suitability for a range of applications and the universality of their potential use.

Many of the ideas used have the desired impact and clearly convey their message. Others exaggerate the technique to such an extent that what started as an ingenious device becomes an overcomplicated gimmick which not only loses its own credibility but by implication jeopardises the reputation of the sponsored material. The illogicality of an all-aluminium, or all-steel, or all-plastic house or car body can hardly impress a reasonable potential buyer. He would rather see an equally ingenious but more purposeful demonstration of how these materials fulfil their role of benefiting real-life-products which in turn will benefit him.

Visits to industrial exhibitions by the general public and particularly by group excursions and schools are regarded as a great nuisance and impediment by what is euphemistically called the trade who frequently voice their annoyance in the technical press. From a marketing point of view, the educational aspect of exhibitions seems sadly neglected.

A group of young potential future customers who are obviously undergoing some form of education relevant to industrial markets, must surely present a medium term marketing target for many industrial products. Apart from that, quite a number of industrial products would benefit in the market if they were presented in a fashion by engineers disdainfully described as *popular presentation*. Such a presentation would also benefit some specialised trade buyers who augment their half-knowledge of technicalities by pomposity and price bargaining.

The addition, where practicable of popularised versions of industrial exhibits combined with pre-exhibition invitations to selected technical colleges and trade schools could yield a more tangible and lasting marketing impact than that apparently expected from a display of semiclad but otherwise uninteresting live embellishments of the stand.

Reception Elements
The elements listed under the heading of reception elements are an indication of functions rather than a requirement for actual physical facilities. As functions they are important and should be taken into account irrespective of the size or complexity of the stand. If yours is only a small stand with the display element taking up most of the space then reception, conference and interview facilities will be physically non-existent, but a careful selection of stand personnel will enable you to entrust these functions to one person specially talented in that respect. Such a receptionist can do more for your visitors than a most luxuriously equipped reception area manned by brightly smiling, but on the whole half-informed or buck-passing personnel.

Visitors' reception can be a loose leaf-book for recording details about visitors, it can also be a reception desk with several receptionists in attendance and direct telephone connections to other stands of the same exhibitor and to his headquarters. Conference and interview facilities can range from a few chairs and tables to a complete suite of rooms on a floor above the stand. A modest conference room where a visitor can be served with sandwiches and coffee or a cold drink which he can consume in comparative comfort could do more for your image and goodwill than a lavish supply of alcohol. You may need that as well, because customers come in all shapes and partialities, but if you take the trouble to ask, instead of automatically assuming that everybody needs a drink, you will be surprised by the relief of many to be able to choose some light refreshment instead. At one exhibition stand a special effort was made to reduce to a minimum the use of bread and rolls, and to provide a choice of non-fattening savouries. The fame and memory of that stand among higher rank expense account executives persisted for three more exhibition events. It was the most cost-effective public relations exercise ever known.

The stand office is an essential function of your exhibition activities. Here too it is the function which is important not the actual frame. An efficient stand manager, an experienced secretary, a tape recorder and a portable typewriter, inquiry forms and loose-leaf books of the same standard size issued to stand personnel with instructions to adhere to the one-page-one-subject rule can produce a record of exhibition activities and a dossier for follow-up action superior to a sophisticated enquiry card system operated by a multitude of bored helpers hired for the purpose from outside. In recent years customer enquiry cards made their appearance on exhibition stands together with attractively uniformed 'research assistants'. They persuade visitors and somewhat indiscriminately chosen passers-by, to fill in so-called customer interest cards which bear all the hallmarks of a surprisingly un-marketing exercise. They are so obviously designed for the convenience of the analyst rather than for the customer-victim, that one is inclined to fill in the remark: researcher research thyself.

Stand Facilities

Stand designers and the executives instructing them could be perhaps persuaded to rely less on, at best, purely intuitive attitudes and often simply on an accepted routine when dealing with so called natural functions which are in fact ergonomic problems. The exhibition stand is a shortlived but crowded habitat of exhibits and people. The performance of people, which can be assessed and predicted by behavioural and biological measurements, is crucial to the effectiveness of the exhibition effort.

Apart from all personal equations and the absorption of marketing principles, that performance will also depend on the nature of the stand facilities.

The mechanical and physical elements of stand design, such as benches, tables, counters, the position of literature racks, the access to exhibits are all elements which, when designed for a purpose, make life on the stand easier. When treated as an afterthought they do not only hinder stand personnel in their main task, but they also display their inefficiency to observant visitors. The deep bottom drawer at the back of a display counter proudly claimed as clever utilisation of space, and in fact, the source of back-breaking exercises because it is too low and so deep that the weight of leaflets jams it in its place, is one example. The slotted rack for leaflets placed in front of the stand counter and below waist level is another. It enables passers-by to take leaflets without the stand personnel being aware of it. There is nothing inherently wrong or underhand in that—but for the stand personnel the main task of making personal contacts and of ascertaining visitors' needs is made more difficult.

Publicity Material

The subject of sales and technical literature and other publicity material is discussed in the chapters on publicity and intelligence. The policy of literature distribution from the stand and the selection of recipients and targets will determine the method and the arrangement required. It is very important to include in the instructions to stand designers not only quantities and types of literature, but also details of the underlying policy so that apart from space requirements such elements as accessibility to visitors, encouragement, restricted distribution and similar considerations can be taken into account.

An *open display* is readily accessible to visitors in the form of single items or a folder with a selection of items. In a fixed, covered display leaflets or other items are firmly attached to a display board preferably protected by a transparent cover. The individual items can be identified by reference numbers and, depending on strategy, can be requested verbally or by means of a request form in which the name and other details of the visitor are noted. The request can be met at the stand, or by post after the exhibition, or by a combination of both methods. Outdoor stands require special provisions, their scope again depending on your aims and distribution targets and also on local climatic conditions. An economic method of distribution is a weather-proof *fixed protected display* and distribution on request.

Whilst some of the accessories for literature can be of modular design and serve several exhibitions, storage provisions for larger quantities are usually included in individual stand designs.

Art Patronage

Art patronage is one of the areas which could enrich many a stale exhibition scene. The use of plastic panels, vacuum formed plastics, the combination of light, movement and sound in art works, or perhaps pop art works, should give some inspiration to publicity practitioners in industrial undertakings. When abstruse sculptures created by the application of metal welding and brazing techniques and by the use of glassfibre materials move from sophisticated art galleries to the fronts of buildings and to courtyards of palatial headquarters, surely exhibitors of industrial products could do more than just adorn their stands with a row of flower pots. There are notable and some-times spectacular exceptions mostly on stands of large corporations in the chemical and plastics industries. On the other hand some pseudo-advanced banalities in encapsulation and what is intended to be funny personification of components are examples of how not to use basically good ideas.

A neglected source of such artifacts are the apprentice schools of industrial firms.

In one particular case an advertising agency engaged by an exhibitor in the copper tube business, acquired some very good items of copper tube sculpture from an artist abroad. They did not know, and no one told them, that the firms' apprentice school in co-operation with the local art college, produced prize-winning designs of no smaller merit than the imported items.

Exhibition Stand—Case Study 4.

The stand is sometimes the reflection of the source of information which was most active or most co-operative with the stand designer. In one case a stand was required for an exhibition in an export market in which the exhibitor had experienced serious service problems. A new service manager had been appointed there recently to overcome the troubles and it was decided, very sensibly, to call in the new service manager, so that his interests should be taken into account. As fate would have it this service manager had consider-able practical experience of exhibitions, probably more so than the also newly appointed export sales manager who was functionally responsible for partici-pation in that exhibition. The requirements of the service manager were stated in great detail and with so much appreciation of local exhibition conditions that everybody heaved a sign of relief, and it was left entirely to him to instruct the stand designer.

The result was a very good stand displaying spares, service tools, locations of service depots in colour transparencies, and a dummy dressed up in regulation overalls. Three service engineers were in attendance. The product, a horti-cultural cultivator was on display, but in a somewhat shamefaced manner, as if apologising for its existence. An analysis of visitors to the stand revealed that 4 per cent showed interest in the stand because they had trouble in the past in locating spares for their cultivators, 17 per cent because they experienced undue service delays, 16 per cent were under the impression that the ex-hibitor is a service organisation dealing with all makes of cultivators.

During the nine months following the exhibition the sales of spares in that territory increased by 63 per cent, the number of calls for service rose by 121 per cent, but this included 31 per cent of trivial calls mostly for equipment in the guarantee period.

Check List 16. *MATERIAL STRUCTURE OF THE EXHIBITION EFFORT*
(page 152)

Check list 16 is concerned with non-personal elements of the exhibition effort which provide the basis and background for personal elements listed in check list 18. In addition to the most important material elements—the exhibits—and the stand, 'other locations for exhibits' can contribute to the effectiveness of the exhibition effort. The motives for exhibiting may call for sepcial techniques of exhibiting and the feasibility of using them may have to be checked against the facilities and services provided at a particular exhibition.

Check List 17. *MATERIAL ELEMENTS OF EXHIBITION STANDS*
(page 153)

Check list 17 deals with the focus of exhibition activities—the stand. The requirements of individual exhibitors and the opportunities offered by individual exhibitions range over such a wide spectrum of size, cost, design and sophistication that a check list can provide no more than an indication of what needs to be checked, initiated or dispensed with. The display elements will be the expression of the motives for exhibiting. The subject of publicity elements is dealt with fully in twelve check lists 20 to 31 but the stand must provide the physical facilities for storage and effective distribution of publicity items.

The activities of the stand personnel (*check list 18*) must be supported by, at least adequate, but preferably by very efficient material facilities. The best qualified stand personnel (*check list 19*) deserves the best auxiliary facilities to enable them to exploit their talents to the full. Numerical or quality gaps in the stand team may have to be compensated by suitable supporting material elements.

The reception of visitors serves the basic purpose of the exhibition effort of establishing personal contacts and conducting them effectively. The range of interests, ranks and personalities of visitors which can be expected at an exhibition stand, will determine the nature of the facilities required to provide a cost and time effective reception background.

	FEATURES EXHIBITED:	
	Exhibits:	
	products	
	product ranges	
	applications	
	processes	
	techniques	
	services	
	Capabilities:	
	research	
	development	
	projects	
	design	
	consultancy	
	Concepts:	
	technological	
	intertechnological	
	interdisciplinary	
	LOCATIONS	
	individual stands	
	pavilions, kiosks	
	stand or booth in collective arrangement	
	projectors	
	cinemas	
	stands of other exhibitors	
	open air area stands	
	special locations	
	locations outside exhibition site	
	TECHNIQUE OF EXHIBITING	
	static displays	
	moving displays	
	demonstrations	
	tests	
	static models	
	animated models	
	visual and audio-visual presentations	

Check List 16. *MATERIAL STRUCTURE OF THE EXHIBITION EFFORT*

	Display elements	
	exhibits	
	showcases	
	literature	
	other display elements	
	Visitors reception elements	
	reception	
	conference room	
	interview rooms	
	refreshments/bar	
	cloakroom	
	washing	
	Literature display	
	open display	
	assortments/folders	
	individual items	
	fixed protected display	
	reference numbers	
	request forms	
	dispensers, hall stands	
	dispensers, open air stands, weather proof	
	Literature distribution	
	open choice	
	restricted choice	
	invitation to take	
	invitation to request	
	from stand	
	to be sent on	
	special distribution	
	Bulk storage	
	special facilities	
	self-erecting packs	
	quantity check	
	Stand facilities	
	office equipment	
	rest room	
	kitchen	
	washing	

Check List 17. *MATERIAL ELEMENTS OF EXHIBITION STANDS*

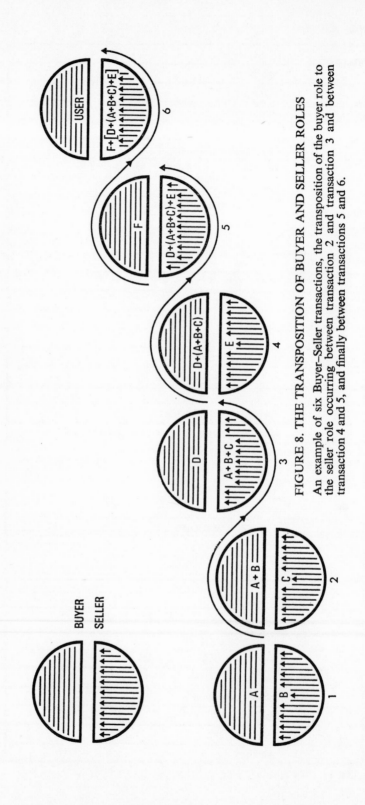

FIGURE 8. THE TRANSPOSITION OF BUYER AND SELLER ROLES

An example of six Buyer–Seller transactions, the transposition of the buyer role to the seller role occurring between transaction 2 and transaction 3 and between transaction 4 and 5, and finally between transactions 5 and 6.

17. Transposition and Confrontation

The most significant marketing characteristic of industrial products is the fact that the majority of them are used in connection with some other industrial products, so that all producers and sellers of industrial products are at the same time buyers of other such products. In this *transposition process* some industrial products pass through several phases of incorporation and a considerable time span can elapse between the date the product is first manufactured and the date it reaches the ultimate user.

Many industrial products move through several industrial markets or across horizontal or vertical layers of the same industry. In their travel some lose their identity on the way from the first product to the ultimate user. In some cases this is a requirement of the buyer, in others it is the unavoidable result of incorporation or assembly.

Very often the final user of a complete industrial product becomes aware of the conflicts and dilemmas arising from the incorporation factor only when he is forced to compare the publicity promises made for the complete product with disclaimers of responsibility for its components made in small print in the warranty.

Nowhere are these characteristics of industrial products more effectively demonstrated than at exhibitions. In a concentrated space and time buyers and sellers, customers and users, complete complex products and simple components, auxiliary equipment and accessories, materials and services, all meet, all are displayed and all clamour for attention.

A simple version of the transposition process is illustrated in Figure 8.

Buyer *A* is the manufacturer of an auxiliary power unit. In the first transaction of the transposition process buyer *A* acquires a component from seller *B* and incorporates it in a subassembly of his own make. In the second transaction buyer *A* obtains a clutch, which completes one version of his auxiliary power unit. In transaction 3 the first transposition takes place, *A* becomes a seller, supplying his power unit to buyer *D* who is an engine manufacturer. Buyer *D* then obtains in transaction 4 a power take-off coupling from seller *E* and incorporates it in his complete engine assembly. In transaction 5, the second transposition takes place when *D* becomes a seller supplying his engine to buyer *F*, a manufacturer of industrial tractors. In transaction 6 the third and final transposition takes place when *F* becomes a seller, supplying his tractor to the user.

The final *confrontation* of a buyer and a seller and the placing of an order, is the expression of the fact that at that particular instance a need of the customer has been satisfied and one of the cardinal aims of marketing has been achieved. At an exhibition of industrial products the frequency with which the placing of definite orders takes place and the nature of these orders varies considerably depending on the nature of the goods and on the preliminaries which preceded the exhibition.

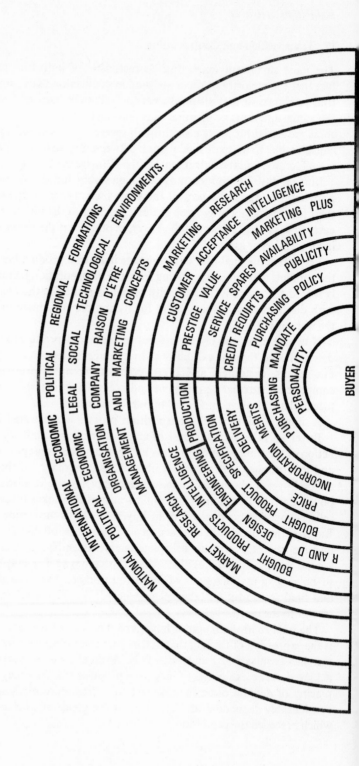

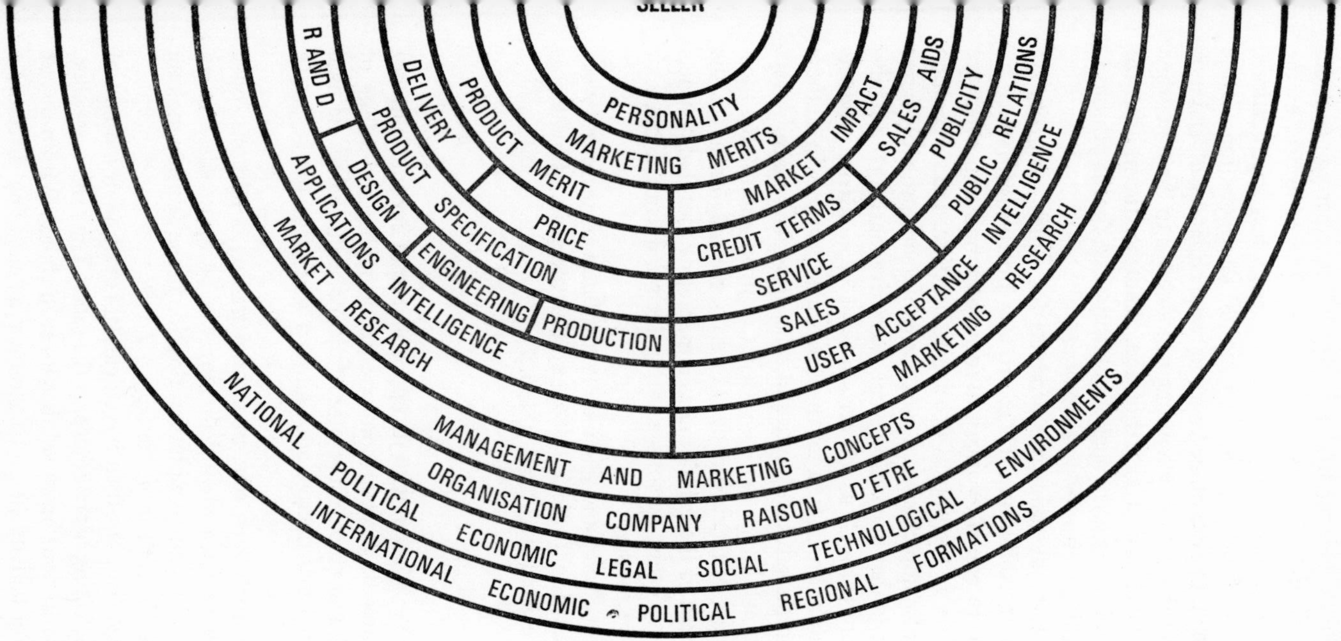

FIGURE 9. PERIPHERAL INFLUENCES OF THE BUYER-SELLER CONFRONTIATON

The buyer-seller confrontation is subject to peripheral influences which collectively shape the final marketing merits of the product offered by the seller, the purchasing mandate of the buyer and when filtered through the personalities of the seller and buyer, determine the compatibility of marketing merit and purchasing mandate, culminating in an order.

The headlines which announce the placing or securing of spectacular orders also vary in the veracity of their reports. It all depends whether you consider the signing of a document in the presence of press photographers as the placing of an order, or whether to you the moment when specifications, deliveries and prices were finally agreed after months of negotiations, is the actual order placing date. On the other hand, in some countries official purchasing agencies go to the length of extending negotiations to the time when they can be formally concluded at an exhibition. Whatever the motives for this procedure, it certainly has a great deal of publicity value for the exhibition and can act as a persuading factor for participating.

There are, of course, many industrial products for which contracts are negotiated and signed at exhibitions. There are also situations in which an exhibition stand reverts to one of its ancestral forms and industrial goods are sold off the peg. Amazingly the objects of such transactions are more often than not large pieces of complex special purpose equipment probably never seen or heard of before in that market. In some restrictive markets the exhibition is the only medium through which certain types of industrial products can be sold so that exhibits are chosen for that particular purpose. In all these cases a final confrontation between buyer and seller has taken place, in fact or symbolically. At an exhibition the buyer-seller confrontation is the most frequent personal contact element, but by no means the only one. It is the strength and special merit of the exhibition as a marketing tool that contacts are made with so many other persons exerting their influence directly or indirectly on that final encounter.

The different functions, roles and personality attributes of these influence wielding people are listed in Table 5, p. 86, and the categories of influences which they can exert are listed in Table 8, p. 166.

Peripheral Influences

The environment of the exhibition with its opportunities of encountering not only the orthodox functions directly connected with buying and selling of industrial products but also most of the other functions influencing the final decision to a greater or lesser degree, adds another marketing dimension to these encounters.

One of the factors involved is that in normal trading conditions, once subsidiary influences have been identified, they can be approached in an order and in a sequence compatible with their position in the decision making process and with the weight of their influence.

At an exhibition the visitor, mostly a buyer, can still exert a fair amount of control and choice in selecting his counterpart the seller. The exhibitor-seller, apart from the direct invitations he issued, has no such choice. Within one or two hours of exhibition activity he can encounter a managing director, a service engineer, an irate user, a buyer, a designer, a chief engineer or on occasions two or three persons from the same firm. They all can exert their near or remote influences on final buying attitudes.

It is suggested that they exert *peripheral influences* which can affect the marketing merit of industrial products offered by their sellers and the purchasing mandate for industrial products needed by their buyers.

A diagram of peripheral influences is shown in Figure 9. It makes no claim to completeness and as it attempts to be as generally valid as possible, it may not fit situations which are either simpler or more complicated than the one depicted. It is hoped that it will provide a guide for much better efforts.

The semi-circles which represented the buyer and seller in Figure 8, now form the inner focus of two semi-circular sectors in Figure 9. The upper sector represents the buyer and the lower the seller. The transaction can take place between two firms of the same or of different national provenance.

The upper semi-circle contains the quarter-sectors of the buyer's manufacturing and sales functions, the lower the corresponding functions of the seller. The perimeters of the two semi-circles form the international and national boundaries of the buyer's and seller's corporate activities and they exert their peripheral influence on the definition of his business and of his corporate raison d'être. The next semi-circular ring-sectors represent the influences of management and marketing concepts which penetrate to all sectors of activities.

Although nominally the functions of production and sales now separate, their influences in the end penetrate to the semi-circular ring-sector of marketing merits. So far we have considered the inward penetration of peripheral influences. Influences will be also exerted in an outward direction and between neighbouring or remote sectors.

In an ideal situation all the various functions would exert their influence in an orderly manner guided by appropriate policies and with a power related to their importance.

In real life personality filters will operate throughout the organisation with the additional disturbances created by departmental conflicts.

One could say that the rate at which peripheral influences can penetrate to the inner focus will depend on the 'density' of the sectors which they encounter on the way. When they finally penetrate to their respective inner semi-circles they influence the marketing merits of the seller's product and the purchasing mandate of the buyer. However, before the final encounter and matching of merits and mandate can take place, they also have to pass through the personality filters of the seller and the buyer.

18. Exhibition Stand Personnel

'In these degenerate days' we oft hear said
'Manners are lost and chivalry is dead'
No wonder, since in high exalted spheres
The same degeneracy, in fact appears   *—from a Lewis Carroll verse.*

Exhibition Stand Manners

By participating in an exhibition you are extending a public and general invitation to all interested parties to come and visit you. In many cases you supplement that public impersonal invitation by asking organisations or firms to visit your stand and you are also extending personal invitations to specially selected persons. Apart from all business and public relations considerations and the benefits which you expect to derive from them you have as, an exhibitor, the plain obligations of a host. The way you treat your visitors becomes thus a matter of good manners which should consciously range from the full business treatment given to a customer or potential customer, to the polite but nevertheless firm dismissal of the long-winded nuisance visitor.

Moderation in the treatment of visitors, whatever their importance, is not only inherent in good manners, but also helps you to husband your resources. In some situations good manners must be raised to the level of diplomacy and extra-cautious tact employed so as not to offend historical, political or hierarchical susceptibilities. If the substance of good manners is consideration for others, and if these others are visitors to your stand, then good manners become good marketing practice, and that, after all, is the main purpose of the exhibition exercise.

As management techniques are generally improving and moving towards professionalism, so should the management of exhibiting. It is surprising to note that many organisations which take the decision to participate in an exhibition on the basis of current management precepts and allocate the material resources for an effective display, stop short of the fundamental task of ensuring the effectiveness of the stand team. The failing is either in the selection or in inadequate preparation or both.

Indifferent or absent stand personnel, inquiring visitors leaving stands with a massive supply of literature but without being asked for their name, lengthy social chats between neighbouring stand personnel or among personnel on their own stand, so obvious to outsiders because all involved are sporting their name badges, stand personnel retiring to the hospitality area or to the hidden parts of the stand—all these and some other manifestations of this failing are there for all to see, to comment upon and perhaps to include in the assessment of the exhibitor, or of his image.

To hand a visitor a sheaf of leaflets and to dismiss him with a paternal smile, saying: 'you'll find all data in these' is tantamount to saying: 'you have wasted your time and money coming to our stand, you could have obtained the same information for the price of a postcard, telephone call, or a reply paid numbers card'.

On the other hand, to force a somewhat unwilling visitor to listen to a description of exhibits which is no more than a verbose repetition of the catalogue entry is to waste his time and yours. The obvious question is when to do which. The answer is briefing, experience and most of all intelligent observation. One or two questions will soon disclose the seriousness of the interest and the difference between a rubberneck, a remote prospect, a seriously interested potential customer and a snooping competitor.

In the absence of such briefing the technical shortcomings of stand personnel are not wholly their own fault, but even the most tolerant observer will blame them entirely for their own personal failing in good exhibition-stand manners. In many cases the composition of the team on an exhibition stand is the result not of planning and purposeful selection, but of haphazard last minute arrangements or of internal manoeuvring for overseas service of volunteers, who imagine that nightclubs are natural extensions of exhibition stands.

Executives of exhibiting firms when questioned *before* an exhibition about this particular organisational task will readily concede its importance, and will regard it as self-evident that due attention should be paid to it. When confronted *after* an exhibition with evidence of failing, the response depends to some extent on whether the interviewed executive actually visited the exhibition or not. The response can range from offended incredulity to assurances of strong corrective action and improvement in the future.

It is interesting to note that failures of that aspect of the exhibition effort can be observed as much on stands of large firms as of medium and small ones, although on large and elaborate stands these shortcomings are perhaps not so obvious or not so glaringly displayed as on smaller stands.

Lack of attention to visitors and passive rudeness by high-powered executives from headquarters can occasionally be observed during visits to the stand. There are, of course, those *real* chief executives who on a busy stand take on any duty required but, unfortunately they are not very numerous. It was a heartwarming experience to see a well-behaved junior clerk save the reputation of a bumptious executive by offering to an obviously interested but tired visitor a chair on the stand. It was late in the day and the keen executive seeing just one more visitor keeping him from the prepared drink asked the junior to dismiss the visitor and tell him 'to come back to-morrow'. It was later learned that the man in question was a deputy minister responsible for approving tenders which this exhibitor had recently submitted. It also transpired very much later, that being the man he was, he noticed the whole manoeuvre but took it in good humour. It is also sad to relate that the executive did not mend his ways until his company was taken over and he had to mind his manners in a new management environment. Stand personnel cannot be expected to be accomplished psychologists or socio-psychologists, nor

F

should they be expected to be cunning manipulators. But for the effective performance of their tasks and for the achievement of set goals they need to be very good persuaders. To round off their skills they should be acquainted with the customs, conventions and codes of conduct of the environment in which they operate. In the Middle East the practicing and expecting of strict punctuality will gain no particular merit points and insistence on it, or reproaches about it, can cause conflicts and otherwise unexplainable setbacks.

By the same token delays and postponements accompanied by transparently lame explanations will incur no penalty points.

In Scandinavia punctuality is regarded as a natural ingredient of good manners which although not in itself laudable, when transgressed can release reactions of disapproval ranging from a grave frown for minor offences, to a temporary break in negotiations when fixed time appointments are not strictly kept.

The Exhibition Stand Manager

If an exhibition effort is to succeed in its aim and reach its objectives, it must be effectively managed. Whether the person entrusted with the task is described as a stand manager or stand executive is immaterial providing his duties and responsibilities are clearly defined and his powers and authority firmly established. It is comparatively easy to define the function of the stand manager in theoretical terms. It would be enough to say that his function is to manage a properly motivated and properly briefed team in a well organised and effectively controlled manner. In practice the motley environment of the exhibition in which the task is carried out, the sources of conflicts, the demands on stamina and patience which are an inherent part of it, create anything but normal operational conditions. It follows inevitably that the ability to cope with an unusual situation requires more than usual qualities.

The structure of an exhibition and its external and internal environments were discussed in previous chapters. The exhibition in which you decided to participate was selected because its marketing merits were compatible with your exhibiting motives and your stand was also designed to serve these marketing motives. Similarly these motives govern the selection of your stand personnel and your stand manager and that selection is a critical element in the series of decisions which you have to make. No amount of publicity nor the most impressive stand can do what an exhibition marketing team can and should do.

Before defining the duties and responsibilities of the stand manager and his team, the importance of the pre-exhibition preparation must be stressed.

The clear statement of the exhibiting motives and strategies form the essential basis for the stand manager's brief and programme of activities.

The human material resources at his disposal should be defined in detail and it is most advisable, although not always possible, that he should take an active part in the preparatory stages of the exhibition effort. To what extent all these postulates can be realised will depend as much on the general scope of exhibition activities undertaken by your company, as on the efficiency, effectiveness and flexibility of your organisational structure. An exhibition stand is the wrong place in which to throw in a learner at the deep end and to hope that by the end of the day he will become a swimmer. In a stand team there should be a majority of experienced personnel and it is of course a basic tenet that the stand manager should be experienced.

The stand manager will also select a deputy, not necessarily formally but in fact, and use the opportunity of the exhibition to teach and train him for future duties.

Good manners, tact and diplomacy are also essential attributes of personal relations within the stand team which can consist of persons of different rank within the organisation, of a mixture of personnel from base, expatriates and foreign personnel.

The main burden of maintaining good behaviour rests with the stand manager and as he has to perform a great number of basic stand tasks as well, his is by no means an easy job.

Qualifications of a Stand Manager

Organising ability is a natural requirement qualified by the addition of special *adaptability* in foreign locations of unusual character.

Knowledge of the marketing motives for exhibiting is the basis of the exhibition effort, but for the stand manager this knowledge will include the *background policies* which led to the motives. This will enable him to deal with awkward problems and perhaps with visitors of higher executive rank. A knowledge of the exhibition host country is desirable, but there always has to be a first time in any country, or a first time for any stand manager.

Tact and diplomacy is a basic qualification for a stand manager, as without these attributes he cannot perform his duties. He has to give an example to stand personnel and, in addition, to visitors from outside and from his own organisation. He has to exercise tact and diplomacy towards exhibition authorities, cleaners, technicians, hall supervisors, the press, officials and special visitors.

Ability to delegate must be assumed as already tested in his internal role in the company. At the exhibition it is perhaps more difficult to exercise as the choice of a delegate is limited.

Ability to relax. The ability to relax can be there, but the opportunity could be lacking unless the ability to delegate is fully exercised.

Stand Personnel Duties

The marketing tasks of the stand personnel are defined by the motives for exhibiting. The actual duties and their allocation to stand personnel is a matter usually decided in the pre-exhibition period particularly when comparatively large teams are selected. Alternatively, if the team is familiar with the exhibition, the stand manager can make the final allocation of duties just before or at the exhibition.

In the hectic conditions of an exhibition the allocation of duties must be flexible, and such flexibility will also benefit the all-round experience of the team. However, the flexibility of allocation of duties does not absolve from the requirement of classifying the duties according to their importance. The classification method will vary greatly, depending on the nature of tasks, the exhibits, the type of business, but in the first place on the motives for exhibiting. One method is to define:

> routine stand duties
> desirable activities
> external activities
> special activities

Routine stand duties are those for which stand personnel was trained, in which they were instructed, of which they have knowledge and experience. Most stand duties revolve around the establishing of personal contacts with visitors, and in greatly simplified form they could be summarised under four headings:

> Invite visitors to your stand
> Inquire about their needs and interests
> Inform them of what you can offer
> Impress them that what you offer will bring them benefit

Like most slogans, these too can mean as much or as little as is read into them.

The invitation to the stand could be no more than a polite gesture, but it can be also a lengthy conversation with a potential customer. The inquiry about the visitors' needs can be a brief note on an inquiry form or alternatively it can mean several pages of specifications and a set of drawings.

Another way of indicating the relative importance of duties is to describe them as:

> main duties
> secondary duties
> supporting duties
> auxiliary duties

They can be further distinguished by their location as:

> own stand
> other stands
> exhibition site
> extra mural

The motives for exhibiting will provide an indication of the audience aimed at, in other words of the appeal targets, which can be customers or users or visitors wielding direct or indirect influences. The motives for exhibiting and the incidence of visitors with different interests will indicate the features of exhibits or services which require emphasis.

Stand Personnel Qualifications

The list of stand personnel qualifications shown in Check list 19, p. 176, is only an example of items which could be checked. You may already have full details of the educational background, training, etc., of your personnel and all you need to assess are attitudes to exhibitions, or perhaps contacts of an employee who recently joined your team. On the other hand you could draw up an entirely different list specifically adapted to one particular exhibition effort.

Visitors—from the exhibitor's point of view

The variety of visitors and the possible permutations of their corporate and individual personality traits pose a special problem in the unique exhibition situation.

Here a relatively small contingent of stand personnel is exposed to a much greater number of visitors with different interests, occupations and ranks, with different degrees of competence and influence. The encounters take place in a small confine of space, often in crowded conditions. The opportunities for generating conflicts are extensive.

Visitors can act as observers only, as partners in a person to person confrontation or in both roles. The manner in which they act out their roles depends on their individual personality and on the motivation which brought them to the exhibition. As far as the exhibitor is concerned person to person contact is a primary aim of his exhibition activity and it is therefore important for him to appraise the actors in the play which will be enacted on the stage of his stand.

The intelligent exhibitor can to a large degree assess the personality traits of the personnel manning his stand—after all, the choice and selection was his. But what kind of persons will they encounter, how will they establish rapport with them, what kind of dialogue will develop, what strategies of behaviour should be used?

The social behaviour and social techniques of visitors will vary as much as the social and ethnic groups from which they come and, at important international exhibitions, the variety will be very great indeed.

However, from a marketing point of view the organisational background of visitors and the motivation for their visit provide the most significant guidelines for a *dialogue strategy*.

The information intake capacity of visitors depends on a combination of environmental and behavioural factors emphasised in their effect by the

BUYING INFLUENCES		
CHARACTER	CATEGORY	FUNCTION
buying	customers	decisive direct: placing orders decisive indirect: initiating orders
recommending	customers	non-buying personnel (peripheral)
advising	consultants others	outside advice, comparative tests independent assessments
selecting	customers	technical, commercial, reciprocity
screening	customers	comparison (products of equal merit)
advancing obstructing	users	direct, intermediate, end use
		contractors, operators, installators, inspectors
	publications publicity media	editorial, comparisons test reports, surveys

STATUS FACTORS		definite, present, future, lapsed, indefinite, future, potential
TIME FACTORS		definite, present, near future, future indefinite, future, distant future

TABLE 8. BUYING INFLUENCES OF EXHIBITION VISITORS

concentration in time and space of the exhibition, previously mentioned.

The information output capacity of stand personnel is similarly affected with the important difference that by judicious staff selection, training, and by the provision of proper stand facilities and aids, the capacity of the stand personnel can be maintained near the optimum attainable level.

In a high *customer density* exhibition, stand personnel will be subject to considerable physical and mental strain during the whole working day. Often times which normally would be rest or break periods, will be disrupted or taken up by work.

It is advisable, even if at times difficult, to insert some rest periods into the schedule. A stand manning arrangement which provides sufficient personnel to allow for work rotas and rest periods, on the face of it requires a higher budget allocation but in the end is more cost effective.

Table 5, p. 86, indicates the categories and individual functions and some personality traits which stand personnel can encounter. The influence of personality traits and attitudes is sometimes questioned, but long experience has taught that a delayed flight, rain soaked shoes and an oncoming cold can make all the difference between an order now and perhaps in three months' time, as much as the 'legitimate' factors of discrepancy in the specification or a difference in price.

Table 8 gives examples of possible variations in buying influences, peripheral influences were discussed on page 158.

Instruction, Training, Forms

To be able to cope with the quantitative and qualitative variety of visitors previously discussed, the stand personnel must be very versatile indeed and such versatility can be achieved only by purposeful special training tailored to the general and exhibition marketing objectives of your company. The ramifications of the required versatility and therefore of the training programme can range from a short briefing session of experienced personnel to a full time training course conducted internally or attended externally. If you have an extensive exhibition programme you can compile records of instructions and experiences in an exhibition manual, but only if you are determined enough and have the resources to keep it up-to-date and to ensure implementation.

In the instruction and training of stand personnel it is important to stress the point that in person to person contacts at exhibitions, any one at any time can find himself in the role of the solitary representative of the company and what it stands for. On stands sparsely manned this is quite often the case and to be courteous in manner and cautious in pronouncements is not always easy under stress or at the end of a tiring day. But the easy way out—the excuse often heard 'I am only an assistant, the chief will be here tomorrow' is a sign of bad training at base, or of a defect in stand management, or both.

The use of forms for noting the details of enquiries varies in practice and depends to a large extent on the organizational structure and quality of the exhibitor, and the personality filter through which such formalised elements have to pass. In the world of industrial products generally and engineering products particularly, the use of formalised elements is a serious issue.

It may be going too far to start with the educational background and methods of teaching which contribute to the state of art of receiving, noting and sending of received technical information in an industrial marketing environment. It is however sufficient to trace the path of any one of hundreds of incomplete or garbled inquiries, even orders, and then to retrace the return path of queries, delays, misunderstandings and recriminations—to find lack of schooling, or sheer subject illiteracy as the basic cause of trouble.

The omission of one critical dimension, of a detail of material compatibility, of accuracy required or dimensional freedom allowed, any of which it would take only a minute or less to establish and to note, can be very costly. The fact that the costs of such omissions are difficult to assess or perhaps that they are taken as a natural ingredient of industrial activities, only covers up, but does not do away with their iniquity. If you are a small but specialised firm and your customer who made the inquiry is a large corporation you may have a difficult task to penetrate their bureaucratic jungle and to get hold of a specification clerk or junior draughtsman who is responsible for that small but important detail.

Large projects in an advanced stage of completion have been known to wait for days to establish the correct position of an ominous decimal point, complicated machinery had to be dismantled because no one suspected that an essential detail could have been omitted. The plea is therefore made to stand personnel to take their notes with care and, to management, to provide stand personnel with aids which will make their task easier. There seems to be a false notion around that to make scrupulous notes on proper forms or in notebooks is the occupation of pedestrian minds whilst the nonchalant scribbling on the backs of envelopes is the sure sign of superior mental powers.

It really does not make sense to travel to a far-away exhibition at great expense, to work hard, to make excellent contacts, to come back with an order rating a press notice in an exalted newspaper, and then to spend hours on telex messages and telephone calls to clear up details. It is cheaper, and impresses the customer as well, to stay over after the exhibition for a day and to return home fully briefed.

Despite the increasing acceptance of marketing concepts, the penetration of marketing attitudes into all spheres of an organisation must of necessity vary in degree.

In all organisations, whatever the degree of penetration, there will be functions which due to their special duties or skills are more remote from direct marketing functions than, for instance, sales or publicity.

The motives for exhibiting and the resultant strategies or the choice of exhibits may require the inclusion in the stand team of personnel from these somewhat remote areas. In such cases it is not enough to issue them with instructions to pack their bags and go and see what they can do. It is essential to imbue them with the marketing aims of their function and prepare them for the exposure to the different kinds of interrogators which they will encounter at the exhibition. Designers, draughtsmen, research and laboratory technicians, chemists, clerical staff, can be called upon to perform stand duties, either because their presence is important or perhaps because there is no one else available.

In many cases their superiors may resent the temporary loss of their services, even when convinced of the marketing justification, or more so if they are non-believers in exhibitions.

An exhibition provides a good occasion to preach the marketing concept gospel in these more remote areas, to the benefit of all.

Long Duration Times

At exhibitions with long duration times, particularly if they are geographically remote from the exhibitor's base, the manning of the stand presents special problems. This applies particularly to general trade fairs and exhibitions. Local sales organisations, branches or agencies can be called on to assist in the manning of the stand, but unless there is definite knowledge available of the persons who would be assigned for the task, this can be a risky procedure.

At international exhibitions with a strong influx of visitors from many countries there might be a conflict of interests between the local agent and a buyer from a third market, particularly if delivery times and perhaps prices and discounts are a problem. On the other hand if the emphasis of the exhibition effort is on the local, regional or national market of the exhibition host country, well screened and well instructed local personnel can be a great asset to a stand team.

The inclusion of local personnel in the exhibition team can provide a good opportunity for their sales training and on many occasions headquarters personnel can learn a lot by judicial observation of local practice, reactions, customs and prejudices.

Contacts between executives on different levels of responsibility carried out in the informal, and of necessity co-operative, atmosphere of an exhibition can be of great value to current and future relations. The establishing of such relations requires a conscious effort by executives of higher rank. The rewards are not only a more effective exhibition task performance, but also the opportunity to assess the capabilities, strengths and weaknesses of those involved.

Languages

The value of talking to a visitor in his own language needs no special advocacy, except that in the environment of an exhibition it receives added emphasis of the overall importance of person to person contacts. The correct understanding of the needs and requirements of customers and potential customers is just as important as the added power of persuasion which it gives to the conduct of negotiations.

At international exhibitions the minimum requirement is a knowledge of the language of the host country and, if possible, of one more additional language which is important in the particular situation.

Surveys of the importance of different languages in commercial, technical and scientific activities are valuable guides for international corporations with world-wide interests. From the point of view of an exhibitor the emphasis is not so much on the objective ranking of any one or more languages, as the relevance of that ranking to his marketing objectives and to the exhibition task currently in hand. The nationality and linguistic aptitudes of expected visitors, particularly of potential customers will provide a guide to the language requirements of each particular task. If your own language is one which is widely understood, do not assume that a heavily accented version of it, or a local dialect, will be comprehensible to your visitors. The use of regionally coloured idiomatic expressions or local figures of speech will not have the same meaning, if understood at all, as at home.

Sectors of commerce and industry often develop their own jargon, some large organisations use their own phraseology liberally dotted with internally meaningful initials and word symbols. They are all very bewildering to outsiders.

Using your foreign customers' language is a matter of courtesy and of good business practice, but when you have only a poor command of it, the courtesy is of more than doubtful value and as a business practice it can do more harm than good. A foreign language as such is not an asset unless it is backed by knowledge of the subject and an understanding of the customers' needs. To include in your team persons only because they know a foreign language has serious limitations. The effectiveness of such a linguist is in direct proportion to the size of your team. The smaller the team, the less effective the linguist will be. If your team is fully manned in accordance with your exhibiting strategy, then the linguist can be very useful as assistant, as interpreter and for helping in social duties.

Knowledge of your customers' language is also most helpful in informal personal contacts and at delicate discussions in which the presence of an interpreter could be embarrassing or unpolitic. If you rely on foreign nationals from branches, agencies or subsidiaries to provide the linguistic capability on your stand, make sure that the personnel selected know your own language as well, so that communication is possible between them, other stand personnel and visiting executives. This will apply particularly to personnel on a medium level of responsibility, as it must be assumed that senior executives know the language of their principals.

Exhibition Activities (Customers)—Case Study 5.

A marketing executive defined the following three types of customers who are likely to visit the stands of the company participating in a number of specialised industrial exhibitions and indicating the attitudes which the stand personnel should adopt:

'*Potential future customers.* The numbers that will visit our stand will depend on your preparatory work, on the number of personal invitations we have sent out to prospects, on the number of special calls which our sales engineers made and generally on our publicity and direct mail efforts. Apart from the special attention which they will receive on the stand, you will suggest to them a visit to our works whenever they are in the area. You may even invite a decision making executive of a really important potential customer to visit our works at our expense.

'*Lapsed customers* will constitute a small group unless special efforts were made to attract them to the stand. Among them will be some who perhaps are not as pleased with the change as they expected. Handled tactfully they are candidates for a return to the fold. Persuasion has to be exercised and be seen to be exercised to give them a justification for reversing their course once more.

'*Present customers* should be numerous because they will all know about our stand from our invitations, from press announcements, from the special note in our current advertisements, from stick-on labels in our correspondence, or because we are usually participating in exhibitions which they usually visit.

'They deserve full attention, perhaps they should meet some of our executives with whom they usually have no contact. Are there any new names in their buying or technical departments?

'They should be given special but tactful attention.'

Exhibition Activities (Stand Personnel)—Case Study 6.

Industrial exhibitions were the subject of a seminar in which the lecturer identified three basic attitude types of stand personnel:

'*Negative* types don't believe in exhibitions, they consider exhibiting or visiting exhibitions as a tiresome, time-wasting and generally unproductive activity. They only attend exhibitions when forced to do so by the sales department rota or by some other form of official compulsion. They perform their duties with a minimum of exertion. They sometimes seek confirmation of their disbelief in exhibitions, by commiserating with tired visitors and asking at neighbouring stands whether they too consider it all an infernal nuisance. They usually report that nothing much happened at the exhibition.

'*Passive* types are usually sales managers or export managers of small or medium firms, who think that they are overworked and their office is understaffed, and sales engineers who think that their territory or area will be neglected or open to competition (disregarding the fact that most of the competitors are also exhibiting).

'When management considers that design or engineering specialists should attend exhibitions, some of the more desk-bound or bench-bound think that all important work will stop during their absence—forgetting that nothing like that happened during their last illness. On the exhibition stand they perform their duties fairly effectively although without any special enthusiasm, this they leave to their exhibition-mad colleagues. Their reports are somewhat formalistic, sometimes patronising, and contain statistics of the number of visitors to the exhibition, etc., copied from exhibition bulletins.

'A few of them, after attending several exhibitions realise that there is more to it than they thought and in time they become converted to active participation.

'*Active* types know that participation in exhibitions is a normal marketing activity. They make provisions for attending by arranging their other activities accordingly, they take considerable trouble in preparing their supporting materials, they inform customers and other interested parties about the dates of their attendance, they co-ordinate their attendance with other colleagues.

Their reports are usually concise, they emphasise the importance of the contacts made and they recommend follow-up action'.

Exhibition Activities (Customers' Attitudes)—Case Study 7.

A stand manager concluded one of his briefing sessions for his stand team, held on the eve of a mechanical handling exhibition, with the following words:

'We have discussed our new equipment and the strength of two new features, we have also talked about what we can expect from our competitors. I think that we are quite well prepared for the ordeal but I would like to stress once more the importance of probing into our customers' needs. You have your inquiry forms. Please pay special attention to the items marked as critical. Just for those who are new to this exhibition I should like to make a remark or two about our present and potential customers. Among the lapsed, present and potential future customers who will visit our stand there will be at least three typical categories and one rare one requiring special attention.

The negative attitude type:
'They are almost inarticulate when required to define their needs in a positive statement. They hint at them indirectly in complaints about the short-comings of our equipment. By judicious questioning you may be able to extract some vague remarks as to what, in their opinion, the equipment should do. In reply to your deliberately provocative question how *they* would improve our equipment a few may have some suggestions, many will plead "I don't know" and some will reply with varying degrees of smugness: "that's your business—I am only interested in buying the right piece of equipment at the right price".'

You must display considerable patience with negative types and guide them gently towards a decision. You could suggest or perhaps write out a pro-forma order and ask them whether the types, quantities, and delivery dates are what they had in mind. In the end they usually respond to a concrete proposition. With some it may be advisable not to press for a decision, and to suggest a return visit to the stand, but only if you have found out that they are not leaving the exhibition at once.

The neutral attitude type
They are, on the whole, fairly satisfied with our machines, but then they con-sider our main competitor's machines to be probably just as good. Their needs are mostly in the areas of prices, discounts, deliveries. As to the future—they will probably require about the same type and quantity as last year—perhaps 5 per cent more, or perhaps 10 per cent less—who knows—it depends on their sales.

With neutral types you must be factual, you must also have ready answers to any questions on comparisons with competitive equipment and if tactically necessary, but only then, you can prove your points by referring to our equipment comparison dossier. If they are potential prospects make sure that they have received all data, ask whether anyone else in their organisation should be sent details, inquire about best times for a personal follow-up visit.

The positive attitude type
They have definite ideas about our equipment and its virtues and vices and their relative importance. They will give you definite, sometimes detailed indications of their present and future needs. Of course, some may completely redesign our equipment in a way which would make it virtually impossible to manufacture economically, but even their out-of-the-way ideas may contain something more than the grain of salt with which you will take them.

Discussions on performance in the field, endurance and service and spares facilities will find their ready ear. If they say that they are going to place an order they usually mean it and you can respond by saying that you in turn will make out a provisional works order to ensure delivery. What is more you should make out that order and at the same time make the necessary arrangements for an early follow-up visit to secure confirmation.

The prominent company type
Visitors from large companies come to our stand in all shapes and sizes. Some are buyers with limited powers, some are executives with a decisive voice in the business. They mostly know exactly what they need and if they had any dealings with us before, we also know what they require.

There is only one type you have to watch and that is the small man in a large company. He grows taller with every hour he spends at the exhibition. He hints at colossal orders at low prices and even bigger repeat orders next year.

He expects lavish entertaining, but he will be evasive about his status in his firm and never carries a visiting card. He can take up to an hour of your time and although he does most of the talking, you soon feel that it is not you, but himself he is trying to convince. If you can manage it without being too obvious, pass him on to our competitors.

> Negative, neutral or positive—they all are, or could be, our customers. Please note what they have to say—be good listeners and poor interrupters.

	Features of Appeal **Targets**	
	customers	
	users	
	primary	
	intermediate	
	end	
	indirect influences	
	operators, installers	
	service, maintenance	
	installation, contractors	
	Features of Exhibits	
	design	
	appearance	
	weight	
	performance	
	economy	
	operation	
	Features of Services	
	operation and training of operators	
	maintenance techniques and maintenance contracts	
	service	
	availability and training	
	spares	
	availability, recognition, packaging and storage	
	distribution, prices, discounts	

Check List 18. *STAND PERSONNEL ACTIVITIES*

This Check list is concerned with the strategy elements of exhibition stand activities. The motives for exhibiting (*check lists 8, 9, 10*) will govern the selection and ranking of features of exhibits and services which will be presented to visitors and also of the categories of visitors which should be the subjects of special attention.

Thus in some market situations the presentation of service availability and training can be ranked as 'most important' when visitors are end users, whilst the features of operating techniques and training of operators may command a higher priority in others.

Check List 19. *STAND PERSONNEL QUALIFICATIONS* (pages 176–177)

The basic qualification requirements of stand personnel are determined by the motives for exhibiting and by the exhibition strategy. This check list provides a means of checking to what extent these requirements can be met and what measures need to be taken to compensate any shortcomings. Technically qualified personnel may need linguistic support. Special or local exhibition experience, if coupled with suitable personality traits, may indicate that an allocation of executive duties should be made, perhaps even disregarding formal seniority considerations. Personality traits of newcomers should be noted for future reference, the need for special training observed, exceptional talents encouraged.

	Educational Background	
	general	
	professional—technical	
	special (lecturing, demonstrating)	
	languages	
	Training	
	marketing	
	sales	
	service	
	exhibitions	
	languages	
	Exhibition experience	
	this exhibition	
	other	
	exhibitions	
	countries	
	stand duties	
	executive	
	routine	
	special	
	First time experience	
	exhibition host country	
	abroad	
	in this role	
	Contacts	
	in exhibition host country	
	in exhibition location (town, region)	
	with customers	
	exhibition sphere of influence	
	local	
	international	
	with other exhibitors	
	with exhibition authorities	
	Personality	
	manners	
	appearance	
	presence	

Check List 19. *STAND PERSONNEL QUALIFICATIONS*

	self-confidence	
	general attitudes	
	adaptable	
	irritable	
	co-operative	
	stand attitudes	
	orderly	
	indifferent	
	negligent	
	attitude to exhibition environment	
	enjoying	
	accepting	
	hostile	

Check List 19. (*continued*)

19. Publicity and Public Relations

Publicity, advertising and public relations are subjects so extensively resear-
ched, analysed and documented that it seems superfluous to add still more to
the vast amount of information available, even if the context of exhibitions
would offer a valid excuse. The ubiquity and penetration of advertising has
made it so widely known that almost everybody feels that, if not an expert, he
is at least very well informed. It also has been pointed out that the all-pervading nature of advertising contains an inherent self-promoting element so that
in some cases the awareness of advertising as a product is greater than the
awareness of the advertised product.

Some exhibition stands bear witness to the promoting of the promotion
syndrome* and devices intended to attract attention to an exhibit, manage to do
so very effectively, except that they mostly attract the wrong audience, and even
that audience remembers later the devices very well and the exhibits not at all.

An exhibition stand and an exhibition environment is such an excellent
vehicle for all forms of publicity and public relations, that one would expect
to find at exhibitions as a rule the best and most effective manifestations of the
art. Unfortunately this is not so. The exceptions are more frequent than the
rule. To an observer the fact that a marketing function which is entrusted to
specialists does not fulfil its task must point to a basic weakness in the conduct
of marketing activities or at least to a failure to apply marketing criteria to a
typical marketing function.

Industrial Publicity at Exhibitions

Whatever functions can be attributed or denied to industrial exhibitions there
is no doubt that they are publicity and public relations media par excellence
and that in the industrial market place no other media offers to these two
functions better or more complete means of expression.

The elements of publicity can be displayed to a large, appropriate and mostly appreciative audience and distributed to well chosen recipients. The very
subjects which publicity usually publicises on paper can be seen in body,
touched, tested, heard and smelled. Audiences can be counted in thousands
and by visiting exhibitions they express their wish to be informed and to
receive the message which it is publicity's task to give them.

Public relations also have an excellent field in which to operate. The stand
and its exhibits, visits of exalted persons, an international audience, official
receptions, lectures, products of scientific significance or new to the market,
executives, ministers, press conferences for both the technical and daily press,
film shows, tests, demonstrations, medals, awards, news bulletins, radio and
television. All these are their domain.

From the exhibitor's point of view the importance of publicity is that in
addition to its main exhibition activity it has crucial duties to perform in the

* See page 53, Exhibition Catalogues.

pre-exhibition and post-exhibition periods. In the pre-exhibition period it is actively involved or closely connected with stand design and the preparation of all routine and special items of publicity required before, during and after the exhibition. The task of selecting and inviting prospective visitors, publicising of participation and all items in check lists 27–31 indicate the importance of the function and of the marketing impact it can make.

In the post-exhibition period publicity participates in the follow-up actions and is concerned with publicising special successes, orders, awards and other achievements of the exhibition effort.

From a marketing point of view we have a unique situation. The exhibition as a universal marketing tool offers opportunities for performing an impressive range of marketing tasks and it is at the same time an exceptionally good medium for two of these tasks—publicity and public relations. Their task in turn is to support all other marketing functions. It sounds almost like a classic example of holism, or even more of synergism defined as a condition under which two agents working co-operatively have an effect greater than the sum of the two taken independently.

The required co-operation is often missing.

A few examples from a very large selection of observed shortcomings will illustrate the point.

At an international exhibition of great marketing merit, the exhibitor, a leading manufacturer of typewriters, offered a leaflet describing his range of alphabets for a great number of languages. The translation of the leaflet in German, the language of the exhibition host country, was full of grammatical and orthographic errors.

One would be justified to assume that the exhibitor's publicity department had in their files, as a matter of routine intelligence, a collection of competitors' catalogues from which the correct translation of technical terms, let alone grammar and spelling could be easily copied.

At the same exhibition the public relations executive of a very large firm appeared on the day of opening and left in the afternoon leaving behind a number of press releases and photographs with instructions to the stand personnel to deliver them to the exhibition press office piece by piece at daily intervals. The fact that a few days later a trade mission of particular importance to that exhibitor was due to arrive, carried less weight than the return home for Sunday. His attendance on Saturday was (expressed by him in appropriate public relations language) a sufficient sacrifice on the altar of corporate loyalty.

A trade journal reported the following about the group effort of a Trade Association and a group stand of 18 firms participating repeatedly in an important international exhibition:

'. . . and provided a multi-lingual brochure/folder revealing vastly more information than visitors have ever enjoyed before, although through no fault of theirs only six of the 18 firms participating in the joint display had contributed to its compilation. And fewer still had thought it worth while to see that the Fair Press Office, a sumptuous suite thronged with journalists from all over the world, was suitably supplied with the promotional material it should have had.'

This last example of ineffectual use of available publicity media is the more surprising as the firms concerned were in fact in the data processing, reproduction and business equipment industries, an industry, one would think, intimately concerned with effective communication.

Publicity when dealing with industrial products, should be equipped to cope with the problems created by the producer-seller-buyer *transposition characteristics*, with problems of incorporation into other products, of the time-distance factor, and of the potential loss of identity. Industrial products can range from simple nuts and bolts and complex miniature precision components to giant earth moving equipment, rolling mills, power stations equipment.

Because of this diversity of range, size and value it would be wrong to generalise about how best to equip publicity to enable it to deal with these problems effectively.

There are, however, two elements of basic marketing intelligence which can be applied to almost all industrial products—the *technological status* of the product and its *area of applications*.

The fact that these two elements are also the cornerstones of the industrial marketing concept is in line with the definition of publicity as a marketing function.

The two marketing elements will help publicity to identify targets and will indicate the strategy of approach. The identification of all known potential publicity targets and the selection of an optimum target range is an essential prerequisite of any publicity activity. For an exhibition effort the identification of targets assumes an even greater importance, as all publicity activities are performed in a limited space of time and there is no opportunity for corrective measures, for repeat actions or for second phase improvements. In supporting the ephemeral exhibition effort, publicity has also the task to provide visitors with information of a more permanent nature. I should assist them in remembering and recalling what they have seen. In short, at an exhibition publicity must do even better than it normally does.

We are dealing with industrial exhibitions and therefore with industrial publicity which relies to a large extent on technical information for the matter of what it produces, a matter which it then dresses in its own manner. This *technical information* comes originally from technicians, mechanical, electrical, civil and chemical engineers, draughtsmen, designers, research, development and application engineers, service engineers, technologists, scientists. Depending on the size and structure of the organisation, the information may come directly or indirectly from technical sources, but even if it is filtered through marketing functions or more likely sales functions, the background, the basic data, the substance of the information have a predominantly technical content. In some organisations the information has to travel all the way up to the highest reaches of the executive floor before it can come down to the more modest levels of publicity. In others lack of interest or even disdain in higher quarters encourages direct lower level contacts, which then occasionally offend against policies of which they are unaware. The *filters of approval and correction* are many and varied and sometimes at odds with each other.

In the industrial market both exhibitions and publicity suffer from the same attitudes of apathy and misunderstanding of their industrial marketing functions and most of all from amateurish do-it-yourself misuse dressed up as enlightened acceptance.

The existence or absence of attitudes is a concern of management and it would be easy to say—if proved necessary let management change these attitudes, it is after all their responsibility. In the field of industrial products the technical content of any activity makes it imperative that an atmosphere should be created in which attitudes are not only modified by influence from outside the technical side of the organisation but generated from inside as well. In other words *technicians* in the widest sense of the term should be made aware of *marketing concepts*.

An examination of these attitudes is unavoidable in any discussion of industrial marketing techniques.

Let us now for the sake of simplicity use the collective name of engineers for the previously mentioned, but by no means complete, set of technical informants and let us examine their relationship to publicity.

The Engineer and Publicity
In the effective performance of his task, in the solution of his problems, in the acquisition of knowledge, the engineer relies on communications with his technological environment from which he obtains information about materials, products processes and services directly connected with his field of operation and about new discoveries, innovations and improvements in his immediate and related spheres of interest. At the same time the engineer is, directly on indirectly, deliberately or unintentionally, the source of similar information for other engineers. Much of that information is given and obtained in the form of overt publicity, but most of all other information contains at least some elements of *allusive, concealed or inferential publicity*.

The three main channels of communication on which the engineer relies in his work, the channel with his *functional environment*, the channel with his *market* and the channel with his *technological environment*, all have a publicity content.

When publicity is discussed with engineers it soon becomes clear that what in fact they praise, denigrate, allocate a budget to or cut down to size, is not publicity in its wider sense, but only advertising and mostly just technical press advertising. Public relations are not really regarded as publicity, exhibitions are a special case and mostly a nuisance, catalogues, leaflets and such like are stationery, instruction manuals and spares lists are the responsibility of the service department.

The engineer very seldom recognises that almost all direct and indirect communications between him and his environment contain elements of publicity.

A well conceived house style and an effective trade mark can be very good publicity and are designed for that purpose. An evasive reply to a complaint, a badly printed drawing, inadequate technical details of a specification, all these can be very bad publicity—although not intended to be any publicity at all. A speedily despatched additional instruction sheet, a clearly detailed installation drawing, a polite and explicit letter can be very good publicity actions even if not consciously executed with a publicity effect in mind. Packaging which not only contains the industrial goods despatched, but also protects them from damage, eases recognition on store shelves and encourages proper treatment, produces just as good publicity, as an efficient polite and well-informed telephone operator generates good public relations. Most of these items make their direct or indirect appearance at exhibitions as well.

The ultimate success of publicity is determined by the soundness of the marketing concepts on which it is based and by the expertise with which the publicity effort is executed. But in one important aspect publicity differs from other marketing functions. In performing its allocated role, it proclaims loudly and publicly to all it can reach, what it does and how it does it. At the same time, even when it assumes the most factual and authoritative form, publicity is no more than a promise.

Quality, performance, accuracy, endurance, cheapness, ease of use, good service, even prestige by association is promised by publicity on behalf of the engineer. The effectiveness of publicity depends in no small measure on the engineer honouring the promises given by publicity on his behalf. The conflicts arising from that situation are numerous. Publicity will try to see in the industrial product attributes which the engineer considers as greatly exaggerated, the engineer will emphasise factors which to publicity have no publicity value. They both use the term 'commercial' to criticise each other. The engineer reproaches publicity as being too commercial, publicity throw up their hands in horror at the utter non-commercialism of the engineer. The results are often very interesting. In one situation publicity despairing of receiving an attractive, even if realistic statement from the engineer, attributes to an industrial product the meaningless virtue of being 'manufactured to the highest imaginable accuracy', in another the engineer evades his metrological obligations by informing publicity, with a slight hint of derision, that his product is 'finished to commercial limits'—whatever that may mean.

Engineers and Publicity Practitioners

The art or craft of publicity, according to some of its exponents aspiring to the status of science, is an expertise and the performance and execution of that expertise is best left to the specialists of the profession. In their ranks—in accordance with laws of normal distribution—there will be some who are very talented, some who are very experienced, not so many who are both and a great many whose main hallmark is mediocrity. The same law applies to engineers. Both professions will have of course their quotas of incompetence, but these need not be considered here.

To be effective industrial publicity must rely on the co-operative effort of two professions, and the result of that co-operation will depend to a large extent on the quality of the partners. Good professionals in industrial publicity have by definition an appreciation of industrial products and industrial problems, they are also conditioned and trained to deal with difficult informants. Engineers on the whole are rather difficult to deal with, particularly when imbued with a self-righteous if unfounded feeling of being always factual, precise and objective.

When dealing with his own problems the engineer is almost invariably involved in finding compromise solutions.

Competing requirements of high accuracy and low production cost, strength and low weight, good finish and reasonable price, accessibility and compactness all these and many others involve the engineer in the process of reconciliation of conflicting demands of optimisation of decisions, of compromise. But when it comes to dealings with other professions the engineer's attitude becomes stiff and unbending. He joins the 'all or nothing' school, he demands absolute numerical proof supported by an impressive array of figures behind the decimal point, he requires accurate predictions of behaviour and performance. Co-operation between publicity and engineering is such a natural requirement that there should be no need to emphasise it. But the experiences of long established specialised agencies indicates what widely spread surveys confirm, that such co-operation is rather the exception than the rule. In some cases there is no recognition of the requirement, in some only one side or the other feels strongly about it, in others there is a marked indifference or even declared animosity. Indifference is probably the attitude most difficult to correct as it is usually well disguised by a mantle of operational respectability known as 'everybody doing his own job'.

Lack of interest or negative attitudes between engineering, sales and publicity can stem from either side, when it exists it is a symptom of causes mostly traceable to deficiencies in management techniques which cannot be examined here. There is however no doubt that the indifference of engineers to marketing concepts is an important contributory factor.

The engineer considers the publicity practitioner as a somewhat erratic individual, slightly mad, given to exaggeration, listening only with half an ear to interesting stores of great technical difficulties heroically overcome, and of complex problems brilliantly solved.

The slightly haughty scorn and the reluctantly faint praise mixed with an implied disparagement of any commercial activity with which technical engineers treat sales engineers is meted out to publicity practitioners with much less reluctance and much greater gusto. After all there is always the possibility that there is at least a grain of truth in the assertion that if there were no sales engineers there would be no need for technical engineers. In his heart of hearts the engineer thinks that it is fairer to say that if there were no technicians there would be no sales.

But surely publicity is not really necessary. Perhaps it is useful in certain circumstances but not when you have a sound industrial product, well known to all interested users. Besides even if it were necessary, it should be more factual, less vague and give more technical details.

The publicity practitioner considers the engineer as too much wrapped in detail, mostly concerned only with his immediate technical problems and seldom capable of seeing his own efforts as part of a larger marketing operation. When asked to approve publicity statements about his product, which may border on the superlative, he is full of reserve and fairness to competitors. But when asked whether his products are vulnerable to failure or whether user complaints are justified, he asserts that his products always—well nearly always—perform as required, and that there are no—well hardly any—complaints from users.

When asked for a graph with a performance curve, he will hand to publicity a half faded dye-line print, on which the only legible words read—'subject to revision'. He remarks that the print is out of date but that a new one will be issued as soon as the current series of tests will be completed. When pressed for a date he will reply—as soon as the new test equipment is installed—which is rather indeterminate, as it depends on other engineers supplying it. Temporary test results are available but they are not suitable for publication.

Exhibition Organisers' Publicity

The quality and impact of publicity given to the exhibition by its organisers in the pre-exhibition period is a factor which influences the attendance of visitors and indirectly the participation of exhibitors. Effective publicity efforts initiated by the organisers can greatly assist exhibitors in attracting visitors. Many organisers supply publicity material to exhibitors for use in their own invitation activities. Exhibitions of a duration time of more than four to five days are also advertised during the exhibition period, particularly when the general public is admitted to industrial exhibitions either during the whole period or on special days.

The publicity facilities which exhibition organisers offer to exhibitors can influence the number of visitors who come to their stands and the ease with which these stands can be located. Such facilities may also assist in publicising the exhibitor's successes, achievements, awards and prices and provide publicity support for post-exhibition follow-up actions.

In several countries the daily press devotes a considerable amount of space and special issues to important exhibitions, providing opportunities for exhibitors which quite a few of them sadly neglect. It is the task of publicity to assess the suitability and effectiveness of the received material and to co-ordinate their own efforts with those of the exhibition organisers.

House Journals

House journals vary so much in contents, make-up and quality that their suitability for stand publicity and public relations purposes must be judged entirely on individual merits for stated objectives. If it is your objective to persuade your recipient that the organisation places great importance on welfare and your household journal can bear witness to that, then it is suitable, but for that purpose only. If it features sales and export achievements with the usual emphasis on personal attainments it may be useful in some locations and not in others—again depending on its quality and on the recipient.

Technical bulletins, guided by definite editorial objectives and handed to selected recipients are excellent means of informing your audience of your achievement in applications, usage, research and development, as the case may be. The literary character and quality of a house journal is of course a matter of taste and expressed preferences can be only personal ones. It is however indicated to study the strata of your recipients from a professional status and ethnic point of view, so as not to be tactless or facetious, because sometimes, what is received with a grin and a chuckle in one place, in another may cause bewilderment or disgust.

Sometimes fears are expressed that too effusive technical bulletins inform the competition of potential opportunities. The answer is that if you are not already one step ahead of competition then it is too late anyhow.

Activities and Production Check Lists

In keeping with the statement made in the chapter on engineers and publicity practitioners that publicity and public relations are best left to experts, the activities and production check lists are drawn up for the purpose of noting what could be done and not what should be done.

In the time allocation budget the activity and production elements would be related to the four time periods of routine, pre-exhibition, exhibition and post-exhibition. The assessment of time requirements for the various geographic destination will provide the first correction factor.

Recipients with actual or potential exhibition interest will probably deserve priority treatment. The relative importance of indirect promotion recipients and indirect information recipients will be determined by your individual requirements. It is also feasible that from your own point of view some recipients should change roles from promotion to information or vice versa.

Sales and Technical Literature

A plea is made on behalf of industrial products destined for international markets. Industrial products are fortunate in that they can use an almost universally understandable ideographic language for the presentation of their shapes and functions. It is the language of sketches, technical drawings, schemes, photographs. The use of expressive drawings, diagrams and action photographs in catalogues and service manuals not only dispenses with costly and often faulty translations but also creates goodwill. The format of service manuals is also important, it should be adapted to standards existing in the country of destination and where appropriate stain-impervious paper should be used. It is important to realise that sales literature, drawings, specifications, plans, schemes are on many occasions the first item your customer or prospective customer receives from you. They are in a way your ambassadors and you only need to check your own reactions when you receive a well printed and well designed letterhead or a badly reproduced, smudged and difficult to read drawing, to appreciate the implications. Guarantees of performance or quality may need a legal check in new territories, price lists and quotations may require an up-to-date check of the currency conversion rate. Literature or special items for public relations functions may need a last minute assessment of the economic or political situation or perhaps the inclusion of a special achievement. Direct mail will be probably used in the pre-exhibition period as one of the invitation elements and in the post-exhibition period in the follow-up action.

The influence and environment elements indicate whether you retain your own style irrespective of the destination, in which case you need to check compatibility with local restraints (social, legal) and of taste and custom. If on the other hand you decide, for good marketing reasons, to comply with the style of the destination country, you should check whether you are really adopting a genuine style, or only an ineffective imitation which can give more offence than the retaining of your own style. The subject of languages is dealt with on pages 55 and 169.

Most publicity elements involve creative work and it is just as possible to produce excellent publicity on a moderate budget as it is to produce indifferent or even bad publicity on a very generous one.

Public Relations

One precept for public relations is that they should create a climate in which all other marketing functions can operate to the best possible effect, another coined by a cynical and obviously disillusioned writer describes the task of public relations as extracting the maximum of reputation from a minimum of achievement. What once, in less sophisticated marketing times, was goodwill, prestige or plain reputation has now become an image. The reputation once attached to the name of an inventor, a pioneering entrepreneur or a commercially successful enterprise has become the corporate image. The quality associated with the trade mark or brand name of a product has become the product image. The building of reputations has moved from the early flamboyant intuitive efforts of patent medicine manufacturers to contemporary image building. Marketing psychologists and motivation researchers discovered that what they already knew about ordinary consumers, namely that they are human beings, also applies to buyers of industrial products. Being human means that when making buying decisions, the buyer of industrial products apart from rational requirements of performance, technical suitability, price, delivery, etc., may also seek in a product emotional values of security, see in it sexual symbols, expect from it a boost to his ego and altogether be influenced by the image of the product, of the manufacturer, of the supplier, of himself. One of the difficulties of assessing the implications of these apparently qualitatively valid observations, is the quantitative relationship of the rational, economic and technological factors to the emotional ones. Another difficulty is the complexity of the industrial products buying process, which in many cases may involve not one or two, but five, six or more buying influences and decisions. To make things even more difficult, these several buying influences are vested in people with different social and technological backgrounds, placed in different strata of executive power and of course with different individual proportions of rational and emotional ego.

An interesting semantic sidelight is thrown on the subject by a manual of public relations techniques with the title 'The Engineering of Consent', and by public relations practitioners who speak of 'Social Engineering' and of 'Yes Engineering'. Thus engineering assumes the meaning of persuasion, mind moulding, conditioning of reflexes, manipulation. Whether this is a compliment for engineers or an indication that engineering in the minds of public relations practitioners is linguistically more respectable than manipulation, is perhaps best left to the new discipline of psycholinguists. There is hardly any aspect of public relations which needs a more accurate definition of individual requirements and about which it is more difficult to generalise than that of the optimum corporate and product image.

In the ideal situation the product image will be determined by the company's overall marketing strategy and by the role which the particular product or range of products plays in that strategy. New products or products resulting from a diversification programme may pose special problems and so does entry into new technological or market territories. Marketing, publicity and the establishing and maintaining of an image, whether corporate or product, is a continuous and live process which should be developed, carried out and modified in harmony with and response to the environment in which it operates. Changes in the technological state of art of the field concerned, in the social, economic or political climate, in user requirements or methods of production, can affect that strategy which requires constant alertness.

Mergers, take-overs, international configurations, changes in management or financial structures, exert their own special influences on corporate and product images. Service requirements of products orphaned by mergers or of troublesome products acquired by mergers, re-arrangements of distribution outlets and overseas agencies, intrusion into the family of products of erstwhile competitors with a history of claims and counter claims are some of the factors which can upset an established marketing routine. The basic requirement is that the image building action should be planned to serve a declared purpose, to make a desired impression. The engineer can contribute to that planning by analysing the engineering factors involved in the new situation not only from his own design, production, application point of view, but also from a wider marketing perspective. Once more the engineer should have an open attitude of mind and an understanding for the fact that all marketing functions are of importance even if the techniques used are as exotic as those used by public relations.

Public relations on their part should try to understand the difficulties of the engineer when faced with such terms as the rationalisation of human emotions, concretisation of abstract qualities, psychological penetration factors and others.

Faced with these bewildering terms from an alien discipline he withdraws into his shell from which it will be difficult to extract either him, or some useful information. Public relations must not be too quickly discouraged by such behaviour, which their resident psychologist will readily explain.

To many engineers public relations activities appear as strange phenomena which in their inner thoughts they consider even more superfluous to serious industrial endeavour than the somewhat unproductive but apparently indispensable sales activities and the definitely parasitic advertising efforts. After all, public relations are practised most prominently in the field of consumer goods and these are of no interest to true engineers, except perhaps when they act in the role of consumers. Yet whilst many of the products classed as consumer goods or consumer durables (cars, refrigerators, vacuum cleaners, etc.) are technically complex articles with a high engineering content, their sales are promoted predominantly on the strength of price, appearance and other non-engineering features. By virtue of their sales these products exert an important influence on the economic life of a country and of course affect the livelihood, salary levels and standing of all engineers directly and indirectly engaged in the industries concerned.

In quite a few engineering enterprises profits from consumer goods activities support less profitable 'real' engineering ventures. Once again, irrespective of justified or unjustified attitudes of approval, apathy or hostility it behoves the engineer in his own interest, to understand and to know what public relations can do and what they should do in terms of benefits for industrial products, for products with engineering content and for engineers who design, make and service these products.

The public relations function assumes special importance when the motives of exhibiting include the two defensive functions of redeeming a tarnished image and counteracting prejudices, antagonisms, hostility (*see Check list 9, p. 82*). Closest co-operation between all concerned in the matter is essential and it is not enough for the person charged with the public relations exercise, to be assured, by others, that there really is an improvement or that there are no valid grounds for prejudice. To discharge his task effectively he must personally put himself in the position of a critical audience and ask his colleagues some searching and perhaps unkind questions until he can be sure himself that he can believe what he is going to preach. Such probing is a difficult undertaking which at first may create a certain amount of animosity. But as tact and diplomacy can be assumed as part of public relations' stock in trade, once the objectives are understood, co-operation usually follows. If it is found that the redeeming exercise is justified, then public relations can do their job so much better for being fully informed. If it is found that the exercise would be premature, it will be recognised that, what might be called, a negative public relations action was avoided and further loss of prestige averted. The above remarks are prompted by several experiences which varied in the severity of after-effects, but where in all cases the first abortive redeeming exercise had to be even more redeemed by a second one.

Publicity—Case Study 8.

At the conclusion of an exhibition abroad the stand manager asked how he ought to cope next year with the following problem:

> On a Sunday, half-way through the exhibition period, he was faced with a horde of 15-16 year old high-school boys who denuded the stand of very expensive catalogues.

The elements of the problem were put as follows:

> School excursions on Sunday were a feature of the exhibition.
> It would be below the dignity of the firm to put catalogues out of reach.
> How can one save expensive catalogues, and yet extract some benefit from the visits of schools.

The following suggestion was put forward, accepted and planned for the following year:

1 print a cheap but graphically effective one page leaflet specially designed for the purpose,
2 design a simple leaflet dispenser so constructed that only one leaflet can be taken out at a time and that a certain amount of effort is required to do it,
3 print self-copying invitation cards requesting a visit to your stand in which 'schoolboy/girl XYZ was so interested' allowing space for name and address of invited person,
4 hire two senior students from the local technical college for the Sunday on which excursion is due,

5 instruct the two senior students as follows:

   5.1 observe school boys/girls approaching stand and speak to those who take leaflet and proceed to inspect exhibits

   5.2 ask the following questions:

       what do you intend to do when you finish school?

       if study—what subject?

       why are you interested in this product?

       would your brother, sister, parent, relative, be interested in this product? what are their positions? (to be asked only if impression is gained that the question is acceptable)

       would he/she be interested in visiting the stand?

   5.3 hand to those responding, one, two or three (not rigidly enforced) invitation cards and ask them to insert name and address of the person interested in visiting the stand.

In the event two excursion groups from two local technical colleges visited the stand, but this time they were accompanied by a lecturer who acted as guide and interpreter.

The final result was:

115 names of persons were recorded to whom invitation cards were issued. During the next four days, 41 visitors came to the stand with these invitation cards. The most prominent included: four top executives of potential customers who stated that normally they would not have come to the exhibition, but were puzzled by the invitation; three local government officials, who stated that they were honoured by an invitation from a foreign exhibitor (in contrast to their own compatriots who did not bother); three technical college students who contemplated export careers in that industry. Furthermore the exercise resulted in:

A public commendation from the exhibition authorities, who learned of the scheme when approached for complimentary tickets.

A request from the two technical colleges for educational (sectional drawing) posters of the exhibited products.

It would have been nice to report that some orders resulted from this exercise but that was not the case. However, two years later one of the technical college students applied for admission as a trainee, was accepted and eventually became application engineer for the firms' export market.

The total cost of the exercise was:

hire of two students as stand attendants £20, cost of leaflets £35, total £55.

This 'junior' P.R. exercise became a feature of a number of subsequent exhibitions, and was copied by two indigenous exhibitors.

Check Lists 20–23. *EXHIBITION PUBLICITY AND P.R. LITERATURE AND MATERIALS* (pages 192–196)

Check lists 20, 21, 22, 23 deal with publicity and public relations literature and materials of general, special and supporting character. The number of subjects (*check list 20*) can be extended to include products for which individual leaflets are required, but even for general catalogues the listing of subjects and the motivation of their choice is a useful reminder of the marketing aims which they should serve. A review of general and special exhibition items will reveal the availability of existing and the need for new or modified material. This availability can be checked against the despatch time elements of check list 25.

	General Sales and Technical Literature	
	Subjects described:	
	products, components, materials	
	processes, techniques, services	
	capacities, capabilities, concepts	
	range of subjects	
	exhibits only	
	total market range	
	total activity range	
	Main literature elements	
	sales dominant	
	technical dominant	
	combined sales and technical	
	Auxiliary/supplement elements	
	technical data sheets	
	detailed	
	simplified	
	drawings, sketches, photographs	
	product (dimensional)	
	installation	
	assembly	
	incorporation	
	photographs	
	individual subjects	
	albums of subjects	
	Special Exhibition Literature	
	stand location (map, guide)	
	invitations to visit stand	
	individual exhibits (pamphlets, leaflets)	
	special features/modifications	
	particular market suitability	
	new exhibits	
	introduction	
	technical details	

Check List 20. *GENERAL AND SPECIAL EXHIBITION LITERATURE*

	prototypes		
	special offers		
	lists of available items of literature		
	requests forms for literature		
	to be obtained on stand		
	to be sent later		

Check List 20. (*continued*)

	Supporting Marketing Elements	
	guarantees	
	performance	
	life	
	quality	
	compliance with standards	
	compliance with regulations	
	testimonials	
	approval authority	
	performance	
	endurance	
	customers	
	users	
	price lists	
	quotations	
	customer requirement forms	
	technical details	
	dimensional	
	quantity and delivery	
	Service and Spares Facilities (maps, lists)	
	location of facilities	
	international	
	national	
	regional	
	local	
	manuals	
	service	
	maintenance	
	operation	
	installation	
	spares	
	lists	
	selection charts	
	price lists	

Check List 21. *SUPPORTING MARKETING LITERATURE*

		Indirect publicity literature	
		reprints	
		editorial articles	
		learned/scientific papers	
		reports of symposia	
		independent assessments	
		press reviews	
		technical bulletins	
		scientific/theoretical	
		research and development	
		practice/applications	
		popularising	
		textbooks	
		technical data pocket books	
		general purpose	
		special purpose	
		conversion tables	
		Literature for public relation functions	
		company reports	
		company activities brochure	
		house journals (internal/external)	
		special exhibition issues	
		press releases	
		Direct mail literature	
		routine destinations	
		pre-exhibition destinations	
		post-exhibition destinations	

Check List 22. *INDIRECT PUBLICITY, PUBLIC RELATIONS AND DIRECT MAIL LITERATURE*

G*

Publicity Materials	
for exhibiting activities:	
models	
static	
animated	
transparencies	
films	
sound	
combinations	
sound film	
sound transparencies	
posters	
for stand use:	
memorandum pads	
note books	
exhibition diaries	
badges for:	
stand personnel	
visitors	
gifts, souvenirs	
non-utility	
utility	
accessories	
office, writing	
professional	
personal	
leisure use	

Check List 23. *EXAMPLES OF PUBLICITY MATERIALS*

Check Lists 24–31. *EXHIBITION PUBLICITY, P.R. AND INFORMATION, PRODUCTION, DESTINATION, DESPATCH ELEMENTS, LOCATIONS AND DIRECT AND INDIRECT RECIPIENTS* (pages 198–206).

These check lists are concerned with the production and make-up elements of publicity materials, with their geographic destination and despatch times, with their locations at the exhibition and outside it. They deal with direct and indirect publicity and public relations and with the different categories of publicity and information recipients.

	Sales and Technical Literature	
	general purpose design	
	special purpose design for:	
	selected markets	
	industries	
	countries	
	exhibitions generally	
	individual exhibitions	
	texts	
	separate subjects	
	combined subjects	
	in one foreign language	
	multi-lingual	
	format	
	exhibitors home standard	
	international standard	
	special	
	make-up	
	catalogues	
	brochures	
	pamphlets	
	sheets	
	covers	
	folders	
	wallets	
	selfbinders	
	ring binders	
	quality	
	typographical	
	graphical	
	paper	
	make-up	
	packing	
	for transport	
	for exhibition storage	
	for exhibition dispensing	
	for added publicity	

Check List 24. *PRODUCTION ELEMENTS OF LITERATURE*

	availability of material	
	existing material	
	modification required	
~	new material required	

Check List 24. (*continued*)

This check list is concerned with the production and make-up elements of publicity literature. The design purpose and texts are governed by marketing considerations of subjects (*check list 20*), the format and make-up are mainly affected by recipients (*check lists 28, 29, 30, 31*) but also by destination (*check list 25*) and location (*check list 26*).

The format is important for foreign destinations. Packing, when considered in time, can assist the handling of publicity material on the exhibition stand.

	Geographic destination	
	exhibitors home country	
	recipients' home countries	
	exhibition host country (EXHC)	
	countries associated with EXHC	
	economically	
	politically	
	special relations	
	geographic neighbours	
	countries relevant to exhibitors' markets	
	Despatch time	
	routine times	
	preparation period	
	pre-exhibition period	
	exhibition period	
	post-exhibition period	'

Check List 25. *GEOGRAPHIC DESTINATION AND DESPATCH TIME ELEMENTS OF PUBLICITY*

When the selection of publicity and public relations literature and other materials is completed the feasibility of producing them in time for the exhibition effort can be checked against the destination and despatch time elements of this check list. The destination headings can be expanded e.g. in place of the headings 'recipients' home countries', several actual countries can be inserted. The location of recipients of promotion and information (*check lists 30, 31*) can be then co-ordinated with the country and time headings of this check list.

By allocating merit ratings to e.g. destination countries, priorities and realistic production and despatch times can be established.

	Exhibition site	
	approaches	
	entrance	
	exit	
	ground/area	
	halls	
	site fringes	
	site neighbourhood	
	Exhibition stands	
	exhibition halls	
	own stand	
	other stands	
	open air areas	
	: own stand	
	other stands	
	Lecture theatre/cinema	
	own stand	
	other stands	
	exhibition site	
	outside exhibition	
	Other exhibitions	
	competing in/with:	
	market	
	time	
	place	
	attraction to visitors	

Check List 26. *EXHIBITION AND OTHER LOCATIONS FOR PUBLICITY ELEMENTS*

This check list indicates the different locations for publicity elements which are either already available or are specially produced for a particular exhibition. If the exhibition site offers attractive locations for models or posters (*check list 23*) which are available, this check list can be used for a cost comparison of different display locations. If another exhibition in which you don't participate, competes for your visitors, you may require special posters or leaflets to attract them to the exhibition in which you participate.

	Direct personal participation	
	press conferences	
	important visitors	
	group visits/missions/delegations	
	authorities	
	exhibition events	
	organising	
	participating	
	guest	
	Indirect personal participation, guidance, delegation	
	exhibition/extramural events	
	demonstrations/tests/trials	
	film shows	
	lectures	
	congresses	
	conferences	
	symposia	
	special visits	
	receptions/dinners/parties	
	cultural events	
	personnel at exhibition	
	stand personnel	
	visiting company personnel	
	executives	
	lecturers	
	staff	

Check List 27. *DIRECT AND INDIRECT PERSONAL PUBLICITY AND PUBLIC RELATIONS FUNCTIONS*

This activity check list distinguishes functions in which publicity and public relations personnel take an active personal part and those in which personal participation is indirect. Indirect participation may require the briefing of a delegate to a conference or, if he is that type, not only briefing but also accompanying him and attentively listening for the sound of dropped bricks. On the other hand stand personnel may be quite capable of taking on some of the publicity or public relations functions in which case implied or formal delegation will meet the situation.

Check List 28. *DIRECT AND INDIRECT INTEREST RECIPIENTS OF PUBLICITY AT EXHIBITIONS*

When the review of general and special publicity and public relations elements is made by means of check lists 21, 22, 23, 24, the items selected should be checked against this check list so as to ensure that all potential recipients at the exhibition will be served by suitable material. This check list may reveal the need for special items which perhaps were not required in the past for a similar exhibition.

	Other exhibitors, direct interest	
	customers	
	users	
	suppliers	
	contractors	
	operators	
	Visitors, direct interest	
	customers	
	users	
	consultants	
	suppliers	
	contractors	
	operators	
	Visitors, indirect interest	
	officials	
	reporters	
	exhibition surveys	
	market/marketing intelligence	
	exhibits/products intelligence	
	Exhibition organisers	
	administration	
	catalogue	
	publicity	
	Exhibition facilities	
	official press bureaux	
	news bulletins	
	exhibition gazette	
	reception offices	
	visitors	
	exhibitors	
	officials	
	important visitors	
	information facilities	
	offices	
	stands	
	special	

Check List 28. *DIRECT AND INDIRECT INTEREST RECIPIENTS OF PUBLICITY AT EXHIBITIONS*

	Exhibitor's internal marketing functions	
	internal divisions/departments	
	associated companies	
	subsidiaries	
	agents	
	distributors	
	wholesalers	
	retailers	
	Exhibitor's external marketing activities	
	customers	
	users	
	consultants	
	suppliers	
	contractors	
	operators	

Check List 29. *RECIPIENTS OF EXHIBITION EFFORT INFORMATION OUTSIDE EXHIBITION*

In addition to recipients of publicity material which are expected at the exhibition you may find it advisable as a matter of marketing policy, or of courtesy, to provide Information about your exhibition effort to your own organisation or to interested parties even if you know that the recipients are not likely to visit the exhibition.

Check List 30. *EXHIBITION EFFORT PROMOTION—RECIPIENTS OF INDIRECT INTEREST*

Check lists 30 and 31 indicate recipients of indirect interest who should receive promotional and information material concerning your exhibition effort. These two check lists will enable you to examine the suitability of the items to be sent to these destinations and to avoid the indiscriminate despatch of bundles of costly material which due to its bulk is often relegated to the waste paper basket instead of serving its promotional purpose.

	Confirming houses	
	Export houses	
	Purchasing agencies	
	government	
	semi-official	
	trade/industrial interests	
	Trade missions	
	official	
	trade/industrial	
	permanent	
	visiting/special purpose	
	Development agencies	
	regional	
	national	
	international	
	Financial services	
	banks	
	investment	
	credit	
	leasing	
	Trade promotion/information/advisory services	
	Trade information bureaux	
	national	
	international	
	Trade centres	
	national	
	international	
	Press	
	daily	
	trade	
	technical	
	News agencies	
	general	
	specialised	
	Trade directories	
	Catalogue compendia/services	
	Data supply services	

Check List 30. *EXHIBITION EFFORT PROMOTION—RECIPIENTS OF INDIRECT INTEREST*

	Chambers of commerce	
	national	
	international	
	Embassies	
	diplomatic posts	
	commercial posts	
	Authorities	
	government	
	local government	
	regional	
	municipal	
	Associations	
	trade	
	professional	
	Learned societies	
	Educational establishments	
	universities	
	technical colleges	
	trade schools	
	training centres	
	Publishing houses	
	Libraries	
	general	
	specialised	
	Approval/standards/certification institutions	
	Test/laboratory/survey establishments, societies	
	Special interest bodies	
	consumer protection	
	industrial safety	
	public safety	
	environment	
	users associations	
	operators associations	
	Tourist offices	
	official	
	national	
	specialised	

Check List 31. *EXHIBITION EFFORT INFORMATION—RECIPIENTS OF INDIRECT INTEREST*

	Travel agencies	
	official	
	private	
	air lines	
	navigation	
	rail	
	Hotels	

Check List 31. (*continued*)

20. Exhibition Intelligence

An exhibition intelligence task is the application of *organised curiosity*. As exhibiting or visiting are marketing functions, exhibition intelligence becomes in fact, a marketing intelligence function, usually initiated and organised by marketing research who also sort, evaluate and analyse the obtained material. Many marketing intelligence tasks would be best performed by specialists from marketing research or perhaps even by a special marketing intelligence function, but there are complex engineering products, sophisticated conceptual systems, complicated chemical formulations which require an intimate knowledge of their properties to be able to discern the differences, the changes, the faults which could be the subjects of an intelligence task.

Exhibition intelligence can be assigned to an outside organisation, carried out by internal resources, or by a combination of internal resources and outside assistance.

Internal personnel and time resources have their limitations even in organisations with large marketing research departments, let alone in medium and small firms. The accomplishing of intelligence tasks becomes thus a matter of delegating it to personnel engaged on other duties. In the context of a busy exhibition this can impose severe strains and affect both stand duties and intelligence tasks adversely.

The requirements for intelligence tasks must be therefore included in the personnel and time budget of exhibition activities. Depending on the scope of the exhibiting effort and the exhibition environment this may mean additional stand personnel or at least additional junior personnel to provide the necessary assistance and relief, or alternatively personnel primarily engaged on intelligence and only assisting in stand duties. The danger is often stressed of using sales personnel for intelligence tasks because of lack of objectivity and potential conflict of interests. That sales personnel is most frequently singled out for these doubts, is understandable on several counts. Firstly, sales operations in the field are a natural source of intelligence and sales personnel is engaged in these operations. Secondly, intelligence tasks are often misinterpreted as marketing research tasks, when the doubts would be justified, thirdly in the industrial products sector, service engineers, maintenance engineers, operators and others, could be just as well charged with intelligence tasks and the same objections of bias and conflict of interests raised. However the problem of objectivity cannot be confined to personnel outside the marketing research function or even a special intelligence function.

Even highly skilled and experienced researchers will show different degrees of objectivity. Let us take the case of two research assistants assigned to the same intelligence task. Don is a member of an independent market research organisation, George a member of his company's market research department.

Apart from personality traits, different educational background and training, in the real world, as distinct from the textbook world, the objectivity of

Don in his role as outsider, may be affected by his loyalty to his organisation, or to his private ambitions. George in his internal role may be affected by departmental jealousy, by wishing to outdo the outsider, by wanting to prove himself. Of course it need not happen and both may be willing and anxious to co-operate to the greater glory of the task in hand.

When there is a mixture of research and other personnel of the same organisation similar conflicts can arise. Market research departments are sometimes resentful of a possible infringement of their preserves, if some of their duties are delegated to others. Sales departments are apprehensive about the encroachment on their territories and on their contacts with customers by market research. The segmentation, empire building, bureaucracy and departmental rivalry which can be found in any organisation large or small must be taken as normal and only then can counter-measures be taken.

The performing of intelligence tasks by specially assigned personnel, not involved in stand duties, has very great advantages. The stand provides a good base of operations. An exhibitor has access to information and data not available to visitors, the assistance in technical matters by specialists, interpreters by clerical staff, even the opportunity for rest and refreshment may greatly ease the intelligence task.

The concentration of *intelligence targets* at an exhibition and the opportunity to accomplish the task in a set time usually fully justifies special assignments on time-person-expense grounds alone. Cost effectiveness, a great saving in time, valuable experience, are mostly additional benefits.

Visitors undertaking intelligence tasks are on their own, and must rely on their own systematic preparation. They can obtain such assistance which the exhibition organisers provide and can perhaps find a friendly exhibitor-customer or supplier who is willing to extend his hospitality. However as debts of gratitude are the most difficult ones to repay—caution is indicated.

When delegating intelligence tasks to personnel visiting exhibitions or to stand personnel, it is important to assess their capacity and capability to perform the task. The personality, experience and knowledge of the person may not be compatible with one type of task, but ideally suited to another. The task may appear too trivial to one, or too strenuous to another.

What must be avoided at all costs is to treat intelligence either as something which is 'to be done when the time is available' or as a duty which 'is at least as important if not more than anything else you do'.

If the task is only of marginal importance, then why waste the time of a person otherwise engaged? If it is all that important, it deserves the efforts of a person specially assigned to it.

Another pitfall to be avoided is to invest an intelligence task with a false glamour by describing it as 'a bit of market research really' and adding a benevolent pat on the back for good measure.

Many an environment and location of an interesting intelligence task is much more glamorous than that of a dull, slogging piece of desk research legitimately described as market research. If conditions require a modicum of public relations before you can achieve your objective, why not stress the 'intelligence' which is required to perform the task, the opportunity of extra knowledge, nay expertise, to be acquired, the satisfaction of tangible immediate and reportable results.

Each situation will require individual treatment but the basic precepts are the same:

> definition of intelligence task aims
> preparation, instruction and provision of task aids
> designation of minimum and optimum task goals
> selection of personnel compatible with tasks.

The quest for absolute objectivity although desirable in itself should be somewhat tempered in the definition of aims. Although the basic requirement for acquiring factual data and noting factual information must be clearly stated, room should be left for the reporting of some non-objective information providing it is marked as such, for the expression of opinions if declared as such. An exaggerated demand for objectivity may generate an inclination to present all collected data as objective, or to select only such, which will pass the test.

If people can be persuaded not to be afraid to say in a report 'in my opinion' and then express that opinion concisely, a great deal can be gained. Apart from other considerations, subjective pronouncements of impressions and observations will reveal personal prejudices, preferences, aptitudes, frustrations and powers of judgment which eventually can be checked against facts. The resulting assessment of the personality traits may be very important for future assignments. The programmed tasks of an executive visiting an exhibition will have an inherent or self-assigned intelligence content. If his role is that of a visitor only, the intelligence element will be related mainly to his immediate interest and depending on his personality and his other interests, extended into other areas. If he visits an exhibition in which his organisation participates, the intelligence element will also cover the exhibition stand, the performance of the stand personnel and the effectiveness of the participation effort.

A systematic preparation for a visit to an exhibition can be assumed at an executive level of responsibility, but intelligence tasks are usually left to ad hoc decisions. This is due partly to the fact that at executive level intelligence tasks are rarely defined as such and partly due to a widely accepted view that 'one will not know what to look for until one gets there'. It is also sometimes thought, consciously or subconsciously, that to prepare specially for an activity which has to do with 'intelligence' may reflect unfavourably on one's own. Only a live performance of an intelligence task in the company of such an executive will convince him, of the synergetic effect of executing an intelligence task intelligently, in other words, with proper preparation. This preparation may mean no more than a few brief notes about the subjects to be observed and the people to be met, or it may run to a full dossier of products, designs, competitors, customers and the points about which intelligence is required.

If no special intelligence tasks are planned, a deliberate, even if modest intelligence effort added to normal duties will amply repay the effort. It will provide background and colour to exhibition activities on which reports may be later received. It will enable the executive to add his personal impressions not only to the subject of the reports, but also to the image of the people who wrote them.

From a general management point of view it is important not to isolate the intelligence function as one performed only when required. *Intelligence vigilance* should be preached and instructed as an integral element of any marketing activity, to be practised by everybody with varying degrees of emphasis regulated by the importance of current main tasks.

Intelligence Interviews
Interviews with customers, suppliers, users or any other respondents are easier to arrange at an exhibition than in the normal course of business. There is at an exhibition an atmosphere of an easy exchange of views. The danger of alienating respondents by probing questions about competitors or customers is much less likely at an exhibition where the comparing of competitors is a natural function. Operationally the exhibition offers unique advantages. You know that your respondents will be at the exhibition for a set time, you can revisit them to check on information received, you can repay the courtesy shown before, by imparting interesting information. If you are fortunate enough to perform your intelligence task with the backing of an exhibition stand, you can perhaps request the support of a specialist in an interview, where his qualifications are more compatible with those of the respondent you intend to interview, then yours. Stand personnel could also give you assistance with linguistic or social skills. The importance of intelligence tasks deserves a remark about technicalities. Intelligence is a systematic discipline and requires the making of notes and records. If we start with the basic element of notes made on paper the plea is made not to use large cumbersome clipboards more suitable for stock-taking in a general merchandise stock room than for a task which whilst probing must be tactful, whilst intruding should remain unobtrusive. At the other extreme the making of notes on odd bits of paper when interviewing a senior executive can give the impression that you are not really so very concerned about what he has to say. A whole range of sophisticated aids is available starting with loose leaf books, through pocket tape records to miniature cameras. The aids should be not only suitable for the task but should also comply with legal restrictions and

regulations of individual exhibitions. The issues of ethics, espionage and design stealing are the realm of individual or corporate conscience.

Language Problems

Intelligence tasks at exhibitions held in foreign countries with difficult or unfamiliar languages can present a problem. The essence of intelligence tasks is not only a matter of noting facts but also of registering shades of meaning and interpreting understatements and exaggerations. When such difficulties are foreseen in time it may be possible to employ local, preferably bilingual, personnel to perform the task at the exhibition.

The bilingual requirement is to ensure good understanding between the instructing researcher and the person charged with the task. When properly instructed university or technical college students, engaged in studies with some affinity to your problem, or free-lance journalists dealing with your area of interest, can perform intelligence tasks very successfully.

Exhibition Merit Intelligence

Exhibition merit intelligence is a valuable aid to a merit rating study. In exhibition conscious organisations such intelligence is obtained as a result of definite instructions, on the basis of detailed questionnaires, or in the form of memoranda or reports. It comes from many sources, from stand personnel attending exhibitions, from members of the staff and executives visiting exhibitions and also from outside sources such as press notices, trade journals, official reports, etc. On the whole information gathered on a non-systematic basis suffers from the deficiency that is either too general or too particular in one detail or altogether too superficial, to be of real value. Often it is collected by individuals on an ad hoc basis and regarded by them as their own property. It is then a question how much of it is reported back, and how useful such personality filtered information is to the organisation receiving it. It is not unknown for such intelligence to be regarded as a personal asset, a means of building a reputation for being an expert in a market or territory.

Press reports vary considerably in value. Statistical data which should be clear and outstanding are often lost in the folds of a chatty text or given in a form more puzzling than revealing. Photographs of brightly lit attractive stands do credit to the stand designer, but say nothing about the lack of ventilation, the smell and the accumulated rubbish which in fact made attendance an ordeal.

In the absence of comprehensive merit rating data about an exhibition, an examination of available exhibition intelligence may have to serve the purpose of selection. In the present state of the stock of objective information about exhibitions it seems imperative to use each opportunity to collect exhibition intelligence from as many sources as possible.

Your own staff visiting exhibitions or in their role as stand personnel, when suitably briefed should be best qualified to gather such information.

It is however important that the task of collecting exhibition intelligence should not infringe on the main task whatever that may be.

Comments of customers, competitors and independent observers are valuable, provided they are categorised and weighted according to their origin and possible bias.

It is sometimes necessary to extract the few intelligence items significant for your particular need from a mass of details of varying quality and veracity, on the other hand one or two cogent comments on a particular aspect of an exhibition can influence your decision to participate.

Technological Intelligence
The technological environment of an exhibition was discussed on page 112. Technological intelligence tasks are directed towards selected targets within your sphere of interests, for example:

    improvements and innovations
    manufacturing techniques
    needs for new products or processes

Technological intelligence tasks are best performed by specialists. In the case of the above three targets these would come from research and development or design, production, market research functions. Although the requirement of systematic preparation is valid for technological intelligence tasks as much as for any other, there is a different attitude in the execution of the task. The observation and probing is more free-ranging and at the same time more discerning. Imagination plays an important role in relating the intelligence gathered to your own skills and resources and when technological intelligence is subjected to the test of market research and long range forecast analysis it can also trigger off promising speculative developments.

A typical and rewarding technological intelligence task is the identification of gaps between the technology available and the technology actually used in your sphere of activity. However, before initiating a 'gap identification task' you should carefully assess the merit of the exhibition in that particular respect. A general industrial exhibition in which several branches of the technology in which you are interested participate, is a suitable medium; a highly specialised product-oriented exhibition will yield better direct product intelligence material, and only by inference technology intelligence material.

An unconventional not quite systematic approach to intelligence can also yield results if used by persons of suitable talents. To see something better done not in his own field, can on occasions show an imaginative designer how to short-circuit a more elaborate procedure. The shortcomings of competitive products can provide an early warning of potential pitfalls.

State of Art Intelligence

The state of art intelligence is closely related to technological intelligence except that it mostly concentrates its attention on the achievements of a defined object rather than on its environment. Where technological intelligence is inclined to be synthetic, state of art intelligence tends to be analytic. It can be applied to single products, to a system of equipment, to a process or to a function. A state of art intelligence task must be carefully organised and there is no room for deviation from the brief. All collected observations and data should be objective facts, any information thought valuable but not objective should be declared as such. It cannot be stressed too often that a requirement for objectivity does not exclude all other information but only insists on prefacing it with the appropriate adjective.

Sales and Technical Literature

The acquisition of sales and technical literature of competitive products and of products related to your direct and indirect marketing interests is a basic intelligence task which should be performed as a matter of routine not requiring special instructions. When stating that requirement it is assumed that your personnel is sufficiently steeped in the marketing concept to know that the ramifications of your market are not confined to what you make, but defined by the need you serve.

All sorts of unnecessary ruses are often used to obtain your competitors' literature whilst all that is required in most cases is to offer him yours in exchange. If you are the one reluctant to part with publicity material in case it falls into wrong hands, you are mistaken on two counts. Firstly, you are denying your publications their name and their case for existence, secondly, any determined competitor need only use the help of a friendly customer to obtain all the material required. To a discriminate inquirer trade associations and specialised information bureaux can also provide supplementary and sometimes very interesting material.

Although the acquisition of sales and technical literature completes the intelligence task it is only the first step in its exploitation for marketing purposes.

The material will be received, sorted, indexed and when called for analysed by the market or marketing research function, and most important, arrangements will be put in hand to keep the material up-to-date.

Product Intelligence

The additions, refinements, changes in appearance, colour, shape and functions of products are more easily detected at an exhibition, when immediate comparison with other products is possible and when an observation already made can be repeated, an omission corrected, and impression noted and, if necessary, confirmed.

User Intelligence

When your exhibits are industrial products which are auxiliaries, accessories or other built-in components, user intelligence is an important task.

Quality or performance is often judged by the user subjectively and as a result of other factors than the actual properties of the product. An excellent accessory can be judged unsatisfactory because it is difficult to fit or remove. The dissatisfaction generated by the awkward handling properties and difficulty of opening of a container is affecting the judgement of the contents. A combination of one very good and one indifferent component is not so serious although it lowers the opinion about the good one. A combination of a good and a bad component invariably gives both a bad name. Systematic intelligence gathering of user attitudes can make a very valuable contribution to product improvement.

General Survey Intelligence

At exhibitions of a high marketing merit the observation of the numerical incidence of an exhibited product or product group can give an indication of market saturation trends, of product ranges, of shortages. Once again it must be stressed, that the task of intelligence is to observe facts and note them carefully. Marketing research has the task to co-ordinate, analyse and to draw conclusions. A report saying 'we have observed a greater number of air-cooled engines installed in earthmoving equipment than last year' means very little in terms of intelligence, except to confirm that such engines are used as before, which everybody knows anyhow.

A report giving the names of 30 models of equipment and the makes of the 27 engines installed in these 30 models, together with technical data of both earthmoving equipment and engines, or including the relevant technical literature, is all that is required.

It is possible to receive the first type of report without asking for it, or because the questions asked were not specific. It is also possible to receive the second type of fully informative reports without requesting it. It all depends how intelligent the intelligencer was. It is comparatively easy to ensure that only the second type of report will be received. A purpose made questionnaire, a sufficient supply of preprinted forms made in a handy format, an indication of minimum and optimum information limits and the result is great satisfaction all round.

National Market Intelligence

National exhibitions not open to foreign goods provide a good field for market and marketing intelligence related to a nationally defined market. A subsequent comparison with intelligence gathered at an international exhibition held in the same country supplements the first intelligence report most effectively. In export viable countries a national exhibition also provides valuable insights into current technical and design trends, and thus into a potential third market competition.

	Personal tasks	
	interviews	
	observations	
	lectures	
	symposia	
	meetings	
	Printed matter	
	sales and technical literature	
	service literature	
	performance data	
	price lists	
	publicity material, company reports	
	Materials	
	samples	
	products	
	components	
	Other tasks	
	attending and/or participating	
	test runs	
	demonstrations	
	trials	

Check List 32. *EXHIBITION INTELLIGENCE ACTIVITIES*

This check list sets out personal and material elements of intelligence tasks which can be conducted as a separate function, as part of stand personnel duties or as functions combined with exhibition visiting activities. When intelligence tasks are combined with other duties, it is nevertheless important to identify the intelligence elements of these combined tasks and to allocate to them merits of importance and priority.

	Intelligence technique	
	internal personnel assignment	
	special task	
	combined with other tasks	
	external assignment	
	non-personal collection of data	
	Exhibition structure	
	quality of halls, display areas	
	services, facilities, amenities	
	standards of organisation	
	Exhibition merits	
	organisers statistical data	
	independent surveys	
	previews, reports, special issues	
	press	
	technical journals	
	other media	
	reports and comments of	
	participating stand personnel	
	visiting personnel	
	comments of exhibitors	
	customers	
	competitors	
	others	
	comments of visitors	
	customers	
	competitors	
	others	

Check List 33. *EXHIBITION MERIT INTELLIGENCE*

Exhibition merit intelligence can be a separate task of an intelligence assignment or part of it. It can be also wholly or partly executed by desk research methods. Whilst general exhibition intelligence tasks are usually motivated by marketing objectives, exhibition merit intelligence should be exercised almost as a natural reflex action, even if not specified as a definite task. This check list can be used to assess the extent of available information, the need for specific action, and the relative importance of the elements involved.

21. Exhibition Budgeting

Exhibitions are marketing tools and thus budgeting for exhibitions should be a part of the general process of budgeting for marketing expenditures. For companies recognising marketing concepts and management accounting as essential ingredients of their corporate existence, the budgeting of marketing expenditures is a natural element of financial control.

In live organisations no single activity can be entirely isolated and treated separately, and many overlapping or cross-influencing marketing functions are difficult to separate. It is therefore not surprising that actual budgeting practices vary widely and that the definitions of what constitutes 'marketing expenses' or 'marketing costs' are even less uniform, and less generally applicable, than those of the more conventional definitions of selling expenses. The accounting systems of many manufacturers of industrial products were evolved to serve the needs of traditional production cost control. They often fail to reveal, and sometimes tend to obscure, data needed for a realistic allocation of marketing expenditures and what is more important for pin-pointing the responsibility for such expenditures.

Apart from logical and functional considerations the allocation of market-ing expenditure items and their budgeting is influenced on some occasions by seemingly irrational but none the less decisive factors such as strong executive personalities, interdepartmental politics, changes in executive appointments, entrenched departmental positions, new executive brooms, etc.

The methods of budgeting for exhibitions vary as much as those of budget-ing for other marketing functions except that budgets for exhibitions are sometimes based on what can only be described as motivations of imitation, faith, hope, hunch and feeling. The most frequently encountered methods of allocating exhibition expenditure practised by large, medium and small exhibitors are the following:

> percentage of the publicity budget
> percentage of advertising appropriation
> percentage of sales promotion budget
> fixed or variable percentage of selling costs
> fixed or variable budgets for stated territories or other market definitions
> special budgets for specific products

Less well defined allocations are made as a result of *ad hoc* decisions based on vaguely stated expectations of inquiries or orders or on an expected response to the launching of a new product. Financial participation by agents, distributors, official or trade bodies also influence contributory allocations.

The degree of financial flexibility with which these allocations are imple-mented, depends as much on the internal structure and strictness of controls of individual companies as on the influence of external circumstances such as cost inflation, competitive pressures, powers of persuasion of interested parties, outside assistance, financial situation, etc.

The most popular of these methods, and at the same time the most facile, and from an industrial marketing point of view least reliable practice, is to consider exhibition expenditures as percentages of general publicity or specific advertising appropriations.

A prospective exhibitor searching for guidance in published sources would also find this method of exhibition budgeting as the one most frequently quoted. Unfortunately, attempts to relate quoted percentages to real values founders on the very wide variations in both appropriations for advertising and the percentages allocated for exhibitions. The fact that publicity or advertising budgets are also based on percentages, mostly of total sales or sales costs, adds another dimension to these variations.

A review of advertising and exhibition appropriations in thirty-nine industrial product groups showed that exhibition percentages expressed a percentages of total advertising expenditures ranged from 5 per cent to 25 per cent, with a median of 11 per cent. The advertising expenditures in turn expressed as percentages of gross sales ranged from 0.16 per cent to 3 per cent, with a median of 1 per cent.

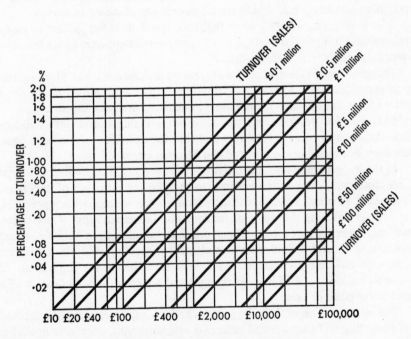

FIGURE 10. EXHIBITION BUDGET APPROPRIATIONS

A graphical presentation of the wide variations in exhibition budget appropriations which are based on percentage values of the sales turnover.

Whilst the percentages for advertising expenditures showed a fairly logical relation between percentage values and product characteristics, the appropriations for exhibitions were influenced to some extent by company size or individual practice but showed no generally valid trends.

A prospective exhibitor, examining one particular group of products would find that advertising appropriations varied from 0.96 per cent to 1.72 per cent of gross sales and exhibition appropriations varied from 3 per cent to 19 per cent of advertising. His notional budget for exhibitions could therefore range from 0.029 per cent to 0.326 per cent of his gross sales.

At a level of gross sales of £2,000,000 and a 0.03 per cent exhibition appropriation, participation in even one international exhibition would be beyond his reach but an appropriation of 0.3 per cent would enable him to participate in three to four exhibitions (*see Figure 10*). The assessment of exhibition expenditure as a percentage of publicity spending, even if useful for analysis purposes, is an inappropriate device for budgeting.

Publicity is a very important marketing function in its own right and it also plays a leading role in exhibition activities. It is nevertheless only one of a range of marketing functions performed at exhibitions. It does not seem to make very good marketing or financial control sense, to budget for a complex activity embracing almost all vital marketing functions, on the basis of a primitive percentage calculation related to only one of these functions.

This is even less justified when that function itself is the subject of many misunderstandings of its role, and of controversies concerning its financial demands and their cost effectiveness.

The sound application of corporate resources demands that a given exhibition expenditure should yield a maximum return or alternatively that a given return from an exhibition effort should be achieved at minimum cost.

Exhibition budgeting means translating the marketing motives for exhibiting into decisions to commit resources and thus the definition of the three basic elements of *expenditure, return* and *cost* becomes a crucial issue.

In theory, generally valid definitions of the concepts of expenditure, returns and costs could be constructed in a form valid for purposes of exhibition budgeting. In practice the prevalent variations in cost accountancy practices, sometimes reaching the point of fundamental incompatibility of principles, not only make the task a very difficult one, but provide a stern warning against construing general definitions which almost inevitably would mean different things to different interpreters. What may serve better are suggestions of possible attitudes and of lines of thought and a plea for the application of a marketing point of view.

The interpretation of these suggestions and the implementation of a method of budgeting will then depend rather on real situations, corporate aptitudes and personal talents, than on theoretical considerations.

What is the size of your organisation, what are its resources and what are the methods of their allocation.

What is the character of the chain of relations between departments, responsibilities, executives and what are the strong and weak links in that chain.

To what extent does your market information, your marketing research, your market intelligence provide you with a rational basis for motivation and decision taking.

What are your methods of taking decisions in situations with a high degree of uncertainty. To what extent is your organisation expense conscious as distinct from cost conscious and how does that consciousness manifest itself in normal conditions and how in crisis conditions.

These are some of the questions which have to be asked before budgeting can perform its task of saying what should be done instead of simply repeating or revising what has been done in the past.

Expenditures

At first sight the term appears self-explanatory and for many items of exhibition expenditure that is so. Charges for stand space, stand erection and dismantling, stand services, consumable items both technical and culinary, all these are direct exhibition expenses which can be allocated to a particular event. Modular or standardised stand fixtures can be allocated to several exhibitions on a pro rata basis. Stand design and stands when appropriate can be treated in a similar way. When it comes to sales and technical literature, gifts, samples, souvenirs, the issue is not so clear-cut. Let us consider the most important and most expensive of these items—sales and technical literature (*see Check lists 20, 21, 22, pp. 192-195*).

Special exhibition literature should be regarded as an exhibition expense, but general, supporting and indirect publicity literature requires closer examination.

It must be assumed that you have a complement of sales and technical literature catering for your markets. If the participation in an exhibition reveals the need for additional quantities, for special issues, for translations, then obviously that need is based on the same marketing motives which decided your participation in the exhibition. The exhibition may have provided the stimulus for translations or modifications, but if your marketing motives have any validity, then these special issues or translations will be used in the existing or potential market in future routine operations and also in operations resulting from and following the exhibition. Furthermore should a situation arise which would prevent you from participating in that particular exhibition, you would have to use alternative techniques to achieve the same marketing objectives and, providing your marketing motivation was sound to begin with, you will need all the material prepared for the exhibition.

Depending on your method of budgeting you can allocate the expenditure connected with these special issues to general marketing expenses in that particular market sector or to any other sales and technical literature appropriation. Only in exceptional cases of one-of-a-kind exhibitions or perhaps participation motivated by singular indirect or remote marketing motives should an exhibition budget bear the whole burden of such items.

Similar considerations can be applied to other items of the material structure and material elements of the exhibition effort (*check lists 16, 17, pp. 152, 153*), because an exhibition should not be regarded as an end in itself, a singular event, but as one of many tools used for performing marketing functions. The fact that exhibitions are usually more effective tools than others should reinforce these considerations.

Stand personnel expenditure

The method of allocation of the monetary expenditure of manning an exhibition stand will depend on your general cost accounting policy, on your salary structure, bonus and incentive plans, commission systems, expenses accounting, profit sharing, contingent compensation and all other factors entering into your overall scheme of gross profit calculations. Opinions, systems and practice vary a great deal. They vary according to the type of business, the size of the operation, management philosophy and attitudes. There is however one common denominator of personnel operations—the time expenditure factor although that in turn is subject to variations of individual ability, working capacity and experience.

If time budgeting techniques are used in your field work, you will have no difficulty in applying them to exhibition activities where they are an indispensable ingredient of the operation.

Auxiliary stand personnel, specially recruited for an exhibition in most cases represent a direct exhibition expenditure although even here there are many special considerations. If auxiliary personnel is required to supplement the linguistic aptitudes of your own staff, you may have to discriminate between the needs of the specific market which provided the principal motivation for your participation and the wider opportunities offered by an international exhibition, i.e. you discriminate between principal and subordinate marketing motives or perhaps between special and public relations motives (*Check lists 8, 9, pp. 80, 82*). The application of these discriminatory considerations to time-expenditures will enable you to allocate appropriate monetary values, to separate them if considerable amounts are involved, to disregard them if the amounts are small or trivial in relation to the overall budget.

Returns

The marketing motives (*Check lists 8, 9, 10, pp. 80-84*) on which you based your decision to participate in an exhibition also determined the nature of the returns demanded from an exhibition activity. Exhibition budgeting should also provide budgets of expected returns, firstly to establish bench marks to be aimed at and, secondly, to enable an assessment of performance.

Motives with 'market share' objectives demand returns in terms of orders, serious inquiries, establishing of new contacts, maintaining or improving of existing ones.

If the making of otherwise 'elusive contacts' is a subsidiary motive then the return demanded is a quantitatively and qualitatively satisfactory number of such contacts and an effective exchange of relevant information. If 'redeeming a tarnished service image' is one of the motives, the demanded ultimate return may not become apparent for a long time, but the demanded interim return can be expressed in terms of numbers of visitors' queries which were satisfactorily dealt with and numbers and quality of visitors who were informed of the improved service.

Some of the returns can be measured quantitatively, some in monetary values. Returns in the form of orders and inquiries can be measured in actual or potential monetary values, other returns can be evaluated quantitatively and qualitatively, but some can be only assessed by subjective judgment. The achievement of returns may be apparent at the conclusion of the exhibition, others mature after a period of time. The achievement of some demanded returns may be entirely dependent on the effectiveness of the exhibition effort, the achievement of others may depend on the effectiveness of follow-up actions in the field, in the office, in the factory. The ultimate success of the exhibition effort—of which the returns are a measure—will depend on the totality and continuity of all involved marketing functions and elements.

Costs

The relation between the budgeted exhibition expenditure and the demanded or expected return determines the *budgeted cost* at which that return is expected to be achieved. The relation between exhibition expenditures incurred and returns in fact achieved determines the *actual cost* of an exhibition effort.

However, some exhibition functions and some expected returns defy direct assessment in monetary or other material values and once again judgment and discrimination have to be used.

You may be able to record and assess the quantitative values of man-time factors as applied to the number of contacts, length of interviews, number of visitors to the stand, enquiries received, literature dispensed, demonstrations conducted, hospitality offered. Complications arise when qualitative factors are involved, particularly if they concern functions other than sales functions.

You may have established reliable and effective criteria for the cost effectiveness of your sales force in the field and on a direct time basis you can compare their field effort with that at an exhibition. But what value do you allot to the assistance which your sales personnel receives on an exhibition stand where exhibits, specialists and service engineers can support and enhance the validity of their statements.

What expenditure in money, time, personnel and material would you consider appropriate to secure 200 interviews with prospective customers. How would that overall expenditure compare with that required to mount an exhibition effort which would aim at the same numerical result.

What value would you ascribe to the greater ease of securing appointments with important customers as a result of personal contacts made at the exhibition.

How do you assess the value of the attendance of a marketing executive, does his presence have a beneficial effect on the performance of the stand personnel, does his authority improve the prospects of securing orders or long term contracts.

There are no generally valid values which could be attributed to these factors in terms of monetary or material gain until perhaps their long term effects become apparent.

Identical exhibition techniques used by two different exhibitors, can generate entirely different effects. Only practical experience, intelligent observation and systematic follow-up actions can in time provide answers to these questions.

There are numerous accountancy techniques dealing with costs and new approaches to old techniques as well as truly new ones, as distinct from merely novel ones, appear from time to time but may suffer from an inbuilt inability to distinguish between expense and cost and between cost control and budgeting.

In the context of exhibitions, effective cost control depends not only on the correct and logical choice of expenditure and return headings and subheadings but also on the allocation of well defined responsibilities, for expenditure and return, to suitable executives. Provisions should be made for a reasonable amount of flexibility necessary in exhibition activities and this will help to reduce the need for formalistic paperwork which so easily can become an operational burden instead of being a tool used for cost control.

One of the budgetary control techniques suitable for exhibitions is the flexible or variable cost method. *Flexible or variable cost exhibition budgeting* is based on the proposition that general marketing expenditures should not be translated to an individual exhibition effort. By definition, fixed marketing costs would not vary within the limits of a marketing time period or within a given market area. Variable exhibition costs, on the other hand, are attributed to the exhibition effort that causes them. They are generated by the expenditure sustained to enable participation in a specific exhibition so as to achieve declared specific results.

The material elements of an exhibition stand and the comprehensive range of marketing functions which can be performed at an exhibition suggest that at least two methods of cost analysis used in engeineering—*value analysis and function cost analysis*—could be applied with good effect to exhibition cost problems. Value analysis is concerned with the identification of basic functions and with evolving new means of performing these functions at lower cost.

However in exhibition activities there are often situations where the same function when performed in two different locations can cause vastly different expenditures, mostly of an unproductive or secondary nature such as travel or transport to distant locations. Whilst value analysis can reveal the relative merits of general functions if some form of cost control is already in operation, function cost analysis is better equipped to deal with individual or special target functions.

Time Budgeting—Case Study 9.

At an exhibition abroad the stand of an engineering company was to be manned by several sales engineers, a marketing executive, a secretary and a stand assistant. The duration of the exhibition was five days, the daily opening hours were 9.30 to 18.00, i.e. $8\frac{1}{2}$ hours.

An estimate of potential visitors was made on the basis of records of existing and prospective customers, market intelligence information, known merits of the exhibition and, most important, on the basis of the response to sent out invitations. An estimated total of 260 visitors to the stand was arrived at and a time budget for that number of interviews was prepared.

Past experience indicated two factors relevant to the time budget. One was that the first and last day of the exhibition were usually 'slack' days and the three days between them were 'busy' days. The second factor was that visitors could be usually recognised as belonging to one of five categories of importance and that different lengths of interview time should be allocated to these categories. The percentual incidence of these categories and the average interview time were known to vary depending on the location of the exhibition, on its duration, on stand facilities and on other local factors, but the following values were accepted as valid for the particular exhibition discussed:

Importance of visitors	*Incidence per cent*	*Average Interview Time minutes*	*Cumulative Interview Times minutes*
outstanding	10%	60	600
great	15%	30	450
medium	35%	20	700
moderate	20%	10	200
marginal	20%	5	100
	100%		2050

TABLE 9. INTERVIEW TIMES FOR IMPORTANCE-CATEGORIES OF VISITORS

The total of cumulative interview times for 100 visitors would be 2050 minutes and for the estimated maximum number of 260 visitors $2050 \times 2.6 = 5330$ minutes.

Taking the estimated maximum of 260 visitors as a guide, the required net interview time was calculated as follows:

Daily exhibition opening time	510 minutes
Preparation, meals, rest periods	150 minutes
Available interview time	360 minutes

The theoretical maximum total interview time capacity would be 360×5 days $= 1800$ minutes, but during the two 'slack' days only 75 per cent of the time would be utilised so that the theoretical total would be reduced to 1620 minutes. Thus to cater for the 5330 minutes of interview times for 260 visitors, stand manning by at least three, but preferably by four sales engineers was required. In view of the attendance of the marketing executive it was decided to assign only three sales engineers for the task.

The three sales engineers had a maximum available interview capacity of $1800 \times 3 = 5400$ minutes, and taking into account 'slack' and 'busy' days a real capacity of $1620 \times 3 = 4860$ minutes.

In actual fact 229 interviews were conducted on the stand and the total time spent on these interviews amounted to 4122 minutes.

The records of visitors to the stand, of their categories and of the actual interview times in the five categories were analysed at the conclusion of the exhibition and a comparison of the actual figures with the estimated ones is shown in Table 10.

Importance of Visitors	Interviews numbers		Average Times minutes		Cumulative Times minutes	
	estimated	actual	estimated	actual	estimated	actual
outstanding	10% 26	18 8%	60	47	1560	846
great	15% 39	32 14%	30	35	1170	1120
medium	35% 91	85 37%	20	18	1820	1530
moderate	20% 52	62 27%	10	7	520	434
marginal	20% 52	32 14%	5	6	260	192
	100% 260	229 100%			5330	4122

TABLE 10. ESTIMATED AND ACTUAL STAND INTERVIEW TIMES

The estimated and actual numbers of visitors and interview times for five visitor categories are compared for an exhibition effort of five days' duration.

The balance of free time between the maximum available interview capacity and the actual stand interview times (5400−4122=1278 minutes, i.e. 426 minutes for each sales engineer) could be utilised only to an extent of 70 per cent as some of the time saving occurred towards the end of the day, or very early in the day. Nevertheless during the available free time sales engineers conducted a total of 16 interviews away from the stand with customers and prospects who were also exhibitors. In the time budget these visits were anticipated but only as an optional activity.

The total number of sales engineers' interviews conducted during the exhibition amounted to 229+16=245 interviews.

A time budget comparison of the exhibition activity of the three sales engineers and their activity in the field was the first step in a cost effectiveness assessment of the exhibition effort.

The market which provided the main motivation for participating in the exhibition had certain geographic characteristics which, combined with the location of customers and prospects, indicated that even with strictest time discipline and effective programming a sales engineer could not make more than four visits per working day. Thus the maximum visiting capacity of three sales engineers during a period of five days would be $4 \times 3 \times 5 = 60$ visits.

Assuming that all visits in the field would have been arranged on a selective basis with a high proportion of 'outstanding' and 'very important' prospects, and assuming further that there would be no cancellations or postponements, an optimistic stratification of the 60 visits would allow for not more than 30 contacts of 'outstanding' and 'great' importance and 30 contacts of 'medium' importance.

By giving the notional field visits the benefits of the most favourable assumptions a number of quantitative and qualitative comparisons were made.

Number of contacts. A comparison of the number of contacts in the field and on the exhibition stand would yield a ratio of 60:229=1:3.8, for a comparison of field contacts with the total number of contacts at the exhibition the ratio would be 60:245=1:4.1.

Contact time. If the comparison between field work and exhibition is made on a simple contact time basis then in the field the three sales engineers would have been in personal contact with their prospects during times of 30×60 min=1800 minutes and 30×30 min=900 minutes, i.e. during a total of 2700 minutes. The comparisons between the different field and exhibition contact times yielded the following ratios:

field contact times to exhibition stand contact times,
2700 min : 4122 min=1:1.5
field contact time to total exhibition contact time,
2700 min : 4922 min=1:1.8.

Working time/contact time. Assuming an eight hours working day in the field and an eight and a half hours working day at the exhibition, a comparison of the effective use of the total working time would produce the following percentages:

total field working time	7200 min	100%
total field contact time	2700 min	38%
total exhibition working time	7650 min	100%
total stand contact time	4122 min	54%
total exhibition contact time	4922 min	64%

Apart from the quantitative time comparison which could be evaluated in terms of expense and cost per contact or per interview hour, there was the qualitative aspect of the two types of contacts. At the exhibition the sales engineer was supported by exhibits, by hospitality facilities and by the presence of a marketing executive. Return visits were arranged, interviews were extended or curtailed—as each case demanded. Even gaps in visiting attendance were usefully exploited. Duties were shared, delegated, times re-arranged, special customers were afforded special treatment. The evaluation of the impact of these qualitative factors and of the effects of follow-up actions was undertaken at a much later date.

Check List 34. *EXHIBITION STAND EXPENDITURE*

This check list deals with expenditure related directly to the exhibition stand which can vary within very wide limits determined by the scope of the individual effort. More detailed items which contribute to that expenditure can be found in relevant check lists. Thus for example stand structure is the subject of check list 17, exhibits are listed in check list 16, publicity equipment in check lists 20, 21, 22, 23.

Check List 35. *PERSONNEL EXPENDITURE*

The check list of personnel expenditure is intended as a means of apportioning emoluments and expense to an exhibition effort, so as to provide a basis for discriminatory analysis e.g. of partial allocation to an individual exhibition, of allocation to direct or indirect marketing expenditure, or to any other appropriate function. Check lists dealing with the activities which gave rise to items of expenditure can assist in such an analysis. The expenditure of 'visiting personnel' attending a scientific congress connected with an exhibition (*check list 27*), is ostensibly an exhibition expenditure, yet in fact would have been incurred just as well if that congress had taken place at another time or place. Intelligence tasks performed by an exhibitor's staff (*check list 32*) could be regarded as exhibition expenditure. On the other hand the opportunities offered by the exhibition may result in substantial savings in an expenditure which such a task would require if performed by other means.

H

	Exhibition Stand Expenditure	
	Stand space charges	
	Stand structure	
	furniture & fittings	
	operational	
	protective	
	decorative	
	Exhibits	
	main items	
	auxiliary display equipment	
	signs, showcards	
	Publicity display equipment	
	Stand transport charges	
	to exhibition	
	from exhibition	
	mechanical handling	
	packing	
	Stand construction charges	
	erection	
	dismantling	
	maintenance	
	auxiliary labour charges	
	General and Operational Expenditure	
	services	
	communication	
	clerical and records aids	
	catering (staff)	
	hospitality	
	security	
	safety	
	cleaning	
	waste disposal	
	ad hoc repairs	
	consumable materials	
	insurance	

Check List 34. *EXHIBITION STAND EXPENDITURE*

	Personnel Expenditure	
	Salaries, Wages, Bonuses	
	Stand personnel	
	exhibitor's staff	
	auxiliary staff	
	Other personnel	
	demonstrators	
	intelligence	
	service	
	Publicity and public relations	
	Visiting personnel	
	Expenses	
	Travel external	
	Travel internal	
	Hotel/accommodation	
	Out-of-pocket expenses	
	Personal equipment	
	special apparel	
	cameras	
	tape recorders	
	other	

Check List 35. *PERSONNEL EXPENDITURE*

	Promotion Expenditure	
	Publicity and Public Relations	
	pre-exhibition expenditure	
	exhibition expenditure	
	post-exhibition expenditure	
	Sales and Technical Literature	
	general	
	special	
	supporting	
	Other Publicity Materials	
	Catalogue Entry and Advertising	
	Gifts, Souvenirs	
	Photography, Cine & Cine-Audio	

Check List 36. *PROMOTION EXPENDITURE*

Similarly to check lists 34 and 35 this check list indicates only some of the main headings of expenditure incurring activities, related to an exhibition effort, without pre-judging their actual cost allocation. Here again the whole series of check lists dealing with publicity and public relations (*all lists from check list 20 to check list 31*) will assist in the detailed analysis and apportioning of expenditures.

22. Preparation, Analysis, Follow-up

The preceding chapters have dealt with the structure of exhibitions and their merits, with the motives for exhibiting and visiting, with exhibition activities and with the budgeting for exhibiting.

The subjects were discussed from a marketing point of view and with the aim of justifying the basic proposition of the study that exhibitions are universal marketing tools. Systematic procedures were reviewed for selecting exhibitions suitable as such marketing tools, and means were suggested how best to use these tools.

For an exhibition effort the motivation and selection is the first link in the closed chain of exhibition elements, the second link is the decision to exhibit, the third is the preparation for exhibiting, the fourth is the actual exhibition activity, the fifth the analysis of the exhibition performance and the sixth the follow-up activity.

There is of course a great amount of interaction between the six elements— preparation activities can influence the exhibition performance, analysis and the results of follow-up activities can affect marketing motivations and the decision to exhibit again. In this chapter we examine the three elements of preparation, analysis and follow-up activities which really only become relevant when a definite decision to exhibit has been taken.

These three elements receive their roles from the other three elements of motivation and selection, decision to exhibit and exhibition activity and without their directives they have no *raison d'être* of their own. It is for this

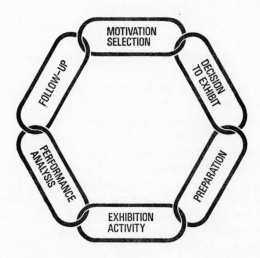

FIGURE 11. THE CHAIN OF ELEMENTS OF AN EXHIBITION EFFORT

reason that the activity and material check lists used in the previous chapters provide the basis for preparation, analysis and follow-up activities. Another characteristic of these elements is that they are least suitable for theoretical treatment as in real life they would be applied to very specific exhibition situations and these can show great variations not only for different exhibitors and exhibits, but even for two successive events attended by the same exhibitor.

Exhibition preparation

It is a commonplace of all theoretical essays on organisations, that preparation is an essential ingredient of any complex organisational activity. Yet in practice one is more likely to find the preparation function relegated to the lower strata of the organisational pyramid, than to see it elevated to the status of an important management service function, which it deserves.

Exhibiting requires preparation not only because it is a complex marketing function, but also because of its intensity and concentration and of its propensity to expose shortcomings. On the other hand the intrinsic value of effective preparation and the resulting economic use of resources employed is enhanced by the extrinsic value of the resulting smoothness of the exhibition operation and the general good impression created.

Depending on the organisational structure of the exhibitor and on the ramification of his exhibition programme, exhibition preparation can mean as little as a do-it-yourself exercise of a small exhibition team, or as much as the operation of a fully fledged special department. The range of preparation activities for an exhibition effort is defined by the marketing motives which decided participation, by the material structure of the exhibition effort and of the stand and by the tasks set for the personnel. Irrespective of the size and scope of the operation, exhibition preparation activities are concerned with the deployment of personnel and material resources during specified activity periods and for specified purposes.

But just as exhibiting should be a part of integrated marketing activities so preparations for exhibiting should be integrated into the general scheme of marketing services. As exhibiting embraces many marketing functions, routine preparations for such functions contribute their share to the special aspect of exhibiting. Preparations for the issue and maintaining of stocks of sales and technical literature and publicity materials, preparations concerned with packaging and transport, preparations for demonstrations, tests, trials, all these can be adapted and extended for the special requirements of exhibition efforts. From a timing point of view exhibition preparations can be related to routine time limits, to the active preparation period, to the immediate pre-exhibition period, the exhibition duration, the immediate post-exhibition period, the analysis time target and the duration of the follow-up period.

Routine time limits for preparations are applied during normal periods of corporate activities.

The active preparation period extends from the time when participation in an exhibition is confirmed by a definite stand allocation to the immediate pre-exhibition period. The *immediate pre-exhibition period* begins with the despatch of the material contents of the stand and its exhibits and ends on the opening day of the exhibition. The exhibition period is obviously identical with the duration of the exhibition. The *immediate post-exhibition period* lasts from the closing down of the exhibition to the completion of stand dismantling activities and removal and despatch of exhibits and stand contents to base or to another destination.

The *analysis time target* determines the time span between the end of the exhibition and the date when an analysis of the exhibition performance is required.

The follow-up is the time span during which the initiatives and stimuli generated by the exhibition effort are implemented at base and in the field.

Preparation activities related to time elements are best illustrated by reference to some of the appropriate check lists.

Check List 5.

The frequency of the exhibition will influence the preparation period between applications for stand space. If the date of the exhibition is movable, a close check must be kept on changes of dates. In some locations cancellations and other changes are more likely than in others. Some competing events may be known a year in advance, some may become known only weeks, or even days, before the opening of an exhibition.

Check List 8.

Changes in assigned tasks and duties may require additional preparation, a close scrutiny may indicate the need for additional personnel or throw doubt on the feasibility of accomplishing the task.

Check Lists 10 and 12.

Changes, additions, cancellations, congresses, symposia, cultural events and special functions can influence drawn up time schedules and may require their modification.

Check List 15.

Changes in official attitudes, e.g. a move from a neutral to a friendly or privileged attitude may require more frequent or longer attendances at official functions.

Material structure preparations

The preparation of the material structure of an exhibition effort is so closely defined by its scope and content that general remarks are of limited value. For one exhibitor attending a number of exhibitions, preparations of the material aspects are matters of experiences brought up-to-date at each event, for another exhibitor participating in as yet unknown events in difficult locations the preparation can assume the dimension of a major operation.

When an exhibition takes place in the environment of an established market, the extent of the necessary preparations can be easily assessed as the features exhibited, their locations and the techniques of exhibiting (*Check list 16*) will be reflected images of the marketing techniques already employed in that market. When a new market is explored (*Check list 8*) or exhibits new to the market are introduced, effective preparation may be a critical factor which could determine the suchfailustre of the effort.

A thorough scrutiny of check list 16 dealing with the material structure elements of the exhibition effort and the supporting publicity and other materials and an examination of the facilities and services available at the exhibition will provide a guide to the preparations which are required and to their timing.

Personnel preparations

The establishing of personal contacts is one of the main tasks of any exhibition effort and deserves the best preparation. The motives for exhibiting indicate the areas in which contacts should be sought, and the most appropriate means of encouraging new contacts, i.e. visits to your stand, can be selected from the relevant check lists.

For alert exhibitors an exhibition of high marketing merit provides many facilities for encouraging visits to the stand, for publicity, for press releases, for invitations to demonstrations, etc.

Meticulous preparatory work is required if these facilities are to be fully exploited both during the pre-exhibition period when persons manning the services are more receptive and less overworked than during the actual exhibition period. The use of check lists to assess the preparations required is shown by the following examples:

Check List 3.
> Suitable material should be submitted in time for inclusion in pre-exhibition publicity, press releases, press conferences.

Check List 7.
> Catalogue entries should be checked for correctness in time for the final catalogue issue, with particular attention paid to new products, translations of texts, addresses and telephone numbers.

Check List 9.
> If support for an agent is one of the motives for exhibiting, the preparatory activities of the agent may need checking, advice or guidance.

Public relations activities may require careful preparation of timing, of suitability of material and checking of compatibility of personnel, even when the exhibition environment is similar to that of your home ground. In locations with marked differences, the preparation could amount to an investigation in depth well ahead in time of the actual activity. Many a distorted image or questionable reputation was established as a result of insufficient preparation or inept adaptation to local conditions. Marketing executives following in the wake of such campaigns have to repair the damage done instead of reaping the expected benefits.

Check List 19.

The need for preparing personnel attending an exhibition for the first time needs no special emphasis. The task of personnel with established contacts can be eased by the preparation of material aids, advance invitations, gifts, etc. The personality traits and attitudes of stand personnel may need checking, correcting or encouraging, particularly if experience of a particular country or exhibition is lacking.

Check List 2.

The geographic location of the exhibition may indicate the need for advice and perhaps for the provision of special clothing appropriate to the climatic conditions, the season of the year or the environment. Exhibition activities may include visits to agricultural, mining or marine locations requiring special clothing. In addition to its primary protective function, the provision of such clothing also indicates to customers the exhibitor's capacity for foresight and planning.

Check Lists 12 and 13.

The national environment of the exhibition may impose certain sartorial demands perhaps not known to newcomers to an exhibition. In some countries at official functions and receptions formal dress is expected, even if not stipulated, and informal one is regarded with disapproval.

Check List 3.

Restrictions on the nationality of stand personnel or of visiting executives imposed as a result of political events or changes in regime can take place after all preliminary preparations were made. In locations prone to such changes vigilance up to the date of the exhibition opening may be necessary.

Check List 9.

When 'thank you' gestures or hospitality to highly placed customers is an exhibiting motive, the status, compatibility and social technique aptitudes of the persons concerned are important.

Preparation of information aids

An important and often neglected aspect of preparations is the provision of aids for stand activities, interviewing, inquiries, intelligence and generally for enabling information to be gathered in a reliable form without being an operational burden. It is the task of the preparation function to examine aids which are available on the market as to their suitability for a specific exhibition event. The temptation to take the path of least resistance is often great and sometimes based on entirely irrational reasoning. In one case it was administratively easier to order 'exhibition record cards' of a commercial pattern in expensive loose-leaf binders, than to justify a request for specially designed and cheaply duplicated cards. The fact that the 'bought in' cards could be charged as 'general stationery' but specially designed cards would be charged as 'exhibition expenses' decided the issue.

The company in question participated in about eleven exhibitions annually, but no one seemed interested in the fact that specially designed and internally produced cards would have reduced the overall annual expenditure of this item by about 67 per cent. In the context of the total budget of eleven exhibitions the actual amount which would be saved was not significant but the operational end results were nevertheless fairly damaging. The commercial pattern cards were for obvious reasons designed for a wide range of applications with an emphasis on consumer goods. Neither the headings nor the spaces for entries were suitable for inquiries concerning the sophisticated industrial products exhibited and when used the cards had to be supplemented frequently by additional pinned on or stapled bits of paper, many of which were eventually lost before they reached the analysis desk.

There are situations where the character of the exhibition location or the type of product exhibited or perhaps the audience aimed at is not suitable for noting too many details of inquiries or interviews. A tape recorder placed in the stand office can provide the means of recording summaries of interviews, comments, impressions, preferably not later than at the end of each span of duty.

The aids provided in one form or another should be examined as to their suitability for record purposes, for analysis and where appropriate for follow-up activities. The ultimate utility test of such aids is in the first place their purposeful design and the ease of handling which together should encourage their use and only in the second place the convenience of reproducing, storing and analysing them. The ideal aid meets both requirements with an equal degree of effectiveness.

Preparation of travel arrangements and formalities

Travel arrangements, visas and other formalities require varying degrees of attention, depending on the location of the exhibition. Whilst in one location the length of time required to obtain a visa determines the starting date for that aspect of preparation work whilst hotel reservations present no problem, in another no visa is required, but hotel reservations must be made 10 to 12 months ahead.

In one case all arrangements can be made with ease from the exhibitor's office by telephone or telex, in another it is imperative to employ but the best of specialised agents dealing with that territory. The task of the preparation function is to find the optimum means of achieving the desired results, and when expedient to abandon the ambition of doing it all without any outside help. For many exhibition locations advance preparation of visits to customers and of other marketing activities scheduled before and after an exhibition can yield substantial savings in time and expenses, providing that a valid marketing goal is the guiding motive for such arrangements. (*See also case study 2, p. 96.*)

Exhibition performance analysis

From an overall marketing point of view the analysis of the exhibition performance is the critical link in the chain of six exhibition elements shown in Figure 11, p. 233. All exhibition activities and all of the material framework in which they are performed represent the theoretical totality of elements which could be the subjects of analysis. In practice a selection of such subjects must be made, as otherwise the extent of the task would defeat its own twofold objective of providing a speedy purposeful guide for future action, and an assessment of the performance of the whole exhibition effort. The exercise of selecting and listing the exhibition elements which should be observed and noted for subsequent analysis in turn creates a salutary opportunity for a critical assessment of the intended exhibition effort.

The need for exhibition performance analysis is widely recognised in theory but in practice it is implemented with varying degrees of insistence and even more varying degrees of success.

In the bustle of a busy exhibition it is difficult to note all relevant observations and details, even with the help of the best aids and accessories. The nature of inquiries, the categories of visitors and incidence and density of visits, all these factors can change from one event to another in a manner which cannot be foreseen.

When exhibiting in new markets or at exhibitions not attended before, even the best pre-exhibition intelligence cannot fully compensate for the lack of experience. In such cases it is good practice for the stand manager, or the executive in charge of exhibition activities to hold a short and informal analysis session at the end of each working day. The relaxed atmosphere of such a session generates an exchange of observations which are still fresh in memory, emphasise problems of a symptomatic nature, reduce single complaints to their exceptional status, and provide warnings for required corrective measures. Modified strategies can be discussed, tensions released, successful approaches can be more generally adopted. Such a session also gives the executive in charge an opportunity to observe the strengths and weaknesses of his staff and indicates where support is required and where initiative can be given a free reign.

However, if their usefulness for subsequent analysis is not to be lost, these free and relaxed sessions should nevertheless have some formal content in the shape of brief notes or recordings of the salient points discussed.

Eight analysis tasks

The first task of the analysis function is the systematic scrutiny of all messages (orders, inquiries, requests for information, opinions, impressions) received and their arrangement in distinguishable action groups related to the motives for exhibiting. The quality of these messages is affected by the fact that at an exhibition they are received against a background of noise, interference and distortion—both in the acoustic and communication meaning of the pheno-mena—fortunately the effects of these disturbances can be reduced by pre-paration and the better the preparation the better the reception.

The range of marketing motives for a particular event will determine the nature of the action groups, their fragmentation, their claim for priority of response and also the selection of messages which have to be allocated to individual groups. The action groups most commonly encountered are the following three in the order of their importance: sales interests, service inte-rests and information interests. Within the individual groups internal priori-ties could be established. Thus the order of priorities for the sales interests group could be: production orders, trial orders, specific requests for quota-tions, general requests for prices. The priority order for service interests could be: warranty problems, general service problems, spares and replacements orders, service and spares inquiries. Information interests could be arranged in the order of: specific requests for product data, request for general tech-nical information. In the course of an exhibition of five or more days dura-tion, orders, requests for quotations and for information can be fully or partially actioned during the course of the exhibition, but it is essential that these actions should be included in the analysis schedule under their approp-riate headings.

The second task, closely connected with the first task and relying to a large extent on the contents of its messages, is the analysis of visitors to the stand and of all other personal contacts. The categories and traits of exhibition visitors are shown in Table 5, p. 86 and their buying influences in Table 8 p. 166. Both these tables provide a suitable background for analysis purposes. Whilst the list of buying influences indicates the most frequently encountered areas of competence, different areas, both wider and narrower, can result from delegation of duties, changes in roles or peculiar internal organisation structures. The position in the company and the rank of a visitor usually enables a correct interpretation of the exerted influence. There are also cases when the influences of two or more visitors are exerted simultaneously and it is difficult to assess the dominant influence. Only energetic follow-up action can provide the answer.

The third task of analysis is the scrutiny (related to the objectives of exhibiting) of the composition and competence of the stand team of the effectiveness of teamwork, of the response to assigned duties, of the correctness or otherwise of the definitions of these duties and of the resulting capacity of personnel to cope with them. Exhibitor's visiting personnel attending for more than a flying visit can contribute to the performance of special tasks and duties both technical and social. The effectiveness of such visits and the suitability of selection is a subsidiary analysis task. The observation of the activities of stand personnel and of their effectiveness is a delicate matter to be carried out with tact and diplomacy but it is none the less an important aspect of performance analysis. The marketing and social behaviour of stand personnel is crucial to the realisation of the exhibiting objectives. But beyond that on the open stage of an exhibition stand and in the more secluded precincts of stand offices or special rooms, the image and reputation of the exhibitor can be influenced by impressions from personal behaviour to a degree quite out of proportion to the status, position and importance of the individuals whose manners and attitudes generate these impressions. Strange roles, unusual situations, tiredness, subconscious or even overt xenophobia, self-deprecating criticism of one's own products, company, country; disinterest, commercial or technical arrogance, odd personal habits, all these and many more are the factors involved. It is not the task of a stand manager to be an accomplished psychologist but a popular paperback on the subject read on the dull journey to the exhibition could give him quite a few hints as to what to look for in personnel behaviour and the reasons for it.

The exhibits are the subject of *the fourth task* of analysis. The main items of scrutiny are the following: the relevance of the exhibits to the stated objectives of exhibiting, their functional and aesthetic effectiveness related to the special marketing tasks of exhibiting and to general corporate marketing aims, the response of visitors, their praise and criticisms, the support which exhibits gave to the efforts of the stand team or their shortcomings or failings in that respect.

A subsidiary task is a critical comparison of exhibits of direct and indirect competitors and the implications of the observations made. Award winning exhibits or exhibits which attracted exceptional publicity both your own and those of your competition deserve critical appraisal.

The fifth task of analysis is an assessment of the exhibition stand under the following main headings: the functional and aesthetic effectiveness of the stand related to: the exhibiting task, to the performance of stand duties and activities, to the corporate prestige and standing of the exhibitor and to stands of competitors.

Once again restraint must be exercised lest the magnitude of the task should defeat its objective, but Check list 17, p. 153, and the detailed discussion of the stand design (p. 143) will indicate the requirements for analysis in relation to the particular event attended.

The sixth analysis task is the assessment of the actual merits of the exhibition attended, in relation to the merit values credited to it at the time when the decision to participate was taken. The check lists dealing with the structure of exhibitions (*Check lists 1, 2, 3, 4, 5, 6*) and with the marketing and environment merits of exhibitions (*Check lists 12, 13*) will indicate the scope and extent of the analysis which may be appropriate for an individual exhibition effort.

The seventh task of exhibition expenditure analysis is usually carried out in response to the established system of budgetary controls exercised by the exhibitor and check lists 34, 35, 36 indicate the items concerned.

The eighth task of the performance analysis of the publicity effort is a specialised activity which should be undertaken with great circumspection. The major role which publicity can play at an exhibition and the resulting responsibilities were discussed at length in the chapter on publicity and public relations. The analysis task should be geared to the actual publicity effort and one important aspect of analysis is the degree to which opportunities for publicity, offered by the exhibition were in fact exploited to the best advantage.

Analysis report

The aim of an exhibition performance analysis is to produce an *exhibition report*. The composition and contents of this report are governed by two factors: the corporate character and organisational structure of the exhibitor and the scope and magnitude of the exhibition effort. A very large corporation can, where appropriate, participate in a specialised exhibition with a modest stand, be it of high quality. A medium size firm relying on exhibitions as a main marketing tool can participate in a number of exhibitions with quite sizeable and elaborate stands.

In one case the exhibition report can be addressed to an executive of a division or perhaps of a subsidiary of a large corporation in another to the chief marketing executive of the firm or to its managing director. One report will consist of a page or two of terse comments and a summary of good or bad results, another will be a complex essay compiled on the basis of an analysis carried out by means of the most sophisticated methods available. At both ends of the scale the validity of the conclusions will be determined by the quality of the data collected and their intelligent interpretation and only to a limited extent by the means by which they were processed.

The methods and techniques which exhibitors could use for processing exhibition data would cover a spectrum which is as wide as the variety of their corporate sizes, wealths and organisational skills. There is however one fundamental requirement of performance measurement and analysis—that the parameters used should be meaningful in their own right and that they should be relevant to the special needs and aims of an individual exhibitor.

Each report should present salient conclusions and recommendations for action under three main headings:

A summary of the intake of marketing messages received as a result of exhibition activities and of their general follow-up implications.

A review of the performance of the stand personnel and of the effectiveness of exhibits and of the stand in relation to the stated objectives of exhibiting.

A review of the effectiveness of the exhibition as a medium for achieving the stated marketing objectives.

The summary and the main body of the report should be concise and should be written—in keeping with marketing principles of regarding the customer—with the recipient in mind. If necessary it should be subdivided into suitable sections, which can be also separated physically so that recipients with specialised interests can be served without burdening them with redundant matter. If the report is compiled from contributions by several persons different methods of presenting the report can be employed. At best the several reports or parts should be submitted to an editor who creates out of the parts one comprehensive whole and also assumes overall responsibility. It is sometimes a matter of mistaken policy, or a case of shunning responsibility, that a collection of separate reports is presented in a form in which the common outer binding is the only unifying factor. Such a collection usually carries open or hidden marks of individual authorship and the contributions are mostly coloured by personal opinions, to the detriment of objectivity and factual reporting. Objectivity in reporting is a discipline which should be taught and practiced, talents in that area are very rare. Many an internal conflict and the settling of interdepartmental scores have their origin in deliberately provocative or subtly distorted presentations of basically indisputable facts. One comparatively tame example will illustrate the point. The following are extracts from three reports written by three persons who followed each other in the rota of stand duties on the same stand.

'. . . as it was known that the exhibition takes place in June and that the hall will be extremely hot, it is surprising that a closed design was adopted and that no provisions were made for air conditioning.'

'. . . our stand was so hot and the air so stifling that it was impossible to conduct normal business'.

'. . . it is suggested that next year it would be advisable to adopt an open stand design, to provide several low speed fans, a refrigerator or ice cube making machine and to arrange for a facility to serve cold drinks to customers and staff'.

The first extract contains a direct accusation of incompetence, the second an exaggerated ('impossible') complaint and only the third one makes a positive suggestion allowing the reader to draw his own conclusions or to ask the appropriate questions. The writers of reports realise it only when it is too late, that their essays are read by senior executives not only for their factual content but also as voluntary confessions of personal talents, failings and attitudes. On the other hand the reason for technically and otherwise deficient reports can be often traced to inadequate preparation and training and the lack of management guidance. Finally the presentation of success analysis in a report is just as important as that of failure analysis. It is imperative to establish the sources and origins of success and failures. The analysis of symptoms, however detailed and penetrating, very seldom provides a prescription for the required cure or for the energetic pursuit of healthy exercises.

Follow-up

The follow-up of an exhibition effort is the activity most intimately connected with the continuous marketing function of contacts with customers and prospects. If these contacts are normally maintained in a regular and organised manner, the co-ordination and inclusion of exhibition follow-up activities will present no problems. On the contrary it can strengthen that function by providing additional interest, by opening new doors and easy access, by creating new opportunities. Publicity initiated in connection with the exhibition, gained as a result of the exhibition effort or timed for post-exhibition impact can also contribute its share to an intensified sales drive.

The follow-up activity directives emerging from the first and second analysis task, i.e. the action groups and their priorities and the analysis of visitors and contacts, should be supplemented by information from records of previous marketing activities so that a final evaluation can be made of priorities and of degrees of importance. This supplementary information is particularly important when it concerns service prone products, built-in products, customers who were supplied with prototypes, in short all cases where previous contacts of technical or commercial importance are on record. Reference to marketing records will also disclose habitual inquirers who year in year out visit the exhibitor's stand, collect some literature, leave their visiting card and indicate their interest in one or two exhibits. A follow-up visit, paid in the course of routine duties, will then disclose whether there is perhaps a genuine interest hampered by internal obstacles or whether it is enough to maintain goodwill by a formal response.

In overseas markets the exhibitor's service or delivery reputation can influence the timing and character of follow-up actions and in some locations background information may indicate that the normal procedure of leaving follow-up actions to the local agent or distributor, will not meet the case and that a special visit to the territory is required. The effectiveness and economy with which human and material resources can be deployed in follow-up activities is thus strongly affected by the capability and efficiency of the information retrieval system operated by the exhibitor.

The techniques used for follow-up activities vary, depending on the exhibitor's corporate ego, on the extent of his exhibition efforts, on the range of exhibits and of course on the motives for exhibiting. When large numbers of visitors express interest in a range of medium priced products which are also extensively advertised, a general direct mail action supplemented by individual approaches to potential large customers will be sufficient. In the case of high value capital goods follow-up action may involve an executive's visit to the prospective customer, an invitation to visit the location of existing applications and an invitation to the exhibitor's works, possibly all at the exhibitor's expense.

Between these two extremes there is the personal letter, the telex or telephonic request for an appointment, the so called personal cold call, or any combination of these techniques. The timing of follow-up actions is as important as the timing of other marketing activities. The requirement for promptness of action is self-evident, but speed alone has no intrinsic value. When speed is applied to a well prepared action aimed at serving individual needs of prospects and customers it produces its own marketing justification. When lip service is paid to promptness by an indiscriminate despatch of stereotype acknowledgments of visits to the stand and a vague promise of later attention, speed is of limited value and is very often counter-productive.

Just as speed and co-ordination of follow-up can earn rich rewards, so tardiness can cause considerable damage. Some exhibitors demonstrate their interest and attention by an attentive immediate follow-up—others, mostly large corporations, by long delays reveal the gap between the modern image implied by their magnificent stand manned by a multitude of well dressed attendants and the sad reality of a heavy-handed bureaucratic response. If the considerable expenditure of resources which is involved in any exhibition effort is to make economic and marketing sense, then follow-up must be regarded as an essential and productive part of that effort.

Follow-up deserves careful preparation and requires efficient execution and integration into the framework of the exhibitor's general marketing activities. It is the last link in the closed chain of exhibition elements (*Figure 11, p. 233*) and the results of follow-up activities can strengthen, weaken or modify marketing motives for exhibiting, they can influence the decision to exhibit and the selection of exhibitions.

	Routine time limits	
	Active preparation period	
	pre-exhibition period	
	immediate pre-exhibition period	
	Exhibition duration period	
	post-exhibition period	
	immediate post-exhibition period	
	Analysis time targets	
	follow-up period	

Check List 37. *PREPARATION TIME ELEMENTS*

The time elements of preparation are significant for all exhibition activities and this check list can be combined with the relevant activity or material check lists in a matrix formation to provide feasible solutions to time problems. In practice the general headings of this check list would be replaced by real time periods and actual dates.

	Stand Elements	
	Exhibits	
	Design	
	Material structure	
	Display elements	
	Reception elements	
	Stand facilities	
	Information aids	
	visitors record cards	
	literature request cards	
	product intelligence forms	
	stand intelligence forms	
	Exhibition Site Elements	
	Extra-mural Elements	
	Administration Elements	
	Stand space	
	Catalogue entry	
	Services	
	Hired items	
	Packing	
	Transport	
	Insurance	
	Security	

Check List 38. *PREPARATION OF NON-PERSONAL ELEMENTS*

The extent of the preparation for all non-personal elements of exhibiting is so closely governed by the scope of the individual effort that the headings of this check list should be regarded as no more than reminders pointing to the areas for which preparation and anticipation is required. More details can be found in the series of check lists dealing with the relevant exhibition elements.

	Publicity and Public Relations	
	Literature and materials	
	stand location	
	other locations	
	Recipients and destinations	
	Personal participation	
	exhibition events	
	extra-mural events	
	press conferences	
	special functions	

Check List 39. *PREPARATION FOR PUBLICITY AND PUBLIC RELATIONS ACTIVITIES*

This check list indicates only the main elements of publicity and public relations which require systematic preparation, with special attention paid to time schedules and advance planning. The series of check lists numbered 20 to 32 deal in detail with this important area of exhibition activities. The preparation time elements (*check list 37*) the geographic destination and despatch time elements (*check list 25*) are particularly relevant.

	Exhibitors Personnel	
	Stand and exhibition site	
	commercial staff	
	technical staff	
	demonstrators	
	service personnel	
	clerical and auxiliary	
	Special task visitors	
	Visiting executives	
	Publicity and public relations staff	
	Auxiliary personnel	
	Interpreters	
	Technical	
	Clerical	
	Catering	

Check List 40. *PREPARATION FOR PERSONNEL*

This check list indicates some of the categories of the exhibitor's staff, for whom preparation is essential for the performance of their tasks or who could greatly renefit from it.

Preparations to be effective must be related to the persons concerned and to anticipated situations and perhaps to encounters deliberately contrived to achieve desired results. Not all situations can be anticipated and some encounters may not take place, but the waste of a superfluous preparation is much to be preferred to the disadvantages of no preparation. Preparations for exhibitor's personnel can be frugal or generous, but they should never be perfunctory. In some cases the scope and quality of the preparation can be a critical factor e.g. in difficult market conditions (*check list 15*), in locations with language problems, when stand personnel has no exhibition experience or when auxiliary staff is engaged.

Check lists 18, 19, 32 can provide more background to the categories and characteristics of the persons involved. The other partners of exhibition encounters are the subject of the complementary check list 41.

		Customers		
		Current		
		Potential		
		Lapsed		
		Users		
		Indirect Influence Contracts		
		Non-buying contacts		
		Suppliers		
		Invited Visitors		
		Other Exhibitors		
		Authorities—Officials		
		Visitors from Exhibitor's:		
		Associated company		
		Subsidiary company		
		Other branch or division		
		Agencies		
		Representations		

Check List 41. *PREPARATION FOR CONTACTS*

This check list is complementary to check list 40. By reviewing the list of visitors expected to visit the stand and of contacts which should be made, the preparations of the exhibitor's personnel can be made to better purpose. Specially invited visitors may require attention not only to business matters, but also some consideration for personal needs or problems connected with the visit. In such cases preparation should be attentive without being obtrusive. At the same time stand personnel should be prepared i.e. warned that some visitors not only expect exceptional treatment but on occasions show no reticence in demanding it. Unfortunately nothing short of a crash course in firm but tactful diplomacy is a sufficient preparation for such visitors. The categories, traits and characteristics of visitors can be examined in greater detail on the basis of check lists 11, 12, 13, 15, tables 5, 6, 8 and Fig. 9.

	Travel and Personal Transport Arrangements	
	pre-exhibition	
	during exhibition	
	post-exhibition	
	Hotel Reservations	
	special requirements	
	location	
	telex	
	secretarial service	
	conference facilities	
	exhibit display facilities	
	banqueting facilities	
	Other Staff Accommodation	
	Private rooms	
	Caravans-trailers	
	Aboard ship	
	Hotel-trains	

Check List 42. *GENERAL PREPARATIONS*

This check list deals with general preparations for personnel attending the exhibition and in special cases for invited visitors or participants in congresses, symposia and other events connected with the exhibition. Pre-exhibition tasks and post-exhibition tasks may need inclusion in these arrangements. Check list 43 dealing with personal preparations can be regarded as a companion check list. The location of the exhibition (*check list 2*) exhibition facilities and amenities (*check list 4*) and exhibition time elements (*check lists 5, 6*) provide background information concerning general preparations.

	Personal Welfare	
	Protection (health hazards)	
	Remedies (personal susceptibilities)	
	Apparel	
	climatic conditions	
	protective clothing	
	Personal formalities	
	Passport	
	Visas	
	Special permits	
	Currency, credit cards	
	Insurance	
	general	
	special risks	
	Letters of introduction	
	Personal aids	
	Visiting cards (foreign language)	
	Phrase book, pocket dictionary	
	Conversion tables	
	Camera	
	Tape recorder	
	Portable typewriter	

Check List 43. *PERSONAL PREPARATIONS*

The supreme importance of personal efforts has been stressed throughout the study. In the environment of an exhibition the effectiveness of performing tasks depends not only on qualifications and aptitudes, but also on the absence of intrusive irritants unrelated to the tasks, but hampering them and on the availability of personal aids easing these tasks.

This check list provides examples of such items. Some are essential some optional but all require attention either by the person concerned or by the exhibitor's ad ministrative function charged with preparations. At first sight the items listed may appear obvious or trivial, but their neglect can cause considerable delays or loss of time. Check list 42 is the relevant companion check list.

	Analysis, Interpretation and Report Tasks	
	Messages and Information	
	sales interests	
	service interests	
	information interests	
	Visitors and Contacts	
	customers	
	users	
	indirect influences	
	Exhibitor's Personnel	
	stand team	
	visitors to exhibition	
	other functions	
	Exhibits	
	effectiveness	
	comparison with competition	
	Stand	
	effectiveness	
	utility	
	comparison with competition	
	Exhibition	
	merits for exhibitor	
	general merits	
	Expenditure	
	Publicity and Public Relations	

Check List 44. *EXHIBITION PERFORMANCE ANALYSIS*

The analysis of the basic exhibition activity and material elements indicated in this check list should yield purposeful directions for follow-up actions and an assessment of the exhibition effort in relation to aims and objectives. Such an analysis need not be restricted to the eight main elements listed, the relevant check lists can provide many more details which could be included if justified by the scope of the effort and by the capability both to analyse and to follow-up.

Conclusion

Before final decisions are taken to initiate or continue an exhibition programme, the marketing executives involved must be convinced of the value of such a programme. Without management understanding and wholehearted support an exhibition programme cannot achieve full effectivenes.. The considerable expenditure involved in an exhibition programme make the exertion of maximum efforts imperative, if reasonable cost effectiveness is to be achieved.

The initiation of a new exhibition programme involves a speculative risk and in addition to measurable and foreseeable factors a high degree of imagination and pioneering spirit is called for.

The continuation or extension of an existing exhibition programme involves a calculable risk which can be gauged on the basis of experience and historical data and their projection into a future programme.

However, past performance should be assessed not only against the results which were actually obtained, but against *results that could have been achieved* by high quality personnel with adequate resources and effective preparation.

Index

Abbreviations: exh = exhibition   exhs = exhibitions

Page numbers of check lists, figures and tables are shown in italics